D0445582

JAPAN'S BUSINESS RENAISSANCE

HOW THE WORLD'S GREATEST ECONOMY REVIVED, RENEWED, AND REINVENTED ITSELF

MARK B. FULLER
JOHN C. BECK

McGraw-Hill
New York Chicago San Francisco Lisbon London
Madrid Mexico City Milan New Delhi
San Juan Seoul Singapore
Sydney Toronto

The McGraw-Hill Companies

1 2 3 4 5 6 7 8 9 10 DOC/DOC 0 9 8 7 6 5

ISBN 0-07-145507-8

This book is printed on recycled, acid-free paper containing a minimum of 50% recycled, de-inked fiber.

To Stephen H. Fuller and Frances Fuller
who first introduced me to Asia and world
MBF

****

To Roger
who supports me through all the Renewal Cycles
JCB

CONTENTS

Acknowledgments

Many people have helped us through the various renewal cycles in our lives as we've moved from being students, to academics, to consultants, to whatever it is we call ourselves today. We owe a huge debt of gratitude to those who have shaped us, supported us, and inspired us. We first thank our mentors. Those who helped us to appreciate strategy and history include: Dave Dyer, Alan Kantrow, Allen Morrison, Mike Porter, Steve Schuker, and John Wells. We learned about the principles of leadership from some of the best thinkers in the world: Chris Argyris, Angel Cabrera, Jamie Higgins, David Kantor, John Kotter, Diana Smith, and Iain Somerville. And importantly, for this book, these men and women taught us to appreciate (and begin to understand a little about) Japan: Walt Ames, Tom Craig, Henry Eyring, John Harlow, Chikatomo Hodo, Maarten Kelder, Eric McCallister, Masakatsu Mori, Yohsuke Nishitani, Ken Ohmae, Richard Rawlinson, Ryo Sambongi, Osamu Sekiguchi, Emmett Thomas, Roy and Wuta Tsuya, Ezra Vogel, Teruaki Yabe, and Michael Yoshino.

We would also like to thank all the clients and colleagues in our firms who have made us smarter and better people over the years. Thanks to our friends, coworkers, and clients at the Monitor Group: Bruce Allyn, Mike Bell, Neal Bhadkamkar, David Boyce, Richard Broyd, Jonathan Calascione, Bruce Chew, Margaret Covell, Jim Cutler, Harriet Edmonds, Jonathan Goodman, Jeff Grogan, Tammy Hobbs-Miracky, Matt Holland, Bernie Jaworski, Steve Jennings, Ron Jonash, Ralph Judah, Vanessa Kirsch, Bob Lurie, Roger Martin, Bill McClements, John Moore, Nikos Mourkogiannis, Bansi Nagji, George Norsig, Neal Pearse, John Pittenger, Sandy Pocharski, Jeff Rayport, Howie Rice, Bob Samuelson, Peter Schwartz,

Rajeev Singh-Molares, Sameer Srivastava, Dennis Stevenson, Alice Warner, and Michael Wenban. And thanks to the very hard workers and very trusting clients associated with North Star Leadership Group: Meredith Brenalvirez, Jeff Cole, Bill Green, Jon Huggett, Alan Larsen, Jonathan Lipsitz, Patrick Lynch, Allen Miner, Mark Nevins, Courtney Rogers, and Mitchell Wade.

In addition, we owe a special debt of gratitude to the people without whom, quite literally, this book would not have happened: Lisa Bandoni, Adam Carstens, Yoshihide Kusaki, Maria Plese, and Melissa Rivers-Teitel. And to our family members who not only support us each and every day of our lives but are the motivation to always try to improve each time we go through another renewal cycle: Roger Beck, Katie Beck, Adam Beck, Elizabeth Beck, Joseph B. Fuller, Alexander M. Fuller, and Linda Jo Froman.

Introduction

In business, renewal is something we all take for granted. Think about it: especially in this era of constant change, what executive would ever admit, to a search committee or market analysts or the press, "Yeah, I'm great at doing the same old thing—I can drive my organization to do more and do it faster. But if we have to change course...I'm not your man." And what employee would ever say, even to herself, "If the world changes around us, this company is doomed." Sure, we can change. No problem. Absolutely.

But can we, really? Do we? How many of us have even seen it done, even once, up close? Hardly any. Because the truth is that most organizations worldwide really aren't good at renewal. To admit that the old ways really aren't working; to throw away the things that got us here; to truly start over...all that is vital to success today, just like the textbooks recommend—but it's not something we know how to do.

And little wonder; the most influential business theories we have—the ones you're probably using now, without even noticing it—assume renewal is either literally impossible, or might as well be. And our deeper cultural training agrees; in our hearts, we believe in one story: *The Rise and Fall of*...the Roman empire...the latest sports hero...our companies...and ourselves. That, not renewal and regeneration, is what we expect. No surprise, then, that that's what we get.

Now that's a bit depressing.

It's also just wrong. There's plenty of evidence that renewal is possible—not just once, but over and over. Companies can come back from the worst depths you can imagine, and not just return to former heights, but go higher than ever. And that's not just an ideal; it's a clearly documented historical pattern. There are examples—lots of them. Even better, there are specific strategies, tactics, and ideas that you can use, in your company, to achieve the same results. Most of us Westerners don't know about them, though, because they come from outside our own culture. One culture, Japan, has consistently reinvented itself for centuries now, overcoming challenges that seemed obviously fatal. Companies, executives, and employees there have absorbed those cultural lessons and made them work in business, again and again, for longer than any of us have been alive. It's a compelling story, with invaluable lessons...and the subject, of course, of this book.

WHY JAPAN?

Unless you're already packing your bags for retirement, renewal equals success. Heck, it equals survival. And if you look the world over for a society, set of companies, and group of individuals who have deeply embedded renewal skills, you won't find any better example than Japan. In its national history, Japan has moved around the renewal cycle several major times. Each time, key inflection points provoke the Japanese into bursts of openness to, and learning from, the outside world. These periods are then followed by long, profitable periods of closing and stability. Right now, Japan is moving into a period of openness and tremendous change. We believe we know what is causing this (in other words, why it has to happen), how it's likely to play out, and finally, what needs to be done to react to it in the right way—whether your point of view is Japanese or non-Japanese. This story—reflected in dozens of individual corporate examples, and in provocative findings from a new international survey—contains important lessons. If you want renewal, in any setting, study Japan.

But Isn't Japan Dead?

Yes, it was in all the papers. But if you look closely, you find that Japan is exhibiting prominent signs of an economy on the verge of rebirth. (You'll know about this one before the journalists.) While indicators are mixed, many important ones are headed up. It may not be this quarter or the next that it becomes obvious to everyone that Japan is back. But in the next few years, we'll all know it. This current rebirth is no accident. Japan has been accomplishing this same basic "miracle" for its entire known history.

And you can accomplish it too, even in your country, even with your culture. Certainly Japan is not the only country with the ability to change rapidly and completely—nor is its pattern perfect. In fact, there are times when Japan's method of revival seems balky and old-fashioned. We can find many of the elements of the mindsets and methodologies that drive Japanese revival in other countries and in companies outside of Japan. And it is clear that Western companies, even Western individuals, can learn the resilient approach that seems to come naturally in Japan. It is not Japan itself, but the core of the Japanese *method* of rebirth and renewal that counts.

By looking closely at Japanese renewal, from its swashbuckling historical roots to the very latest corporate examples, you can understand this method...and adapt it for yourself.

That's what this book is about—understanding this uncanny ability to regenerate, and getting to the point that we can make it happen, for ourselves, in our own cultural setting. This book gets you to that point in a four-part process:

- Part One: Renewal and the Samurai Spirit looks at how renewal happens and how Japan (and its companies) seems to exhibit extraordinary performance over and over and over again. Why should we look at Japan at all? The answer is presented in:
  - Chapter One: The Power of Renewal discusses why renewal drives superior performance.
  - Chapter Two: Fight or Fit introduces a model of successful renewal and the challenge facing all of us.
  - Chapter Three: Bushido offers an understanding of the key cultural element that is the core of Japan's strength.
  - Chapter Four: Businessmen and Bushi describes how an ancient warrior's code directly ties to business, and has for more than a century.
  - Chapter Five: Birth of the Modern Corporate Samurai offers the greatest example of how samurai thinking produced miraculous business results—through an entire renewal cycle.
- Part Two: The Sword takes you inside the famous half of Japan's warrior code—the wisdom needed to wield the samurai sword. The lessons aren't about physical survival; they're about competition, commanding loyalty, and wielding power.
  - Chapter Six: Sword-Wielding outlines the Japanese way of competition, and shows how a thoroughly modern corporate success depends on the warrior spirit.
  - Chapter Seven: Hierarchical shows how to use corporate structure and clear direction from the top to achieve results.

Chapter Eight: Loyal details the kind of loyalty any leader must have—and the kind no leader can afford. It makes specific recommendations on how to build this loyalty, as well as drawing on it for strategic advantage.
Chapter Nine: Eudemonic looks at the flip side of loyalty: what leaders owe to their followers, and how to deliver on that.
Chapter Ten: Youthful faces up to a tough truth: when it comes to renewal, youth is a huge advantage. The good news is that there are ways to attract youth, leverage it, even recreate it for yourself or your organization.

- Part Three: The Pen is about the lesser-known half of bushido...the part that doesn't involve weapons or explicit power—but does win battles (and boost earnings per share). If there is a true "secret" to Japan's success at renewal, it lies in this perspective. This aspect of samurai thinking is outlined in four parts:
  Chapter Eleven: Philosophical shows Westerners why the "philosopher" part of "philosopher/swordsman" matters—even today, in both Western and Japanese companies that no one can ignore.
  Chapter Twelve: Spirited demonstrates how Japanese companies achieve renewal by infusing their employees with a unique spirit.
  Chapter Thirteen: Conservative presents the principles behind organizations that embrace change. In a business world where more than half of all corporate change efforts fail, this is a rare and valuable set of best practices.
  Chapter Fourteen: Grounded shows how successful companies get through the hardest part of renewal—how they let go of their origins and break down patterns that no longer work—without ever forgetting who they really are.
- Part Four: Ronin applies these principles of renewal, seen so far in ancient samurai history and in modern corporate examples, to five challenges that all of us in business will have to face during the next few years:
  Chapter Fifteen: Uncertain shows how to achieve Japanese levels of renewal even now, when the pace of change and degree of uncertainty are arguably greater than anyone has ever experienced.

Chapter Sixteen: Knowledgeable provides answers to a problem every organization faces, and will for decades to come: how to wring knowledge out of all this data…and turn it into results throughout your organization.

Chapter Seventeen: Moral Purpose demonstrates how the best organizations manage to renew the driving force that holds them together, and moves them forward, even when everything seems to have changed.

Chapter Eighteen: China-Facing confronts the problem of working with China—an obvious challenge for Japan…perhaps an equally important challenge and opportunity for the rest of us.

Chapter Nineteen: Entrepreneurs: Finding the Inner Ronin outlines successful ways to bridge the gap from steady-state, organization-man thinking to independent, proactive entrepreneurship—a key element of renewal in most times, and certainly today.

PART ONE

Renewal and the Samurai Spirit

CHAPTER 1

The Power of Renewal

Nothing succeeds like success, the old saying goes. And when people, companies, or cultures are doing well, they tend to ignore what the future may bring. History is littered with stories of successful cultures and organizations who were just a few critical decisions away from sowing the seeds of their own doom—from letting the Visigoths settle on the other side of the Danube (allowing them unfettered access to eventually sack Rome), to Enron assuming its creative accounting measures could somehow be kept from markets, investors, and regulators forever. Both Rome and Enron, while still around today, are now shadows of their former selves to say the least, although Rome is much more pleasant to visit!

Usually entities that suffer such fates forgot or ignored the importance of planning for renewal. The same old way of doing things can't possibly last forever, and these days we're lucky if it lasts a few months. So for both companies and individuals who aren't performing up to expectations, renewal should definitely be a part of the plan. But this lesson also applies to organizations and people who feel like they are at the top of their game. High levels of success don't last very long, unless you've learned to apply the principles of renewal. The ability to constantly revamp oneself, creating not just one but multiple hot streaks over long periods of time, is essential to surviving whatever fate decides to throw your way.

There are many examples of companies who have had real success with corporate renewal. 3M used to make sandpaper—now they make Post-it Notes. Hyundai went from a ship builder to an auto manufacturer. In just over 100 years, Nokia has transformed itself from paper company to industrial equipment manufacturer to the world's largest maker of cellular phones—and a global consumer brand. International Business Machines

(IBM) is now out of the "machine" business almost completely, having sold their personal computer division to China's Lenovo, and the company itself is just fine, thanks.

People are also sometimes capable of remaking themselves—but only a select few can pull it off with panache. Twenty years ago, who would have thought of Governor Schwarzenegger? How has Clint Eastwood managed to transform himself from tough guy actor to sensitive award-winning director? Patti Hearst went from teenage socialite to urban guerilla to recluse. But for each of these celebrity transformations, there are dozens, maybe hundreds, who didn't renew their brands—whose economic success rose and fell with external trends. For an individual performer, of course, that's probably okay. Maybe it even reflects their commitment to a particular artistic vision. But for a company, there's no equivalent of residuals from that one big sitcom letting you live happily ever after. A company that chooses to stick forever with one persona or product line probably dies an untimely death. Certainly, its employees, shareholders, and executives all suffer.

WHY RENEWAL?

Renewal, in other words, is certainly worthwhile. But isn't that one of those "motherhood and apple pie" observations. Absolutely. Yet it is surprising how few organizations are really good at renewal. In fact, the issue is given very little attention in the business literature. Sure, we all pay lip service. Who would suggest that renewal would be bad? Words like *transformation* and *growth* are bandied about, which seem to imply renewal. But even they don't strike at the heart of the topic.

In fact, some of the most influential business theories of the last decade—the ones you're probably using now, without even noticing it—actually seem to have a basic rejection of renewal built right into them. The "Core Competencies" school of management (first put forth by CK Prahalad and Gary Hamel, but then interpreted by just about everyone else) basically recommends that companies focus on the one thing they're best at and get rid of everything else. The usual corporate interpretation of Core Competencies is to shed weaker divisions or whatever might not gracefully co-exist with whatever your best-selling product line is right now. Focusing on what you do better than everyone else will allow you to quickly take control of that market. Yet we know that markets are in constant flux—and as they evolve, new opportunities emerge almost overnight. Domestic television manufacturers gave up on the industry back in the 1970s, assuming television had gone as far as it could go. Now, with flat-panel displays rejuvenating the marketplace, don't they wish they had held on to that piece of the business?

While the recommendations of Clay Christensen's "Disruptive Technologies" school of thought would seem to support renewal, the logic of his argument suggests that renewal is almost impossible. In his theory, Christensen says a new technology will eventually come along and make obsolete whatever it is you're doing, so you must constantly chase after a smaller and higher-end customer base. But ultimately, you will be squeezed against the limits of progress. Do you really want to be Rolls Royce? And with the cycle time for disruption shrinking relentlessly, there's exhaustion to think about—not just for you personally, but for your firm's entire culture. If you fully buy into this view of renewal, take along some pain relievers. In the end, this theory understands renewal not as a natural process, a matter of seasons, but as a gut-wrenching, cathartic, and in the end, almost impossible leap. Every major industry player is just ticking the seconds away until its own demise.

STRAIGHT LINES

So, in most of Western management thought, renewal is literally impossible, or just impossibly tough, to pull off. That view was probably a lot easier to take when progress moved in centuries, or even decades. You might spend a pensive moment thinking about the decline and fall of your particular empire. But you could dismiss those thoughts because, for the most part, the consequences were far away...in corporate terms, somewhere beyond your retirement party. Or, as Keynes put it, "in the long run we are all dead."[1] Today, though, the long run seems a lot shorter. If you're not ready to lie down and die just yet, the standard view of business renewal is a bit depressing.

It's also just wrong. There's plenty of evidence that renewal is possible—not just once, but over and over, no matter how great the challenge. There are specific strategies, tactics, and ideas that can clearly help you renew your company. Most of us don't know about them, though, because they come from outside our own culture.

You'd think that we in the West would be really good with the idea of renewal. After all, the pervasive religious influence in Europe and the Americas is Christianity—which is about nothing if not rebirth and resurrection. But you don't have to go far with this cultural analysis to realize that in

Christianity, renewal is the exception rather than the rule. In our dominant, almost unnoticed culture, resurrection is reserved for God, with cameos from Mother Nature. We humans depend on this supernaturally driven renewal; the earth brings back spring every year, and God eventually comes along to raise us from the grave. But our own efforts, including, of course, our own work, are kind of a one-shot deal.

You don't have to be Christian to have absorbed these assumptions. It doesn't even matter where the assumptions started. The historical fact is that they have permeated Western thinking for centuries. If you grew up in this culture, they've almost surely permeated your thinking as well. Christian thought along these lines is consistent with the logic of math, physics, and even social history that originated in Greece and was adopted and enhanced by the Europeans. Lines are straight, logic is consistent, and matter does not transform itself. Civilizations rise and fall—never again to reach their previous heights. Truthfully, now, isn't that the pattern *you* see in history? Or, closer to home, think about mergers and acquisitions. The experts there would have us believe that companies run through a natural life cycle. Once your firm has run its course, the best you can hope for is to acquire a more successful business, be taken over by someone more successful, or be chopped up and sold off piece by piece. The idea that a company can actually remake itself on a regular basis is anathema. And, again, isn't that what you secretly believe? That the story of a GM, even an IBM, may include returning to profitability...but never again reaching the kind of dominance it once enjoyed? That eBay is simply staving off the inevitable fall from grace?

Those perceptions are etched deep into our psyches. But that doesn't mean that they limit reality (or our behavior). To see the possibilities for renewing your company, you simply need to move beyond our culture. There is an entire world where rebirth and renewal are seen as a more natural and common aspect of everyday life. People outside the United States don't just believe in renewal; they make it happen. You can see, and experience, and understand this world. You can emulate it for yourself. You just have to turn to the East.

Yes, we know; the world is shrinking. And after decades of consulting globally, we know that people and organizations aren't all that different between West and East. But the mindset is. Mindset—and the ability to change it—is key to understanding renewal in both companies and people. In the most pervasive religious beliefs in Asia, reincarnation is normal and expected. Although rhetoric and logic in Western societies have been characterized as linear, in Asia they are more circular. (In the West we think of circular logic as a bad thing, because it doesn't seem to get us anywhere. But Asian philosophies are implicitly more willing to accept that the value of the logic is in the journey, not in the destination. Or maybe non-Westerners just think in more than two dimensions—outside the Cartesian box.) Even Western physics and science are coming around to a less linear way of looking at the world. Quantum physics proposes that objects are able to change their basic characteristics depending on their environment.

So while the basic tools for renewal are available to (and useable by) everyone, some have gotten better at it over time than others—perhaps because their basic instincts about life are more accepting of renewal. In fact, at least one culture (not surprisingly, the one we're going to focus on in this book) has been consistently reinventing itself again and again for centuries: Japan.

THE REBIRTH OF JAPAN

Wait a minute, you're saying. Japan? The society that hasn't made a peep on the world stage since their great crash of 1989? The country whose population threatens to start shrinking any minute? The Asian nation which will soon be dwarfed by fashionable, faster-growing, kind-of-scary China?

Yes, Japan. After years of stagnation, GDP growth is now finally consistently positive, with two consecutive years of real growth in 2003 and 2004 and a great first quarter of 2005. The currency remains strong against the dollar and euro, and foreign direct investment is over $100 billion—double what it was in 2000. "Monetary policy has improved dramatically...the inflation outlook has improved...The banking sector has made considerable progress in dealing with its non-performing loan portfolio. [Companies have been] streamlining operating procedures and shedding staff...allow[ing] profits to rise. Some of these profits have been ploughed back into capital spending, which has also reduced corporate debt. Employment has stabilized, and there are even signs that the property market has bottomed out."[2]

Japan is back—again—and that's the whole point. This is the lesson we can learn from. This is not the first time Japan has seemed to disappear from the world stage. Over and over again, Japan has burst onto the scene, and then disappeared. We'll see that as far back as the turn of the first Millennium, Japan was a thriving, prosperous place. But then it lost its way during the Warring States Period of the fifteenth and sixteenth centuries. As peace took hold during the reign of the Shoguns, Japan revived itself into a center of the arts and boasted a thriving economy. But by the end of the Edo period, the culture was getting a bit out of date. The country transformed itself again, this time during the Meiji Restoration, going from backwater feudal society to world power status by the 1930s. But a long string of military defeats throughout the Pacific, followed by a thorough bombing of the country, put Japan back into the less developed category. However, by the 1980s—once more—Japan was seen by Western scholars "as number one."

Even in the Down Decade of the 1990s, careful observers will note the world's second largest economy never really went anywhere. For a while, most assumed Japan's story was over. A falling birthrate; persistent malaise; a real estate bubble burst; and the breakdown of the Japanese trademarks, such as the lifetime employment system, all seemed too much for the once feared economic giant to overcome.

But if you look closely, Japan seems to have been newly reborn. Nearly all economic and social indicators are on the upswing, and the nation is more confident about its place in the world. Japanese executives are no longer resigning in shame en masse over poor performance. The long string of failed prime ministers seems at an end. The country seems to have found itself again, and people are taking notice.

For the past couple of years, several leading indicators have shown Japan finally "bottoming out" and starting to take charge again in the global economy. First, the long-beleaguered Japanese consumer has finally awakened. "Wages are picking up, stock prices are rising, consumer confidence is recovering and that is having a positive effect on consumption,"[3] according to economist Shuji Shirota. Japanese GDP growth was over 5 percent in the first quarter of 2005, as domestic demand blossomed. Japanese consumer confidence increased nearly 36 percent from the start of 2003 to the start of 2005.[4] Japan's Nikkei index has gained 47 percent from April 2003 to May 2005.[5] And the Japanese unemployment rate has fallen to a six-year low in April 2005, while the U.S. rate stays stuck above 5 percent and domestic job creation continues to be uneven at best.[6]

On the investment side, Japanese firms are matching that exuberance with renewed vigor in formerly moribund categories such as capital expenditures, bank balance sheets, and merger activity. The Ministry of Finance reported eight straight quarterly increases in capital expenditures, rising over 10 percent in the first quarter of 2004 and another seven percent in the first quarter of 2005.[7] Japanese companies are making investments in future technologies, such as wafer fabrication facilities and flat-panel display manufacturers.[8] And the Tankan survey, a measure of Japanese business confidence, reached multiyear highs in 2004, and continues to stay near those levels.[9]

Japanese companies are also looking to buy outside Japan again. Mergers and acquisitions by Japanese firms targeting foreign companies have risen 23 percent in 2004 compared to the previous year, "in everything from producing instant noodles and drinks to selling property and casualty insurance."[10] And the notoriously red-ink–prone Japanese banking sector has finally emerged, Lazarus-like, from the dead, ready to act again on the global stage, as Japan's banking regulators now say Japan's bad debt crisis is officially over.[11]

Japanese car companies are still eating each others' lunch, stealing market share and customers without resorting to gimmicky zero percent financing incentives. In fact, all three big Japanese players—Toyota, Nissan, and Honda—"plan to build factories and hire more employees in the U.S."[12] in the near future, while GM and Ford struggle with overcapacity, have their debt downgraded to junk and lay off tens of thousands of employees. Japanese car companies are still "doing the right things to continue growing in the U.S.," said one fund manager. "They're maintaining good quality of their products, they're enhancing their image, and, lastly, they're expanding local production."[13]

Do you think Japan is going to go the traditional advanced nation route and outsource all its manufacturing jobs? Think again. Instead, Japanese firms continue to set the pace for technological advancement and productivity, keeping Japanese plants booming. Toyota and Canon "have developed integrated manufacturing systems that are far more sophisticated and complex than rivals can manage" and "have learned how best to protect trade secrets that have long made them competitive, often bringing back activities that might otherwise risk exposure to rivals."[14] Sharp has recently opened a brand-new next-generation plant to make television flat panels inside Japan, cranking out products much bigger than those made in older plants. Each new plant "contains its own specialized equipment, all of which must work seamlessly to churn out delicate panels with almost no defects."[15]

Japanese companies have even capitalized on the rise in offshore manufacturing. One Japanese company, Omron, makes sensors and scanners that are used by nearly all other manufacturers. "Factories in China are upgrading their methods, and are buying more Omron devices to help."[16]

Japan is able to invest again principally because of a wave of painful corporate restructurings that at long last appear to have taken effect. "The rise in investment appears to be a direct result of corporate restructuring over recent years, which has helped boost companies' profitability,"[17] said *The Economist* in late 2003. That view became more refined as time passed, as "many of the biggest [Japanese] companies...reduced their debt loads sharply over the past few years [and felt] comfortable funneling profits into fresh capital spending. The resulting demand for machinery, materials and other inputs...in turn boosted demand at other Japanese firms."[18]

JAPAN'S DOWN DECADE

Yet not so long ago, Japan seemed lost in a cycle of endless recessions, political crises, banking and business failures, and a societywide questioning of the entire system. The financial and political press was filled with warnings of a slow deflation that would eventually leave Asia's economy permanently scarred.

After the bursting of economic bubbles in the early 1990s, both America and Japan seemed stuck in twin contractions. But gradually, the United States pulled out, leaving Japan behind, seemingly for good. "Once, Japan invited admiration...now, however, it invites despair,"[19] warned *The Economist*. According to the pundits, Japan had failed "to escape from the economic stagnation of this lost decade...to reform its shaky politics and corrupt bureaucracy, and...as a result to be able to lead East Asia out of its troubles."[20]

This failure to lead in turn led to heart-wrenching stories of formerly high-flying Japanese businessmen, now reduced to jobs beneath their station. "62-year-old Jin Matsushita picks up his mop and bucket and cleans the floors of a housing complex not far from his own apartment on Tokyo Bay.... Until 1995, Matsushita made a more than decent living selling stocks for one of Japan's biggest securities houses.... Today, the company in which Matsushita invested those four decades—Yamaichi Securities—no longer exists. It went spectacularly bankrupt in November of last year. The shares he owns are now worthless."[21]

Western readers were apparently supposed to draw the conclusion that a society formerly touted by the same hysterical press the decade before (Exhibit A being the famous 1987 *Newsweek* cover blaring "Your Next Boss Could Be Japanese") had been rendered nothing but mop and bucket men. Japan was something to be pitied or ignored, not feared or copied.

Some even took it a bit further, championing the triumph of "Western values" and individualism over those inscrutable Asians with their (gasp!) "collectivist tendencies" and "concern for the greater good." As the frequently quoted Japanese proverb put it, "The nail that sticks up gets pounded down." "Promises of lifetime employment and a tidy pension kept corporate soldiers in line...[yet] years of stagnation have planted deep doubts about all that. More and more Japanese believe they are left with just themselves to fall back on."[22]

With this angle came gloating from free-marketers that the Japanese model was just another doomed statist pipe dream waiting to be tossed into the trash can of history. "Remember when people were actually claiming Japan would replace the United States as the world's leading economic power?" chortled über-libertarian Brink Lindsey of the Cato Institute in 2001. "Oops—never mind. Asia's ailing giant has just limped through a lost decade of economic stagnation and the prospects for the coming years don't look much brighter. Meanwhile, the U.S. has reeled off one of the greatest economic expansions in its history."[23]

SEEING A PATTERN

Obviously, economic cycles come and go—one country is up, while another is down, and then back again, without imparting any greater advantage to either. Certainly, Japan was down for a long time, and the United States has been relatively fortunate in the last two decades.

But Japan's current rebirth is no accident. It has been accomplishing exactly these sorts of miracles repeatedly throughout its history. In fact, this latest turnaround is minor in comparison to other rabbit-out-of-the-hat tricks that the Japanese people have pulled off in the past. We will argue in this book that Japan has a natural propensity for renewal that gives it, its companies, and its people a natural competitive advantage compared to the West. But it is not that Japan has a corner on this ability to change rapidly and completely—nor that its pattern is perfect. In fact, there are times when Japan's method of revival seems balky and old-fashioned. Many of the elements of the mindsets and methodologies that drive Japanese revival can be found in other countries and in companies outside of Japan. And it is clear that Western companies, even Western individuals, can learn the resilient approach that seems to come naturally in Japan.

Even if you're not interested in renewal, it is interesting—and potentially profitable—to note that every time in the last two centuries that the West was just about ready to write off Japan as dead and gone, it has come back in a new and more vibrant form. Just when we think a rival Japanese firm is circling the drain, it turns into something we didn't expect it to be—something much more powerful than it was before. Sony was thought to have suffered a fatal blow after betting all its chips on Betamax technology, which eventually lost to VHS. Yet Sony has emerged as one of the world's premiere brands on new technologies such as DVD players, televisions, and, most fun of all, video game consoles.

There seems to be something contained within the Japanese *method* of rebirth and renewal—something greater than the sum of its parts. To fully examine these implications, we need to look at models of change and renewal and the way that Japanese methods and mindsets influence these models. Why doesn't Japan just disappear from the competitive landscape? Why do they keep coming back to challenge Western business standards with such regularity?

WHY RENEWAL?

There are probably a variety of lessons we could have drawn in any book that looks at what has happened to Japan over the past 15 years.

There were structural lessons: how should hypercompetitive industries best mask their underperforming sectors in a national economy, for example. There are lessons in national competitiveness: how to fit within the larger world of countries simultaneously competing for cost advantages and growth potential. There are business-government interaction lessons: how did Japan's economy come to be less "directed" over time by government officials. Japan even offers lessons in applied demography: what it means to be living in a developed nation whose population is not only shrinking in size but is made up of almost as many people over 50 as there are under.

But we believe that the most important lessons to write about—the ones where managers in the West can learn something from the Japanese, and even where the Japanese can learn a great deal from corporate success in their own and other countries—are the lessons of renewal.

These lessons begin with a whole host of surprises. We're already starting to see some attitudes that fly in the face of the usual stereotype about Japanese belief systems. On a survey of Japanese and American businesspeople, we found that Japanese were more likely to respond in ways that one might have thought were more traditionally American. Our Japanese respondents are more likely than Americans to:

- Emphasize strategy rather than operational efficiency
- Adopt systems and practices from other countries

- Feel that companies should be unique and act differently from their competitors
- Want to find new ideas from outside rather than from inside their own firm
- Feel that companies should turn a profit and generate wealth for everyone
- Blame a worker's improper practices on senior management rather than on the individual
- Rely on all-out competition rather than look for alliances
- Believe that their generation is more shrewd than the previous generation
- Break society's traditional norms to succeed in business
- Criticize those in authority when they are wrong
- Want to live in a foreign culture
- Correct a colleague or co-worker even if it means embarrassing them
- Disagree with the statement that "loyalty is the most important virtue in life" (by a huge margin)
- Believe in the usefulness of military-like strategies and tactics in business
- Claim that they are part of a revolution inside their organization

Many of these responses represent exactly the kind of mindset that leads naturally to renewal. And renewal is the essential task facing most organizations today. No matter what industry you're in, low-cost producers are threatening to steal market share from beneath you, and new technologies are threatening to migrate your customers up and out of reach. Relying on simple growth is a fool's game—you might as well forget about ever reaching the top, as someone will always be ready and able to grow just that much faster than you. You have to be able to change the game. That means renewal. And our survey results suggest that the Japanese may be better poised to engage in the process of renewal than Americans.

CONCLUSION

Where do these attitudes come from? How are they emerging from a society that has always been characterized as slow moving, tradition-bound, uncritical, and insular? Is our image of Japanese culture so wrong? Not really. In fact, we believe these are all beliefs that really are deeply ingrained in Japanese culture. Of course, these viewpoints are present in the West also. But there is more to Japan than these elements. In a time of crisis, attitudes and behaviors emerge from Japanese people and organizations that are reminiscent of a very ancient system: the way of the samurai, or *bushido*. These attitudes allow the Japanese to reinvent themselves with shocking vigor...and shocking success. They are the best model we can think of for renewal.

The good news is that it is not only Japanese companies, or even individuals, that can tap into these mindsets and methods. We believe that by disciplining yourself and your organization, anyone can absorb the lessons of renewal from the samurai. The lessons of bushido are important because samurai are adept in almost any situation, in multiple disciplines. They are masters of both the sword *and* the pen. Furthermore, samurai have the proven capacity to change—they are changing right this moment to fit the new demands of the business world—into *ronin*, or masterless samurai, who are able to adapt themselves to new environments and demands. In this book, we will explore the characteristics that are most important to today's modern-day corporate samurai, both those in Japan and those in the rest of the world.

Before we get to the samurai, however, we've got to spend a little time on what exactly happens to produce change and renewal in companies, in countries, and in people. The next chapter is about knowing when it is better to "fight" or "fit," given the circumstances. The answer may not be as clear as you once thought.

NOTES

1. John Maynard Keynes, *A Tract on Monetary Reform*, New York: Harcourt, Brace, 1924, p. 88.
2. "Japan economy: A higher forecast, but without great hope", Viewswire Asia, Economist Intelligence Unit, June 2, 2005.
3. Barney Jopson and David Pilling, "A surging Nikkei, faster growth and supportive policy—is Japan's sick economy at last making a....," *Financial Times*, August 22, 2003, p. 15.
4. Consumer Confidence Survey Summary, Economic and Social Research Institute, Cabinet Office, http://www.esri.cao.go.jp/en/stat/shouhi/0504shouhi-e.html.

5. Stephen Schurr, "Japan bull may be bloodied but it isn't finished yet," *Financial Times*, May 31, 2005

6. Todd Zaun, "Japan's Unemployment Rate Fell to 6-Year Low in April," *The New York Times*, June 1, 2005.

7. "Economists Upbeat on Japan Growth," *The Australian*, June 6, 2005.

8. Yoshiko Hara, "Japan making huge investments in chip, LCD manufacturing—A brisk consumer market spurs funding for IC fabs and display-making facilities," *Electronic Engineering Times*, March 22, 2004.

9. Bryan Bemmer, "Japan's Recovery Looks Like the Real Thing," *Business Week*, April 26, 2004.

10. Arran Scott, "Japan Watch: Corp Japan Makes a Comeback in Foreign M&A," *Dow Jones International News*, June 17, 2004.

11. David Ibison, "FSA Declares Japan's Bad-Loan Crisis Over," *Financial Times*, May 26, 2005.

12. John Lippert, "Top Japanese Carmakers Increase Sales in U.S," *China Daily*, February 16, 2004.

13. Ibid.

14. "(Still) made in Japan," *The Economist*, April 10, 2004.

15. Ibid.

16. Ibid.

17. Japan: Confounding the doom-mongers," *Economist Intelligence Unit*, November 3, 2003.

18. The final piece—Japan's economy, *The Economist*, April 24, 2004.

19. "The Japan puzzle," *The Economist*, March 21, 1998.

20. Ibid.

21. Bill Powell and Velisarios Kattoulas, "The Lost Decade: They dreamed of retirement homes and European vacations—and then the bubble burst," *Newsweek International*, July 27, 1998.

22. Yumiko Ono and Bill Spindle, "Beyond Japan's Lost Decade—Standing Alone: Japan's Long Decline Makes One Thing Rise: Individualism—Soured on Consensus, People Sue, Confront Bureaucracy and Look to Themselves—Be Anglo-Saxon and Succeed," *The Wall Street Journal*, December 29, 2000.

23. Brink Lindsey, "So Long, Protectionism: Good Riddance to Managed Trade," *The Asian Wall Street Journal*, January 11, 2001.

CHAPTER 2

Fight or Fit

Renewal—whether it is personal, corporate, or national—looks much more like a cycle than a straight line. It is sometimes difficult to understand where the crisis ends and renewal begins. Prosperity, it seems, sometimes slips almost soundlessly into poverty. So, of course, Japan's latest economic revival (no matter how impressive and unexpected) might not signal a lasting turnaround. But even if this wave of optimistic revival stopped tomorrow, we believe that Japan's next great success story will come sooner rather than later. The point of this book is not to encourage you to rush out and buy stock in Hello Kitty; the point is that Japan is a wonderful example of a cycle of renewal that has played itself out in people, organizations, and on the national level for centuries. Wherever we are in the world, there is much we can learn from the Japanese cycle as we struggle with our own important issues of change and renewal.

Several times before, Japan has emerged from wrenching changes into huge, unexpected strengths. It is a pattern that tends to take Western observers by surprise. And we have observed that the cultural, economic, and structural forces driving a formidable new Japan are stronger than they've been in a long time. However, whether or not the next few years show Japan in dramatic revival, the patterns and mindsets and methods by which Japan goes through this energizing renewal gives us a model for how change can take place in our own lives.

Throughout history, in both feudal and modern times, Japan has often fiercely opposed change—particularly when such change comes from the outside. Then, almost instantly, Japan seems to reverse course, warmly accepting the outside world. To the outside observer, this might seem unusual. Certainly, it has taken many by surprise. It is not entirely unique;

in many ways, it is not much different from how any number of organizations and national economies deal with change. But when the outside world changes unexpectedly, Japan clings to past strategies and resists embracing a new strategy for longer periods of time. Perhaps this is what surprises observers...even in Japan.

THE RENEWAL CYCLE MODEL

To understand how Japan handles change, let's begin with the fundamentals that seem to be universal. Whether change occurs at an individual, organizational, or even national level, there are powerful parallels in how that process unfolds. We can see this most clearly by analyzing a cycle of change. We originally developed our model for this cycle from historical data of U.S., European, and Japanese corporations from the turn of the twentieth century through the 1990s.

Based on those data, we found that large organizations pass through fairly predictable cycles of renewal. Each full cycle seemed to take somewhere between 7 and 20 years. (There is evidence that during the last 20 years these cycles have shortened to 5 to 10 years, particularly in technology-based industries.) Not unexpectedly, we call this pattern "The Renewal Cycle." At a basic level, our model is a simple four-step explanation of change.

The process begins with two axes. (See Figure 2-1.) The horizontal axis details the *focus* of change—internal (giving everyone funny hats) or external (producing suntan lotion instead of BBQ sauce). When companies increase their focus on internal changes ("what do you mean I have to wear a funny hat?"), they often can't focus as well on external concerns, such as customer satisfaction ("this suntan lotion doesn't taste nearly as good as the BBQ sauce"). Vice versa, when focus is trained outside in the search for new markets, internal processes tend to get lost in the shuffle. Meanwhile, the vertical axis relates to the *size* of change taking place. An organization with large-scale change taking place would be at the top; one with absolutely no changes would be at the very bottom. (It would also be rare.)

The axes combine to create four quadrants, which we have named Gaming, Framing, Claiming, and Taming. Despite our focus on the need for renewal, let us be clear: for most companies, most of the time will be spent in the fourth quadrant: Taming. The focus in Taming is mostly on "bottom-line," cost cutting, and performance improvement. To most of us, this feels like normal times, a steady state, the way things are supposed to be. Together, the three other quadrants describe the process that needs to occur for a company to successfully adapt to a significant change...the kind of

FIGURE 2–1

The Renewal Cycle.

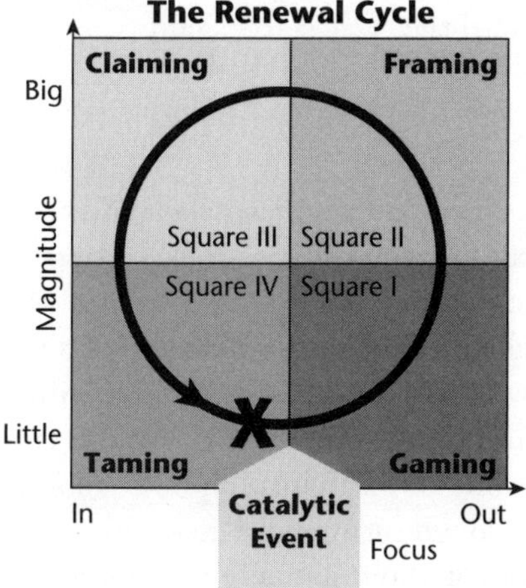

process that makes it impossible to keep doing business as usual…the kind that seems so frequent right now.

CATALYTIC EVENTS IGNITE CHANGE

You will have noticed that people, organizations, and countries don't easily make fundamental changes on their own—especially when things seem to be going well. It usually takes something out of the ordinary to force renewal. We like to call this the *catalytic event*. In principle, this driver can assume different guises. For example, it can simply be the next step in a natural progression, although such progressions rarely motivate change until the resulting circumstances have reached a fairly dire state. The catalyst may also come dressed as an opportunity; although to motivate a fundamentally different way of operating and looking at the world, it had better be extraordinary. In practice, the catalytic event is usually traumatic, or at least highly threatening. A takeover is a good example, or a new competitor, an economic slowdown, even the death of a CEO. These are the kinds of catalytic events that literally force you out of your safety zone, into the realm of the unknown. They change the universe so sharply that to *not* change would be to die. What's more, they are irreversible—you can't go back to the old way of doing things no matter what. This kind of catalytic event is what it normally takes to force any organization to leave the safety of the Taming square. Having made that leap, the company will then move through the remaining three quadrants in a logical sequence, ultimately settling in a new Taming environment...until the cycle starts again.

Square 1—Gaming

How does this sequence work? Well, once you've acknowledged that a catalytic event has taken place (and assuming you have recovered from the initial panic), the next step in the change process is to slowly explore the new world and try to assess what the change really means for you. This is Square 1 of the change cycle, also known as "Gaming." In Gaming, information is key—you at least need to know what's happening. We call this phase *Gaming* because this is a great time to participate in "war games" and simulations. The goal is to think through future behaviors and gather information in support of those actions without actually making major and potentially painful changes. In Gaming, the company does not yet possess enough data about the new environment to make sound choices to support large-scale change. It doesn't know if there really are "weapons of mass destruction" out there or not. And in most situations, the company would be unwise to take powerful action without first being really sure of the facts.

Unfortunately, this phase seldom looks as clear in the moment as it does in retrospect. Times of crisis do tend to breed panic. A catalytic event will create a sense of urgency; it has to, to get you out of Taming in the first place. Heightening this urgency to act are the feelings that naturally arise after a catalytic event: loss of identity, anxiety, even grieving and anger at the security you've lost. It is not surprising that decision makers may respond with an immediate and drastic attempt to transform the organization. Too often, though, such responses are simply ill-considered. It is important to remember that you are only ready to move out of Square 1 when your efforts to gain new information yield less and less. Ideally, this corresponds to a lessening of the negative feeling surrounding the changes and allows you to start getting used to the new reality before moving on. We will show a bit later that while many Western companies are tempted to move too quickly, this is rarely the case in Japanese culture. If anything, the Japanese tend to stay too long in Square 4 and are reluctant, no matter what the circumstances, to move through Square 1 and onto the rest of the cycle.

Square 2—Framing

Organizational leaders who have done their Gaming work well should be more familiar with the new environment and ready for the Framing stage. Framing is when leaders translate their understanding of the new world into an action plan for the organization. During this stage the company is creating its new future; clear and distinct corporate positioning is crucial. Framing is also where firms begin to set external goals. What will you achieve? What are your targets? In Framing, leaders imagine the possibilities and explore the new opportunities set forth by the change, then begin to develop the capacity to translate this vision into reality.

Framing requires focusing on the external, while we explore the limits of the new world the catalytic event has created. The challenge, of course, is that if the environment for one company in an industry has changed, then chances are it has changed for others. Companies that can analyze trends more accurately than competitors and then capture a strong position in the new environment are those most likely to profit in the long run.

Square 3—Claiming

In Square 3 there is still a lot of change going on (the change is "big"), but the focus turns inward. In Claiming, you need to execute the vision set forth in the previous stage. This can only be accomplished through internal change. In order to continue through the cycle, executives must claim the change much like staking a claim to a mine. You must first do the necessary organizational work to make the mine your own, then the physical work to make the mine ready to produce.

People at every level of the organization—or every stratum of society—are usually involved in the claiming stage, more so than at any other phase of the change cycle. And with so many people involved and so many different things happening, this stage tends to feel very chaotic and disorganized. At times, it may seem like everything is going wrong. For every success, there are at least two setbacks. But confusion and frustration are a natural part of putting plans into action. It really is true that the devil is in the details. This is the stage that requires the most work, but the potential payoffs can be enormous.

Japanese corporations have been characterized as slow to make decisions (Framing) but very fast in implementation (Claiming). This is because the Japanese decision-making system tends to ensure that every member of the organization is on board before moving to the next step. In most Western companies, the opposite is true—decisions are made quickly, with plans to get employees aligned during the implementation stage (and, hopefully, induce those not inclined to change to leave the fold). In Western firms, the Claiming stage is a time when internal experimentation and political maneuvering take place—less so for Japanese firms, who took care of most of that in Square 2.

Square 4—Taming

By the time a firm makes its way through the trials of Gaming, Framing, and Claiming, everyone is exhausted. Fortunately, the amplitude of change drops in the Taming period, which is characterized by small, internally focused, and mostly adaptive changes. These changes—really just tweaking around the edges—are far less stressful than the chaos of the earlier phases. Taming is the place for housekeeping, for ensuring that newly installed systems and processes run smoothly, and for making the organization as profitable as it can be. As a company shifts from Claiming to Taming, it moves down the experience and cost curves and profits rise accordingly. No wonder companies like to spend time here.

Even though companies strive to stay in Taming as long as possible—even following a catalytic event—successful organizations must be ready to move on should the need arise. The natural bureaucratic pull toward the bottom left corner of the box (toward increasingly internally focused thinking and less and less change) is enormous. Yet there is only one absolute about Taming: another catalytic event will eventually follow. The most successful companies that are in the Taming phase should, therefore, try to focus equally on internal and external issues. This positioning allows companies to scan the horizon for potential environmental upheaval, while simultaneously making the ongoing internal cost and quality improvements necessary for current financial success.

Getting Through the Cycle

To achieve the greatest possible success, companies must drive through the first three phases of the cycle as quickly as possible in order to maximize time in the Taming phase. To illustrate, note how the best acquisition and alliance candidates often seek out partners that master the new context swiftly, make the right offers quickly, and speed the new entity along. Relationships with customers and suppliers have to be established and managed—again, the victory often goes to those companies that can form these relationships early and exclusively. Finally, any time a company is not in the Taming mode, its costs are higher than they might otherwise be. Companies that can get to Taming first and stay there the longest (while maintaining relevance to the marketplace) will have a competitive advantage over time. The change cycle can be a model to not only help companies manage change but also master it.

Catalytic events—foundation-breaking and irreparable environmental changes—are the death of many companies (witness AT&T's recent retreat from residential phone service, for one). For others, they are an opportunity to thrive.

Our research into corporate responses to environmental shifts or crises suggests that few companies have the skills or confidence to manage dramatic change in a masterly way. We present our Renewal Cycle to help companies thrive on crisis instead of avoid it. Our work shows how companies can take control when a catalytic event occurs, understand the options available to them, and implement those options through a logical cycle of measures. Used properly, the Renewal Cycle methodology will help companies survive and prosper through critical periods.

SOCIAL CHANGE AND THE RENEWAL CYCLE

When we describe the phases in the Renewal Cycle, we may veer into very methodical and instrumental language. But it is important to remember that the process doesn't feel or look methodical. There really is a pattern; organizations, nations, and even cultures evolve through very similar stages. And there really are useful, predictable tactics to help your company move around the cycle much faster by making sure that renewal becomes a conscious effort. But even without such leadership, social change often happens regardless.

For example, let's take the institution of slavery in the United States. Clearly, attitudes, behaviors, and laws about this issue changed considerably throughout the first two centuries of U.S. history. Though there were a number of abolitionist thinkers in the United States even when the Constitution was written, the institution of slavery was so entrenched it was written right into the document. Yet sometime in the mid-1800s there was a catalyst—maybe it was *Uncle Tom's Cabin*, the Dred Scott case, or the new states added to the nation as part of the Louisiana Purchase. Whatever the reason, many people began to imagine a country without slavery. What would it look like? How would it work? What abuses would be left in the past? What new hardships would the country face? These are exactly the sorts of questions asked and answered in the Gaming phase.

Only after an attitudinal tipping point passed in the mid-nineteenth century—namely, public opinion and elected officials in the Northern states who decided slavery had to be abolished—did big changes occur. In this emerging, new environment (the slave-free environment), the Northern states were already very comfortable with abolition, having passed through this cycle earlier. So they turned their attention to their external political environment. Looking back at them were the Southern states, which hated the North's position and threatened to secede as a result. These activities were all done in the Framing stage, as each side prepared for the conflict that began with the Civil War, yet ultimately went long past the surrender.

For the next century, the United States was stuck squarely in the Claiming phase. Even though slavery was formally abolished, the implementation of social systems that would allow African-Americans to interact freely and equally within society was a long and arduous process. Finally with the last "big" changes surrounding the civil rights movement in the 1960s and 1970s, the United States moved into the last phase of Taming on this issue. Now there are constant little tweaks to systems, procedures, attitudes, and mores, but compared to those undertaken from the period of the Civil War until the 1970s, these are relatively small.

So the Renewal Cycle can clearly apply to more than just business. In this book, we'll apply the Renewal Cycle to how Japanese society passed through cycles over the last 500 years that we call "fit" and "fight." The result tells us a great deal about Japan's capacity to surprise almost everyone, and helps us understand what may be coming next.

FIT OR FIGHT

Catalytic events have a way of catching any company or society off guard. None of us are really looking for them. We'd rather stay in Square 4 for the rest of our lives. But forces emerge and shift the power dynamic under our feet. The way that societies react says a lot about their nature. The Japanese have reacted to each cycle in different ways, yet there is a provocative thread of commonality running through them all. Even though the stages of change are the same everywhere in the world, the methods and mindsets brought to bear in each of the squares are quite different in Japan than they are in the West. And those attitudes and behaviors result in a different pace for Japanese renewal.

The core point is that, in a way quite different from other nations, Japan has experienced entire cycles that could be classified as either "fit" (trying to be part of the rest of the world) or "fight" (trying to be uniquely Japanese). For anyone who wants to understand Japanese methods and mind-sets about renewal, this is a good place to begin.

Japan's Inflection Points throughout History

In its national history, Japan has moved around the "fit or fight" cycle several major times. Each time it does so, there are certain key inflection points that provoke the Japanese into bursts of openness to and learning from the outside world. Yet these periods tend to be followed by long periods of closing and stability. Right now we're predicting—or observing the initial indications—that Japan is moving into a period of openness and tremendous change. We believe we know what is causing this (in other words, why it has to happen), how it's likely to play out, and, finally, what needs to be done to react to it in the right way—whether your point of view is Western or Japanese. We also believe (a point we'll get to later in the book) that Japanese history contains important lessons for successful corporate renewal in any setting.

One of the aspects of Japanese history that make it convenient to study is that these cycles are well defined. Except for the cycle after World War II, each of the periods of Japanese history is named after the shogun or the emperor in charge. Let's look at the cycles that have defined Japanese eras of fit and fight.

The Feudal Fight (Tokugawa)

While we could go back even further, a good place to start our review of Japanese historical cycles might be the important inflection point at the beginning of the seventeenth century. The Tokugawa period brought with it the installation of the Tokugawa Bakufu (military government) and the closing of the country to outside influence. The Bakufu came into existence in large part as a reaction to chronic civil war. Even though the Bakufu was preceded by other military dictatorships which consolidated the country and reduced internal fragmentation, it was Tokugawa Ieyasu who consolidated power, leading to 250 years of peace in Japan. This "Pax Nipponica" is regarded by many as the longest continuous period of peace in any nation on earth.

The arrival of Christianity in Japan motivated the Bakufu to act, spurred by the threat of Spanish and Portuguese colonialism in the region. To the Bakufu, Christianity—particularly militant Catholicism—became a fifth column in Japan, especially as its influence started taking over Kyushu, Japan's third largest island. As this progressed, the notion of closing the entire society and taking a "fight" mentality began to take hold. In other words, the strategy came to be one of separating from the rest of the world in an effort to preserve the essence of Japan. Although Perry's famed Black Ships are usually given credit for being the first outside threat to which Japan reacted, it had faced the exact same threat 200 years earlier. Yet the two reactions were entirely different. In the latter case, Japan embraced foreign ways. But during the age of the Bakufu, Japan successfully closed down to the rest of the world, and did not emerge again for centuries.

Meiji Fit Period

The next big inflection point in Japanese society is the aforementioned arrival of the Black Ships. There followed the Meiji Restoration with all of its commercial, cultural, and political manifestations. This was more than simply a commercial "opening"—not only was Western technology adopted but also the trappings of Western culture and military reorganization. The Meiji Restoration was also in many ways a cultural revolution—both in political terms (this age saw the introduction of parliamentary democracy) and media (newspapers were founded, books published, and knowledge distributed broadly throughout the land). Rangaku, or "Dutch learning," was no longer carefully censored. And by the Taisho democracy era of the early twentieth century, Japan was as open as it had ever been—actively pursuing its agenda on the global stage for the first time.

The Expansionist, Imperialist Fight Era (Taisho and early Showa)

During the Taisho era, a new strategy began to emerge. Even though the internal society of Japan became more restrictive, it was not isolationist by any means. Japanese military audacity increased significantly during this era, yet did not receive any outside rebuke. Japan's Meiji and Taisho military advances in Taiwan, Korea, and Russia were all highly successful, and paralleled the Great Game taking place in Europe at the time. Given the information available to the Japanese, it actually made sense for them to believe that they could conquer (with ease) their part of the world.

Because the Meiji era produced such internal fragmentation of Japanese society, the newly powerful military regime in Japan felt that to restore unity it had no choice but to kick the foreigners out yet again. Foreign auto companies were shuttered; foreign media were told to leave. Domestic political dissent was silenced, along with the domestic media. From there it was one slippery slope, from secret police to the end of democracy and, importantly, the end of economic competitiveness and the arrival of media controls. Exacerbated by the Great Depression and economic confrontation with the rest of the world—particularly the United States—tariffs were raised, exports were shut out, and Japanese emigration came to a halt. The Japanese began to view the world as a zero-sum game where only by seizing resources could they provide the fuel necessary to their country's survival. Thus was born the next logical move: all-out attack.

By the 1940s, Japan's obvious belief in itself and its own power was borne out by the fact that General Tojo and other top military advisors had suggested to Emperor Hirohito that they could conquer all of East Asia in just three months—an audacious goal by any measure, and one, not surprisingly, that they were unable to accomplish. In the end it took the Japanese military *three months and one week* to militarily conquer all of East Asia.[1] That ability of the Japanese war machine to deliver results almost to the promised "delivery date" shows what a powerful force they really were. We won't rehash the World War II story here; you've probably seen the movie. But the course that the Japanese were on should have taken them into a very comfortable Taming phase. Suffice it to say, that did not happen. The American resistance to Japan's designs on Asia and the Pacific was much stronger than anticipated. The U.S. victories served as a shocking and paradigm-breaking catalyst for renewal in Japan.

Post–World War II Fit (later Showa)

After World War II, Japan was once again open…but not by choice. Democracy was reintroduced, while past institutions were swept away or made impotent. In this current era, encompassing the last 60 years, we can see all four phases of the cycle at work.

Square 1 was directly after the war but before the Occupation officially ended. At the end of the war, the Japanese economy was utterly in shambles, its people completely defeated and subject to foreign occupation. Yet under economic initiatives such as the Dodge Plan (which stabilized runaway price inflation, fixed the Japanese yen at a conversion rate of 360 to the dollar, and established balanced budgets as a matter of national policy), the Japanese economy was able to return to its prewar levels by 1953.

This Gaming phase allowed Japan to rejoin the community of nations and establish its postwar identity. Clearly, the military expansionism of the past cycle would not be tolerated, so Japan turned to the coming metric of postwar global competition: gross national product (GNP). As the occupation wound to a close, Japan was quietly putting the pieces together for a sustained run at the commanding heights of the global economy.

Square 2 began in earnest after the occupation formally ended and enormous societal reforms were undertaken, turning Japan into a true economic force. Through these reforms, Japan got everyone in society on board with actions resulting in a stronger nation, while doing away with relics of the economy that held back progress. As a result, "land reform successfully redistributed ownership of land farmed by tenants, solving the severe landlord-tenant problems that had long endured.... The labor union movement freed the working groups from the predominant control of enterprise managers to some extent [and] the system of aristocracy was fully abolished, which virtually brought about an egalitarian atmosphere among the general public."[2] During this phase, Japan was saying, "We know what it takes to succeed in this new world order."

As a result of this transformation, Japan raced ahead of other economies. From 1953 to 1973, Japan's real GNP grew on average over two and a half times as fast as the United States, three times as fast as the United Kingdom, and about twice as fast as the other G-7 countries (West Germany, France, Italy, and Canada). Signature events such as the 1964 Tokyo Olympics and the 1970 Osaka World's Fair allowed Japan to show itself to the world as a country reborn.

Japan moved to Squares 3 and 4 in the 1960s to 1970s when its economic dominance really began to take hold on the international scene. Square 3 involved Japan's exporters moving into one industry after another—televisions, electronics, cars—and completely demolishing the established order with efficient production, low costs, and low prices. Japan became every U.S. rust belt politician's bête noire, as jingoistic appeals to prevent the complete destruction of domestic industries multiplied. As the yen began to chip away at the dollar's hegemonic position, Japan now had a place at the table for all major global economic decisions.

Square 4 brought this cycle to a close as Japan's place in the world as an economic superpower was assured. Japanese corporations became some of the most profitable in world history, and used that clout to make a seemingly endless series of foreign acquisitions, for example, Rockefeller Center and Columbia Pictures. Yet sown within that final phase, amidst predictions of the end of U.S. hegemony, were the seeds of the next catalytic event.

During this final phase, the price of land, among other things, had increased so much that the very egalitarianism that had made the postwar economic expansion possible began to unravel. The land surrounding Tokyo's Imperial Palace was said to be worth more than California. Classic paintings by Van Gogh and Picasso were ensconced in Tokyo art museums. Japan's Seagaia golf resort had an estimated price tag of $2 billion. In short, this was not the traditional postwar Japan, where individual sacrifice for the good of the corporation or country is still valued. And of course, things did eventually come crashing down. Two days before the close of the 1980s, on December 29, 1989, the Nikkei hit 38,915. Over the next decade, it would begin a precipitous drop that exemplified all the excesses of the former age, as company after company went insolvent or needed a government bailout.

The Lost Decade Fight (Early Heisei)

Japan's next big inflection point became the lost decade of the 1990s—where the prior model failed to provide the same results, and the search for something new began. After the crash, the Japanese export platform and government-supported economic model had run out of steam. During this period, even though there still existed the same self-referential, inward-looking quality that "Japan as Number One" created, it never carried quite the same intensity.

In a number of attitudinal aspects, this early Heisei period has been a lot like the inward-looking Taisho era. In both times, the early 1900s and the early 2000s, just when connectedness with the rest of the world was getting firmly established, the Japanese seemed to stop thrusting outward. We don't know whether this is because they were self-satisfied, or because Japan finds true connectedness with the outside world quite difficult and not worth the effort. Or perhaps there is just an outer limit to the homeland's tether. Maybe Japan just feels it is losing its identity and needs to pull back when it reaches a certain amount of connectedness.

CONCLUSION

Clearly, the repeated closing and opening of society continues to this day. But the amplitude and severity of each cycle has diminished over time. As we saw, the most complete closing was the Tokugawa Bakufu. The closing after the failure of the Meiji Restoration was less extreme—yet still dramatic in many ways, not least because it led to one of history's great military conflicts. With the end of this most recent cycle, the extremes are almost nonexistent to the casual observer. To our knowledge, no foreigners have been expelled from Japan of late (but foreigners or *gaijin* are almost certain to feel at least ambivalence and perhaps even animosity during their stays in the country).

Each of these fit and/or fight chapters in Japan's history represents a part of a renewal cycle. Japan would go from an effort to fit in with the rest of the world during the Gaming and Framing periods as they focused on the external environment. Then the national character would fall into a seemingly natural fight period as it became more inwardly focused in the Claiming and Taming parts of the Renewal Cycle. Over time, the severity of the cycles has been mitigated, and Japan seems to have increased its level of fit relative to fight. In Chapters 3 and 4, we'll explore how this philosophy developed, and what we can learn from it.

NOTES

1. Sterling Seagrave and Peggy Seagrave, *Yamato Dynasty*, New York: Broadway Books, 2001, p. 15.
2. Ishi Hiromitsu, "The Role of Government in the Postwar Growth Process of Japan," *Journal of Asian Economics*. Vol. 10, Issue 1, Spring 1999.

CHAPTER 3

Bushido: A Cultural History

To understand Japanese attitudes and behaviors around change, we need to understand Japanese history. To understand Japanese history, it is important to understand the notion of *bushido*, or the Way of the Samurai. Over the centuries, myriad philosophies, religious beliefs, and political doctrines have influenced Japanese culture, but the most important and distinct underpinning of Japanese business culture remains the influence of bushido. Why? Because it wraps many of the relevant beliefs, mores, and standards of Japanese history into one neat package of prescribed and proscribed behaviors and attitudes.

One might ask, "How can you capture the important elements of any national culture by looking at one small segment of the social environment?" Good question. But for years, scientists have found that the right cultural sliver can be essential to explaining enormous cultural changes. Max Weber, certainly a founding father of sociology, looked at Calvinism to explain the advent of capitalism. Karl Marx thought that the system of land enclosures (fences) was at the root of world-changing revolutions. We suggest (and we think you'll find the evidence convincing) that the methods and mindsets of bushido serve as a baseline for Japanese behaviors and attitudes around change, renewal, and even success.

(WE CAN BE) HEROES

In a survey of Japanese and Americans in the summer of 2004, over 1,000 respondents in each country were asked to name (in a free-form open response—we didn't give them any names to choose from) their number one and number two heroes, and then to classify them into 17 categories.

The results are telling. They show not only how different the two cultures are but they also show that *bushido* is central to any model of change or renewal in Japanese culture.

Table 3-1 shows a lot of similarities between Americans and Japanese. Respondents from both cultures put a combination of their parents and other family members (usually spouses and grandparents) at or near the top of their hero lists. And many of the other categories (scientists, entertainment personalities, athletes) show similar percentage patterns between the two cultures.

But the differences are astonishing. The single largest category is completely different in both the Japanese and the American culture. For Americans, the most likely type of person to be named as a hero is a government or political leader. For the Japanese, it is a military leader or a warlord.

The Japanese survey literally used the word *warlord*. In the United States, to get across the same basic feeling, the term had to be translated as *military leader*. This translation itself gives us a clue to the differences

TABLE 3–1

CATEGORIZATION OF HEROES IN JAPAN AND THE UNITED STATES

HERO TYPE	UNITED STATES	JAPAN
	(Percent responding among top two choices)	
Head of state and/or government figure	54	17
Father	23	22
Religious figure	21	4
Other	20	44
Mother	16	11
Other family member	13	4
Teacher	9	2
Entertainer	8	9
Inventor/Scientist	7	8
Entrepreneur	7	11
Warlord	7	28
Athlete/Sports figure	5	16
Company leader/Manager	4	11
Author/Poet	3	5
Artist	2	4
Architect/Engineer	1	2
Coworker	1	1

between the cultures. The only way to evoke the same positive, legitimate meaning and emotion that a Japanese feels on hearing the word *warlord* is to transform it into *military leader* in English. If the English-language survey had actually employed the term *warlord*, our guess is that about two Americans would have chosen this as their hero category. In other words, just the words themselves suggest a very different mindset in the two cultures. But the number of people choosing heroes from these categories shows it pretty clearly: Americans want to be like (or at least revere and emulate) government leaders; Japanese want to be like their military leaders.

Many Americans revere the military. But even they seem to admire politicians more. In terms of presidents, our iconic hero is a mere PT-boat commander, John Kennedy, not Supreme Commander Dwight Eisenhower. Americans truly loved Ronald Reagan, who often fought a rhetorical war against communism yet never saw combat himself. They feel much less emotion about George H. W. Bush, who not only was shot down in a fighter plane over the Pacific Ocean at age 18, but also launched a full-scale, clearly successful war in the Middle East against an enemy with real troops, tanks, and ground-to-air missiles. Meanwhile, very few Japanese put recent prime ministers high on their lists—perhaps no surprise since Japanese PMs were only in office an average of 21 months between 1885 and 2001. Instead, it is the ancient samurai leaders of yesteryear who still command the most respect from the Japanese.

You can even see these preferences in the way the two cultures define their heroes. In Figure 3-1 and Table 3-2 on next page, you can see there is definite overlap in the lists of what are classified as warlords and government leaders between the two countries. George Washington, who was in reality much more a military man than a politician, is categorized by Americans as a government leader, not a military leader. Meanwhile, in reality, many of the Japanese warlords were politicians more than they were military heroes. Each culture perceives and prefers its own particular style of leadership and this shows through in the data.

How did these heroes occupy these positions in our minds? Mostly, because we were impressed by the stories we were taught in adolescence, when we were learning about important historical figures. This search for a hero to call our own continues through adulthood, and while it begins in the family, it often turns to popular culture and history, as evidenced by our survey results. When we heard or read about these figures in school, we naturally searched for prototypical figures we could emulate. In adulthood, this "hero quest" guides our choices for whom we love, where we work, and how we deal with change.

Perhaps the Japanese look to old military heroes because their current business and political leaders are so stereotypically political in their

FIGURE 3-1

Comparison of government figures and warlords.

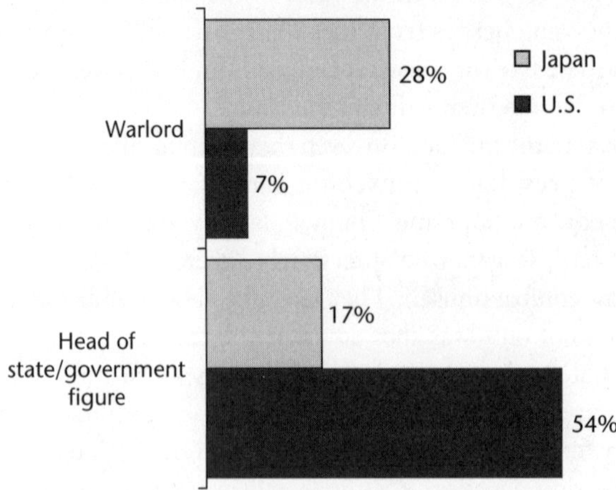

TABLE 3-2

POPULAR GOVERNMENT FIGURES AND WARLORDS
(in order of popularity per country)

U.S. GOVERNMENT LEADERS	JAPANESE WARLORDS
Abraham Lincoln	Hideyoshi Toyotomi
Ronald Reagan	Ieyasu Tokugawa
John F. Kennedy	Komei Shokatsuryo
George Washington	Nobunaga Oda
William Clinton	Ryoma Sakamoto
Thomas Jefferson	Shingen Takeda

decision-making processes. They are known for being slow and plodding, for working to get others to agree with them in their efforts to change. They are the consummate diplomats of corporate and political change. The unbridled individualism found in the image of the samurai chief sitting atop his steed in a field of battle surrounded by tens of thousands of completely loyal samurai—warriors who would without question give their own lives at a command from their leader—is infinitely more appealing. For the modern Japanese "salaryman," lost in the middle of a dense corporate bureaucracy, the powerful shogun is a compelling image.

The warlord-as-hero is still part of the mindset of people in Japan today. And the Way of the Samurai has always played a major role in the way renewal takes place in this society. We think it will continue to be a unique influence on Japan as that society's process of change and renewal continues.

Whence the Samurai?

But a question remains—where did the samurai come from? Why are they so heroic in the minds of our modern Japanese survey respondents? How did they rise to the top of the social order to have such a lasting influence on how a society sees itself and its ideals?

Warriors in ancient Japan were a lot like warriors in feudal societies everywhere else in the world. These were basically farmers and peasants who were hired out to (or were forced into service of) local lords who wanted to defend their lands. They needed an army to do that. And, of course, the bigger the army, the more likely they were to win. By some estimates, as many as one-third of first-millennium Japanese men were serving in the militia of some regional lord. Somewhere along the way, the warriors began to become role models, legends, and heroes in inspirational stories, much like their Roman legion counterparts half a world away.

The final clear signal that these warriors had been accepted in Japan was when the Chinese term *bushi* (meaning "man of arms") began to be applied to a certain type of career warrior. Calling anything by a Chinese word in Heian Japan (ninth- to twelfth-century Japan) was a little like attaching a French word to something in the English world; it makes it so much more elegant. To an English speaker, even snails seem highbrow when they are called by their French name. So conscripts had definitely achieved status when they became *bushi*.

But even as the general category of *bushi* was becoming fashionable, a new, supercharged class of defenders was emerging from among the ranks of Imperial servants. The general name for servants of the emperor was *saburo-bito*. But those who were specifically assigned to guard the Kyoto palaces and who carried swords came to be known by a mutation of their generic title, *saburai*. (Just for ease of pronunciation the "b" in saburai switched to an "m" sometime in the sixteenth or seventeenth century.) Even though it was probably these "imperial" beginnings of the samurai that gave them their important and revered status in Japan, their status was certainly enhanced when they usurped real power from the emperor in the twelfth century, subjugating him (and his royal offspring) under their rule.

For almost 700 years—from 1192 until 1868—the *bushi*, or samurai, were the ruling class of Japan. Yet even within this class, there were struggles. Many early samurai aspired to achieve the title of shogun, a title originally given by the emperor to the military governor of Eastern Japan, but that later came to mean ultimate military ruler of the nation. In an effort to assure as much legitimacy as possible for the samurai rulers, those who received the title of shogun cleverly married their children into the traditional "royal" lines. In fact, most of the early samurai chieftains were connected to the three noble families of the Fujiwara, Taira, and Minamoto clans. This careful nurturing of royal bloodlines continued among the very elite in Japan into the twentieth century. By the early nineteenth century, for instance, most Japanese outside Kyoto didn't even know that an emperor existed. The royal lineages were more associated with military might than with imperial heritage.

During the first half of the second millennium (the Kamakura, Muromachi, and Sengoku eras in Japan), military power, not political maneuvering, really determined status. But after the sixteenth century and up to the Meiji Restoration in 1868 (during the Tokugawa family reign as shogun), heritage began to play a much larger role than military skill. Edo and even the outlying fiefs became "court societies," much like those found in Europe at a similar time in history. The Tokugawa *bushi* have been compared to the courtiers of King Louis XIV in France. Political machinations, not blatant blood-letting, were the power tools of the day. But there is one huge difference—the French were known as effete, artistic aristocrats, while the samurai were supposedly fierce sword-wielding warriors. But in reality, most samurai never wielded a sword in anything more than a show of bravado. The way of the samurai in modern fiction and movies is probably just a caricature of the real way that samurai lived and worked after the Tokugawa shogunate was established. It is the same idealization that has happened in America with the cowboy or the romanticized view of the antebellum South.

What Did Samurai Do?

Apart from any kind of idealization, we can be sure of a few things about the samurai. We can be sure that they did exist.

There were never many of them—they only made up about 6 to 8 percent of the total population at the end of the Tokugawa period—but they were definitely there. And because they had very high status in society, the *bushi* influenced the country inordinately.

We know that they saw their role as protectors of the *daimyo* (feudal baron), the lord's other retainers, their lord's estates, and the peasants who lived and worked in these estates.

We know that they were at the top of the social hierarchy. Confucian beliefs placed scholars and bureaucrats at the top of China's four-level status system, followed by farmers, artisans, and finally merchants. Japan's status system was the same, with the exception of the samurai, who were placed in the top category. It was the samurai who imported and promoted *shinokosho*, the name for the hierarchy in which each syllable represents one of the four classes (you'll recognize the first syllable "shi" as the same as the second syllable of *bu*shi)—in the proper order, of course.

But as members of the top category of *shinokosho*, the samurai also seem to have taken a special pride in watching out for the less powerful. A very paternalistic society emerged that still exists to this day. The samurai were like modern-day police and firefighters. Every day, their duty required that they put themselves in harm's way, protecting other people's bodies with their own.

It is very little wonder that an ethic developed around this job similar to the ethic that develops around most military or public safety professionals: an ethic that says that it is good, even noble, to lose one's life in discharging his duty. The natural contradiction in this kind of job is difficult for people to understand who are not in (or close to someone in) a "protector profession." If you have had a spouse who is a member of the police force or a son or daughter who has gone off to war, you know the question that is always in the back of your mind: "Why should I or my loved ones lose their lives just to protect the life of another?" If the math is right ("My sacrifice will save the lives of hundreds of people"), the dilemma is less profound. But too often the protector is simply trading one life for another (like the firefighter who dies trying to get to that last person trapped in the building). This basic life-and-death tradeoff is the most fundamental of all the dilemmas and contradictions with which the samurai struggled.

There were more concrete dilemmas as well. The samurai were originally and vitally "change agents" themselves...or they were busy defending against change agents. They were warriors hired to expand the lord's territory or tasked with keeping the territory intact. This notion may be at the heart of the quandary many modern Japanese face every day. In their culture today, the Japanese feel a pull to "stay the course," to just sit quietly, to passively resist change. After all, postwar Japan has been a wildly successful economic success. Why change anything? On the other hand, those at higher status levels in Japan must realize that historically it has been up to them to change the society. In this society, no one else is capable of being a force for renewal.

The Way of the Samurai

There is no evidence that the samurai had any particular philosophy or belief system when they first began to appear as a class of warriors. But dilemmas such as those mentioned above demanded that a set of values be institutionalized to help the average samurai cope with the incongruity. And as with most warrior societies throughout history, the *bushi* needed a code for warfare itself: When is it right to kill? When is it wrong? What circumstances require undying loyalty? Which demand perfidy? Even though the *bushi* were half a world away from the medieval knights of Europe (and had no communication with them), the *bushi* codes resemble those of the Knights of the Round Table. And over time these codes expanded from codes of war to a worldview of beliefs and acceptable behaviors by which the *bushi* were to live. As the samurai became less warriorlike and more like courtiers, these rules came to be increasingly important and the warriors more rule-bound.

The samurai code was known as *bushido*—literally, the Way of the Warrior—and it created an environment for change that allowed for those natural dilemmas. As it turned out, bushido is tenacious yet flexible, resilient yet malleable. And it came to be the basic set of rules governing Japanese society. It should be little wonder then that the Samurai Way stands, to this day, as the bedrock philosophy of Japan. And as we'll detail in the next chapter, bushido has its place—even 150 years after the samurai were decreed out of existence—as the cornerstone of Japanese business method and mindset.

Natural Dilemmas

One of the more important facts about bushido is that it is a philosophy of dilemmas and maybe even contradictions. Japan is certainly not the only place in the world to have contradictions and dilemmas at the heart of its political governance process. In most societies, there has always been a tension between warriors and diplomats, the doers and thinkers, the liberals and the conservatives, good and evil. These contradictions form the basis of philosophies, practices, and laws that govern every society on earth. And it is arguable that the contradictions that came about in Japanese philosophy really were intended to make the believer or practitioner of this way of thinking well-rounded and responsive (in a variety of ways) to the world around him.

So much of Eastern philosophy is all about a holistic approach to the world, but this way of thinking seems divisive in its nature. Or does it? It is meant to be an all-encompassing way of thinking and doing. And any whole-life philosophy has to deal with a wide variety of human experiences, some of which inevitably seem to oppose one another. So the belief system has to offer ways of dealing with all of these disparate experiences. Bushido evolved from the religions, philosophies, and native beliefs of the Japanese people. Medieval Japanese had a strong belief in *Yamato Damashii*; many of them were Confucian, some were Buddhist, most worshipped the Shinto gods. Bushido combined elements of each of these, making it easier for the samurai to maintain that paternalistic role.

Yamato Damashii

There are two key philosophical issues that have remained consistent in some form or another from the old Japan. One is the notion of a Japanese spirit. The other is that the Japanese are unique. These two things are related. The Japanese perceive themselves to be unique because they possess this Japanese spirit.

The original, native name for the islands of Japan was Yamato. The ancient and self-defining spirit of the Japanese is known as *yamato damashii* (*damashii*, not surprisingly, means "spirit"). It was a code of valor and a poetics of life. And importantly, this code had both an inherent military heroic quality and an esthetic, moral purpose. This combination of valor and poetics may be the foundation of dilemmas that appear in Japanese thought and action throughout history.

No discussion of the Japanese mindset can afford to minimize the whole notion of Japanese uniqueness. This belief extends so far that, over the years, well-respected Japanese scholars have argued that the Japanese brain is different from the brain of people in any other country.[1] In fact for years, drugs tested on non-Japanese patients were not approved for use in Japan because the government argued that the Japanese body was completely different—the Japanese intestines and stomach worked differently.[2]

This sense of uniqueness is at the center of how Japan deals with the rest of the world. If you've grown up believing you are unique—not just in personality, but physically unique as almost a separate species on the earth—the more you will fight changes imposed by the outside world. This belief has helped the Japanese to master the art of "differentiation" better than most other cultures, at least in the past few decades. Through differentiation, the Japanese keep the notion alive that their products are worth more because there can be literally nothing else like them on the planet.

Three Isms: Shintoism, Confucianism, Buddhism

Another important aspect of Japanese philosophy is what we might call the "three isms." These are important because they arise from the uniqueness that blooms when Japanese native culture cross-pollinates with other cultures.

Shintoism sprang directly from the same wells of belief as *yamato damashii*. The Japanese "spirit" is a spirit—like the Catholic notion of a Holy Spirit—that dwells in the country of Japan, in the Japanese people, and yet seems almost to have its own persona. Every living thing in Japan has its own spirit. And when these things die, the spirit carries on. So Japan is a very small island packed tight with spirits of all kinds of animals, plants, and people, both living and dead.

In some respects, China was the original source of the uniqueness of Japan. Japan's early embrace of Confucianism allowed Japan to incorporate a "foreign" philosophy into their view of self. In embracing Confucianism, they made it their own, but it remained something a little separate. Along with Confucianism came another cultural import from China, but one much more religious in nature: Buddhism. This is, obviously, an Indian import, but it made its way to Japan through China, so there is much more of a Chinese bent to the Buddhist religion found today in Japan.

Confucianism and Buddhism from China were incorporated into Japan's native Shintoism to form an interesting religious mix in the country. This notion of keeping a cross-pollinated uniqueness is completely different from how the outside world has resolved cultural tensions. Japan accepted and incorporated nonnative philosophy and thinking, but then developed them into a philosophy that was quintessentially Japanese. In the West, we have fought war after Holy War to keep new ideas out.

BUSHIDO AND CHANGE

All this talk of religious and philosophical belief in Japan has a point. Through the passing of centuries, the samurai had a unique ability to adopt, merge, and incorporate ideas that at first blush would seem inconsistent and even contradictory. This came to be the Way or the "code" during the Sengoku (Warring States) period—a time of constant war punctuated by short bursts of peace. In the war times, a set of techniques and methods were needed for how to wield the sword, how to win the battle. But this was not enough; a higher-order mindset was also needed to allow some semblance of peace and level-headedness in the middle of a heated battle. But during the short periods of peace, this same code or worldview would have to encourage the proper behavior of the samurai as law-abiding (and law-enforcing) members of a stable society.

Even though Japanese society underwent very rapid spins through the Renewal Cycle we introduced in the last chapter, the samurai withstood it each time to remain on top. During a single lifetime, a samurai was sure to see cycle after cycle of crisis, change, stabilization, and then steadiness for awhile before another crisis and then still more change. Bushido survived—and was in fact strengthened—because it became a philosophy that appealed to both the warrior mind in the middle of a campaign and the civic leader in the months or even years of peace between battles.

CONCLUSION

Human beings seem particularly open to religious and meta-level philosophies at moments when their world is full of change; it helps us deal with issues that seem to be beyond our control. The mindset of bushido served this purpose, giving everyone, in every station in feudal Japan, both a reason to die and a reason to live. The dilemmas in the code were purposeful. They allowed the same bushido to guide people in peace and in war. It became the Way of the sword *and* the Way of the pen. The samurai at the top of the social order became the purveyors of these ideas to the rest of society. From their position at the top, the samurai ideas incorporated into bushido trickled down naturally to the rest of the Japanese people. The most basic tension of bushido is at the heart of much of the philosophy's strength. The poet versus warrior contradiction is built into the Japanese spirit. In fact, it may be essential. The samurai were literally the only people in Japanese society who could wield both sword and pen.

As we mentioned, change cycles are usually characterized by an inflection point—a crisis, a lot of change, a process of stabilization, then finally stability itself before the whole process repeats itself. Because samurai were enabled to drive change, the society did not suffer because of change cycles. In fact, society prospered under their leadership—Japan was for the first time unified, peaceful, and relatively free from outside influences. This holistic yet contradictory method and mindset helped keep the peace for 250 years. In doing so, bushido set itself up as the bedrock philosophy of Japan that still exists today. Just look at their heroes.

NOTES

1. Tadanobu Tsunoda, *Nihonjin no Nou—Nou no Hataraki to Touzai no Bunka* (Translated: "Brains of Japanese—Brain functions and culture of East & West), Daishukan Shoten, 1978.
2. Yomiuri Shimbun, "A wall against new drug approval. Global standard does not apply in Japan," October 21, 2003, http://www.yomiuri.co.jp/iryou/ansin/an3a2101.htm.

CHAPTER 4

BUSINESSMEN AND BUSHI

For centuries, samurai occupied the highest social rung in Japan. At the opposite end of the social spectrum were the lowly merchants, who didn't produce anything, didn't defend anything, merely made their living off the efforts of others. In fact, samurai and merchants in Japan were like Brahmin and Outcasts in India—inhabiting separate co-existing worlds that rarely mingled. But this is a book about business...how could the Way of the Samurai possibly have come to be the Way of the Manager?

BORED IN EDO

The beginnings of the mixing and transference of these social classes started way back during the Tokugawa period, when the Confucian hierarchy was still the absolute ruler of the day. The Tokugawa shogun required that the daimyo, the feudal lords whom the samurai served, had to spend every other year in Tokyo (then known as Edo). They were allowed to go back to their provinces in the alternating years, but there was a hitch. They had to leave their families in Edo all the time. This control-by-hostage necessitated that the daimyo maintain the requisite retinue of servants and samurai security forces in Edo. And over time, many samurai preferred Edo to their backwoods hometowns.

The problem with all these samurai in Edo was that there was really not much to do. The samurai were required to put in just two half days of work a week at the shogun's castle and on the grounds. Uprisings were few and far between, so it wasn't as if they had to protect anyone from the angry masses of commoners in Edo. And since half of the city's residents were samurai, basically, the samurai in Edo were merely protecting each other from each other, rather than from some external invading force.

Erstwhile Warriors

Samurai did enjoy some privileges granted only to them and no one else. Almost everyone in Japanese feudal society could carry a sword, but only the samurai were allowed to carry two swords—a long sword and a short one. And the samurai had the right to cut down anyone in the streets for any reason. This was a practice known as *kirisute gomen* (literally "permission to cut and throw away"). Certainly this was a dramatic privilege, but in the entire, quite extensive written history of Japan there are only a handful of examples of this "permission" being put into practice.[1] And apart from these limited sword-related privileges of being born into a samurai family, there was not much about the average life of a samurai that had much to do with military behavior.

Our modern interpretation of the Tokugawa and earlier samurai is driven by a glorified image of the warrior class that grew out of a revisionist and idealized view of this era. These fictional samurai, as we have learned to know and love them in movies, literature, and other writings, are really a lot more like the samurai of the Warring States Period of Japan. But after the early 1600s, when the Tokugawa Bakufu consolidated power, true warriors found themselves out of jobs. After the shogun quelled the rebellions and declared unified power over Japan, the need for warriors all but disappeared. Sure, the shogun needed men to keep the peace, but thousands of others were simply out of their steady jobs—one of the earliest known examples of corporate downsizing.

Artists of the Highest Order

One of the ways the samurai passed time was with the arts—painting, writing, drama. These are not very warriorlike pastimes, but all of these arts flourished in samurai-dominated Edo. By 1800 there were 120 haiku poetry circles, over 500 bookstores, and varieties of publishing houses. Eighty-five percent of Edo residents were able to read, and the Japanese readers looked for thrilling, exciting novels and stories.[2] Many of the novels that were published in nineteenth-century Japan were swashbuckling adventures of samurai.

It was during this period that Kabuki became a popular diversion. *Chushingura* or *The Revenge of the 47 Ronin* was one of the best attended and most profitable plays of that time. Samurai who had never unsheathed a sword in defense *or* offense thronged to the Kabuki stage to watch a tale that let them vicariously carry out their warrior callings. But this story, unlike other tales, did something more for them, which was probably the reason it became so popular. *Chushigura* convinced the samurai that swordplay was not all that defined the samurai; loyalty was a central trait as well. They left the theater feeling that even if they never were involved in a military campaign in their lives, if they were loyal, then they were true warriors. No wonder *Chushigura* was a hit in Edo; even the lowliest *bushi* could "do loyalty."

Slumming with the Merchants

With all of this extra time on their hands, samurai ended up mingling a lot with merchants. Merchants ran the geisha houses; merchants sold the tea and ran the noodle stands; merchants sold the books and staged plays. And merchants got rich. Some got richer—much richer—than the samurai. And in a tight-knit community such as Edo, the cognitive dissonance between low-status but wealthy merchants and government-stipend samurai must have created some serious tension. Merchants could wear better clothes and live in nicer places, but samurai ranked higher and had lots of extra time. Merchants got rich on that boredom. The merchants couldn't be closed down—they were too important to the stability of the society. So the samurai figured out ways to tap into the wealth of the merchants—either by trading their annual rice offering from their daimyo or borrowing money against their future stipends.

During this entire Edo period, it became increasingly less important to really do warriorlike things, and, as a result, the class system started to blur. That change became clear when Tokugawa Tsuneyoshi was named the Fifth Shogun of the peaceful Tokugawa period. Tsuneyoshi was not trained as a warrior, but as a scholar. He wasn't supposed to be shogun, but some unexpected deaths in the royal line resulted in his ascension to the top military position in the country. Ironically, then, Japan ended up with a shogun who couldn't even win a sword fight—perhaps the ultimate statement of the lack of usefulness for a powerful warrior class during this era.

ENTER MEIJI, EXIT SAMURAI

The catalytic event that brought this peaceful society to an end is marked in most history books by the arrival of American Admiral Perry's Black

Ships in Yokohama harbor in 1853. At that time, America was particularly dependent on whale oil and was therefore most interested in whaling in Japan's waters. Perry's fighting steamships could put any Japanese vessel of that time to shame. Perry demanded that Japan open herself to trade with the outside world. He promised to return in a year's time—either to fight or to trade. The almost bankrupt and greatly outgunned shogunate bowed to the American demands. A year later when Perry returned with nine ships and great pomp and circumstance, a treaty was signed that opened Japanese ports to trade. In all the Renewal Cycles of Japanese history, this was one of the most catalytic of events. It forced all Japanese to confront the outside world. Two centuries of isolation were over.

With this Black Ships event, Japan was forced into the Gaming phase of the Renewal Cycle. In business, Square 2 (or Gaming) is a time when organizations make very few actual changes but rather turn their attentions to the changing external world. Organizations in this quadrant should ask questions like: "What does this new world look like?" "What are the things that we are going to have to change to succeed in this new environment?" "What will our future be?" These are exactly the questions that the Japanese hadn't needed to ask for almost 10 generations. Not only were these questions new; there was no memory in the country of anyone ever having to ask them before—much less how to answer them.

And, as it turns out, they took plenty of time for asking and answering before they turned to framing their new strategy. Perry's ships first showed up in 1853, but it wasn't until 1868 that the new strategy became clear and the country was ready to begin claiming its new future. What happened in those years is a perfect example of how Japanese can change almost everything around them, while keeping the heart of things the same.

SAIGO'S LAST STAND

When the status quo is disrupted in any society, everyone begins to look for ways that they can take advantage of the new emerging world order. This period in Japan was no different. One of the key political power brokers of this time was the samurai Saigo Takamori from what is now known as Kagoshima prefecture. He believed strongly that the emperor should be returned to power and that such a move would only strengthen the power and the dominance of the samurai. Saigo succeeded in his goal—at first. He and his supporters overturned the Tokugawa shogunate, giving power back to the emperor who had for centuries been peripheral to Japanese government and politics. Thus began the Meiji era, as Saigo was put in charge of the military affairs of the nation.

Despite his success, his plan for invading Korea was shelved and advisors to the emperor ended up abolishing the rank of samurai altogether. Saigo left the Imperial Palace in a huff and returned to his native Kagoshima. Deep down, he knew Tokyo was no place for a samurai. In Tokyo, the now-out-of-fashion samurai found themselves the butt of jokes. In a society that revered modernization, samurai customs and practices were considered throwbacks to a feudal era. Most samurai went to extra effort to make sure that they didn't appear to be samurai—they dressed in western clothes and talked about business, economic development, technology, and education. They learned English and German. Those who did continue to dress in kimonos and sport the shaved heads and the braid of hair on the back of their heads were ridiculed, bullied, even jailed.

But in Kagoshima, deep in the south of Japan and about as far away as you can get from Tokyo, Saigo made every possible effort to preserve a samurai society. The community he fostered revered the emperor, but still relied on the principles and beliefs of feudal Japan. He believed a strong Japan could resist the corrupting influences of the West.

But for all of Saigo's efforts to preserve the samurai heritage of Japan, he was actually responsible for the final downfall of the *bushi*. Even though there was an official pronouncement that samurai were no longer important, many parts of Japan still respected the tradition. There was even a good chance a quasi-samurai class might have survived in one form or another. But in 1876, Saigo, with an army of well-trained samurai, launched an offensive against the peasant armies of the emperor. The war raged for about six months. Some 12,000 lives were lost. In the end, the peasants wiped out the samurai. Imperial Japan had been buying modern weaponry from the West for a couple of decades. The sword-master samurai were simply no match for peasants armed with rifles, Gatling guns, and cannons. When the war was over, Saigo committed ritual suicide at the tomb of his master, ending not only his life but also the Samurai era.

POST-SAMURAI BUSHIDO

The question remains: if the Samurai were abolished in the 1870s, why do we think they have so much to teach us? And why are modern Japanese still ranking them so highly on the hero survey?

These are good questions. And we think there are good answers. Obviously, from the hero survey, modern Japanese actually still do revere these historical figures. Part of that reverence comes from Japanese honor for ancestors and today's popularity of reverential novels and movies about samurai. But a more important reason for the primary role that samurai play in the Japanese hero psyche is that the samurai never really went away. They weren't called samurai anymore, but they all stayed in the most important economic and political positions in the country. So did their children, and their children's children. Members of this class were never called samurai again...but they were still in charge.

EARLY CONNECTIONS

Some of that merging of business and samurai began back in the Tokugawa period. There was always a significant percentage of the samurai during the Edo period who were not attached to any particular fief or daimyo. These were known as *ronin* or masterless samurai—dismissed from their posts or left on their own because they were tired of their rather mundane assignments and wanted to find a life with more adventure. In most cases, *ronin* returned to the life of a fief samurai at some point in their lives. But in a few instances, these samurai abandoned their second sword and took on the lives of merchants. Motonari Mori and Nariaki Ikeda were two prominent samurai who became successful businessmen in Edo. Forced to relinquish their samurai status, they both used their influence to become bank presidents, and later, prominent figures in government. By the end of the Tokugawa era, it was already difficult to tell which businesses were samurai and which were from the merchant class.

The period in the Meiji era immediately following the outlawing of the samurai most clearly shows the blurring of samurai and merchant lines. Companies like Yasuda Insurance and Sumitomo Bank got their start during this period—and they did it primarily with samurai ownership, management, and workers. The Meiji period was a time of tremendous entrepreneurialism where everything was turned upside down. The shogun didn't matter any more (in fact, a shogun didn't even exist), an emperor virtually unknown outside of Kyoto was suddenly in charge, Western ideas were all important, and new technologies were everywhere. It must have been a very strange period to live through, much like East Germany in the years after the fall of the Berlin Wall and the reunification with the West. But East Germany was catching up with about 20 years' worth of technological deficit with the West. Japan had been cut off for 250 years.

Even though everything was topsy-turvy, old habits are hard to change—especially since the Meiji Restoration was in many ways so well orchestrated. On the surface, things had changed greatly, especially for mid-level samurai. But for the high-ranking samurai, it was business as usual. In fact, some have suggested the switch from shogun to emperor was no more than a boardroom coup.[3] The emperor was seen by the populace as "god on earth" and the supreme leader of the country. But, in practice, there is much evidence suggesting he remained mostly powerless in the new Japan, subject to the former samurai who had plotted the shogun's demise. And the *bushi*, while gone in name, were never gone in spirit.

The primary difference was that Japan was now open to the West, and was no longer looking to its own history or culture to explain the world. The nation that had seen nothing but itself for over two centuries now looked outside. In that process, during the last 30 years of the nineteenth century, references to bushido all but disappeared. Every cultural aspect of the old era was reviled. But bushido was a lot like wide neckties in U.S. culture—gone for 30 years, then back with a vengeance. Bushido managed to make a nostalgic retro reentrance in Japan at the turn of the twentieth century. But this time it would be reintroduced from the West.

MODERN BUSHIDO

The basic treatise on the subject of the Samurai Way (the one that forms the basis of many of our popular beliefs about samurai today) is a book called *Bushido: The Soul of the Japan*, published in 1899. According to an article by Japanese historian G. Cameron Hurst III, *Bushido*'s author, Nitobe Inazo, was more American than he was Japanese. A devout Christian, Nitobe had been educated mostly in the English language in missionary schools in Japan.[4] Nitobe's book was first published in English, and caught the eye of President Teddy Roosevelt who bought dozens of copies of the book before it was ever translated into Japanese. Roosevelt gave the book to friends and praised it as a great way to learn about Japan. Once the book *Bushido* made it to Japan, it was immediately embraced. A big part of its popularity was that it followed so closely on the heels of Japanese military victories in China and Russia. But Nitobe's bushido was almost more religion than it was military code. It emphasized the virtues of loyalty, honor, and chivalry. In fact, Nitobe's text is rife with comparisons to European knights.

For any Japanese entrepreneur of the late nineteenth or early twentieth centuries, there was still a bushido influence in the not-so-distant past. In the case of samurai-turned-entrepreneurs, it was the bushido they and their fathers learned and applied to a business career in Meiji Japan. But for the businesspeople of the early twentieth century, it was the bushido found in Nitobe's book. These entrepreneurs created very competitive companies in the nineteenth century and in the first half of the twentieth century. They achieved all this entrepreneurial activity from a mindset that drew on a tradition of samurai behaviors and successes.

But no matter how successful these bushido-influenced businesses were in the Meiji and Taisho eras, they became less so in the 1930s. Japan was well on its way to trying to fit into the rest of the world when they were overwhelmed by world issues. Not just the Great Depression, but an entire range of issues—the rise of tariffs in certain industries during World War I, for example—that really catered to the fight mentality. Japan also faced a fear of not having enough resources on hand to care for its expanding population. These changes in the economic environment brought out the "fight" in Japan, as the world would soon discover.

WORLD WAR II

It is not surprising that Japan launched itself so aggressively into World War II. After relatively easy wins in battles in China and Russia, it was probably tough for anyone in the early Showa imperial government to come up with a really good reason why Japan should not be expanding its sphere of influence by military means. The West condensed the explanation for World War II to something ineffable: those samurai Japanese with their warriorlike tendencies just couldn't help but fight. But forgotten was the fact that these samurai hadn't gone to war for three centuries, and they were not as predisposed to war as Americans had been during their relatively brief history. In the 1870s Japan chose not to go to war with the Koreans at about the same time the United States was engaging in an empire-building action in the Philippines. The early twentieth-century Japanese strategy—to forcibly expand their territory and create a "Greater Asian Co-Prosperity Sphere" from Manchuria at the north to Indonesia in the south—was a pretty logical outgrowth of turn-of-the-century Japanese military success. The logic was simple: "It has worked well so far, so why don't we just keep going?"

In all of the buildup to World War II, the concept of the samurai spirit was used by the military commanders both as a rationale for the war and as a way to develop and maintain morale. For the agenda of generals and admirals who needed young Japanese to be willing to die for a rather unclear cause, Nitobe's religionlike version of bushido was a perfect fit. Japan's war commanders adapted bushido into a code that demanded self-sacrifice, courage, devotion, and obedience. They instituted some of the harshest codes for disobedience of any modern army, even for the slightest infractions. Defeat in combat became unacceptable—it was either victory or a glorious death, sometimes achieved by launching hundreds of soldiers into doomed banzai charges against overwhelming firepower. Perhaps most famous among these tactics were the kamikaze methods employed toward the end of the war as Japan struggled to confront the encroaching Allied fleet.

Successful businesses during this period had to buy into this particular definition of bushido. With military actions commanding the attention of the populace and dominating the economic life of the country, there was almost no consumer markets in Japan. All buying and selling were in service of the war, and companies with close family ties to military leaders, such as Nissan, thrived during this period. All superfluous production was eventually suspended in the face of the war machine; textile manufacturing gave way to heavy industry. In 1943, Japan adopted the Military Needs Company Act, which placed companies in certain key industries under government control. Near the end of the war, steel was literally stripped out of houses and other buildings to make more airplanes. Japan tried to extract additional resources from its conquered lands across Asia and the Pacific, but eventually found its basis for production cut off or destroyed.

CONCLUSION

The samurai spirit that dominated Japan during this period was first and foremost directed at military activity. Yet all of that military might was always in the service of economic gain. As soon as the military secured a new territory, such as Manchuria, Japanese companies would flood into the territory to take advantage of the natural and human resources in an effort to enrich the Japanese empire. The distinction between generals and corporate presidents was completely blurred. Military authorities managed mines, heavy equipment manufacturing, and farming tracts all over Asia. These twentieth-century samurai were warrior-merchants. The distinction between the top and bottom classes of feudal Japanese hierarchy had been totally obliterated.

From the Tokugawa era to the Meiji Restoration to the Expansionist era, the ethic of bushido survived and was adapted as Japan went through cycle after cycle. The samurai became rice traders, debtors, bureaucrats, then reinvented themselves as modern warriors carrying the glory of Japanese corporatism across the Eastern Hemisphere. In this process, the evolution of bushido set the stage for Japan's postwar economic miracle. Japan still had its bushido, but the samurai spirit was on the verge of emerging in the service of an entirely new goal—one that would shape both the country's landscape in unimagined ways—in nonmilitary methods and ways of thinking that would dominate the global business world in the last half of the twentieth century.

NOTES

1. G. Cameron Hurst III, "Death, honor, and loyalty: The bushido ideal," *Philosophy East & West*, Vol. 40, Issue 4, October 1990.
2. "Japan: Memoirs of a Secret Empire," PBS documentary, May 2004.
3. Sterling Seagrave and Peggy Seagrave, *Yamato Dynasty*, New York: Broadway Books, 2001.
4. G. Cameron Hurst III, op. cit.

CHAPTER 5

Birth of the Modern Corporate Samurai

Not so very long ago, Japan experienced some of the most wrenching renewal any nation has ever faced. Over the course of 75 years, an empire had arisen out of a feudal nation. That empire conquered nearly a fifth of the globe. Then, in the space of just three years, from Japan's defeat at Midway to its surrender aboard the *USS Missouri*, the empire was gone. Given what had transpired, we might imagine that the revised bushido ethic was written out of Japan's collective memory. After all, it was this ethic that had driven the Japanese to establish dominance in the world. With the empire's defeat, it might have been thoroughly discredited. But it wasn't. The idea of bushido was battered, but not beaten. Though few could have imagined it at the time, bushido would be dusted off and used yet again—with another huge impact on world events.

FIGHTING FOR THE COMPANY

At the end of World War II, Japan was quite literally in ruins. American firebombing had destroyed over 2.25 million homes.[1] Starvation was common. Some local authorities were forced to "suggest that starvation could be avoided by eating mice, rats, moles, rose leaves, silkworm cocoons, and sawdust broken down into powder for use in dumplings and bread."[2] The catalytic event had certainly taken place—but so intensely that, for some years after the war, not a lot of Gaming activity took place. In fact, the primary goal of everyone in the country at the time was simply to survive.

During this period, most Japanese expected that their nation would become a U.S. territory, English would become the national language, and

Japan's identity would be subsumed into a new American reality. That set of expectations readied the Japanese for a complete change in their world view. But the expected change never happened. The emperor stayed in power; most of the military leaders in the war were never brought to trial; and those who were imprisoned for war crimes served relatively short jail terms. After their release, these imprisoned "warriors" were banned from becoming involved in government...so they immediately became the leaders of business enterprises. In effect, they simply took over new armies—ones composed, not of soldiers, but of salarymen.

As the Japanese began to see that their country would not change as much as they had expected, there was a strange and uncharacteristic fluttering between the Framing and Claiming stages of the Renewal Cycle. The Japanese were so eager to get on with their lives that they tried to simply choose a new strategy and start implementing it.

The labor union movement in Japan provides a great example. Labor unions had never been a part of Japanese history, but once the populace believed they should be democratic, a labor movement seemed like an obvious addition to their new world. Although unions were immediately established, no one really knew how they were supposed to work. There were lots of strikes and work stoppages, but it seemed that no one really knew to what end.

In essence, the Japanese had bypassed the more thoughtful, deliberate bushido approach to change—the one where the Gaming and Framing stages of the cycle received a tremendous amount of attention. Instead, Japanese society tried to move into Claiming without a carefully framed strategy, resulting in wasted time and energy while they attempted to sort things out.

It wasn't until the 1950s that the country settled into an effective postwar Renewal Cycle. The strategy of the new cycle was simple, almost elegant: rebuild the country. This was not a strategy of democratization or of equality of the classes, or any of the things that the American Occupation forces had been trying to instill in the Japanese nation. This was about rebuilding Japanese industry, homes, and lives. Similar to bushido, this approach wasn't simply pragmatic; it also carried deep meaning.

No doubt, this strategy got a powerful jump start from the Korean War. The United States stationed its troops in Japan and expected the Japanese to provide supplies, equipment, and provisions for the troops both there and in Korea. These large military contracts allowed Japanese companies to move rapidly into the implementation stage of the cycle (Claiming) yet at the same time never wavered from the strategic goal of rebuilding the country. In contrast to today's prevailing wisdom, the primary goal of these companies was not to take huge profits; most of their profits were plowed right back into the corporations. The goal was to learn, improve, and become a world power again. Japan did just that.

BUSHIDO IN TOYOTA AND SONY

Toyota and Sony are two of the most important corporate successes of post-war Japan. Toyota had always eschewed the government and avoided getting caught up with the military. In the late 1920s, the U.S. automobile business had reached a point where mass production was the norm, and competition among the Big Three was becoming stronger. So General Motors began moving to areas such as Japan, where the auto industry was just starting, and founded GM-Japan in 1927. Kiichiro Toyoda saw the auto industry growing in Japan and took advantage of an international business trip to visit auto manufacturing plants in the United States and Great Britain. The Toyoda family, based on Kiichiro's recommendation, decided to take its prowess in machine building for the textile industry and transfer it to automobile manufacturing. The Toyota motor division was established in 1934, and in 1935, the Toyota Model G1 truck went on the market.[3]

As a rule, Toyota followed the traditional way of the Japanese entrepreneur, and proceeded irrespective of what was going on around it. It's a bit of an irony, then, that it was in fact rescued as a company by the very forces it was trying to ignore. In the early 1950s, procurement orders from the U.S. military made all the difference. Yet the important truth remains: Toyota's success was not because of its close affiliation with the Japanese government, a great contrast to the success of Nissan. Toyota, without a known samurai in the family tree, succeeded because it transferred the bushido enthusiasm that inspired the fight through World War II into a corporate spirit and devotion to company, rather than to an emperor, government, or daimyo.

At Toyota, post–World War II uncertainty was transformed into a modern spirit of bushido that led it to become as efficient as possible, and to dominate the market.[4] Although Toyota's interest in the automobile began in the late 1920s, the Sony story didn't begin until immediately after the end of World War II. Sony was founded by Masaru Ibuka and Akio Morita. Ibuka came from a very distinguished samurai background. His grandfather was a prefectoral deputy governor and the Ibukas were prominent samurai of the Aizu fief,[5] paving the way for this dramatic adaptation of bushido to the corporate arena.

As the eldest son in the fifteenth generation of a family-owned sake and miso dynasty, Morita was unarguably merchant class, but he demonstrated a fair amount of modern samurai thinking as well. Morita had been drafted into the military in World War II. He didn't want to be in the navy, so he ended up as a technical officer working for the Naval Office of Aviation Technology as a radar operator.[6] It was in this capacity, as a member of a task force to build thermal-guidance weapons and night-vision gun sights, that he met Ibuka.

Serendipitously, he was going to his ancestral homeland on a military mission in August 1945 and asked for (and got) a day's leave to visit his family. He informed his commanding officer that if the war ended while he was on leave, he wasn't going to come back. Morita knew full well that when the war ended, his commanding officer was planning to commit suicide (with the expectation that the junior officers would do the same). Although he had been influenced by military discipline, Morita couldn't see giving his life for it, and took this opportunity, instead, to devote his life to innovation, profit, and growth all in the service of rebuilding the nation.

Morita was able to grow Sony into a company with over $70 billion in annual revenues with a continual emphasis on renewal. Sony strove to be continually on the cutting edge of technology, and even though they would occasionally make mistakes (BetaMax, for example), they could always be counted on to right the ship relatively quickly. We'll come back to both Sony and Toyota later in the book, and how they specifically implemented the lessons of bushido that we're about to discuss.

As we all know, however, companies don't just arise from bold visionaries alone. They require a group of men and women willing to put the company before everything and everyone. This group achieved mythical status in postwar Japan, but now may finally be undergoing a change—the omnipresent salaryman.

STRENGTH FROM CONTRASTS

The Salaryman and the Entrepreneur

The odd couple of the salaryman and the entrepreneur really defined the corporate model that emerged in Japan after World War II. The salaryman approach underpinned Japanese economic success in the 1960s, 1970s, and 1980s. This is certainly what was celebrated in the Western management literature that grew up around "Japan, Inc." The success of this model stems from a combination of relatively low salaries, very long work hours, and strong team and group orientation, along with a sublimation of traditional national purpose into moral purpose related to the business. The idea was "Instead of conquering China and serving the Emperor, we're rebuilding Japan and serving the Emperor." It was a very functional model in many respects, but also a model that led to a lot of misery. There was emptiness in the lives of the salarymen, strained family relationships, a very poor quality of life in other respects (the famous rabbit-hutch living arrangement), and too many deaths from exhaustion.

But in this same period, in this same environment of postwar Japan, right alongside the salaryman model, entrepreneurship was also on the rise. In fact, many successful entrepreneurial companies, including Honda, Sony, and Toyota, created their own versions of the salary model. It seems a strange hybrid. But in its strongest forms, this hybrid proved extraordinarily powerful. In the interplay between entrepreneurship and big salaryman-style corporations, the most exciting and successful Japanese companies are not the Mitsubishi Shoji (the trading arm of Mitsubishi) of the world but the Hondas. It is in those types of companies that a fundamentally anticorporation and antigovernment entrepreneurial spark counterbalanced the plodding nature of the salaryman, while capitalizing on his work ethic and single-mindedness.

There has always been more of a spirit of individual entrepreneurship in Japan than the business literature usually acknowledges. Take Sanrio, for example—one of the world's best-known and best-loved brands. Started by Shintaro Tsuji, Sanrio has grown from a simple sandal manufacturer to become a worldwide toy empire. In the 1950s, Tsuji was a government bureaucrat. But he soon became bored with his desk job. He then started selling sandals and other basic products, but found that by taking the revolutionary step of painting strawberries on a pair of sandals, his sales exploded. His mantra became "Sell ordinary sandals and you'll make a dollar. Sell sandals with fancy designs and you can charge five."[7] From there, Tsuji developed his own character-branded products until he hit upon the gold mine of "Hello Kitty" in 1974. Hello Kitty became an instant hit, and turned into a clothing and gift line, theme parks, and media empire. By 2004, global sales had reached $760 million.[8]

At this point, you may be wondering "If the new Japanese model was so successful, then why did Japan crash in the early 1990s?" The success of the salaryman was assured as long as it fit well in its environment. But when the fit with the environment—not only in Japan but also globally—dissipated, the strength of this approach became its weakness.

In the Japanese case of post–World War II economics, the loss of fit wasn't just a decline of external fit with the competitive reality of the outside world. In this long cycle from 1945 to about 1990, it was also that the strategies and structures put into place were self-destructive—in the best sense. By achieving certain goals, the model literally eliminated the need for itself. The salaryman model created great prosperity. That great prosperity in turn created a greater sense of individual self, a desire for self-actualization, and a demand that prosperity provide rewards to the people—if not to the specific individuals who created the prosperity, then at least to their families and their descendants. But the model was not necessarily transferable to the next generation. This parallels the West in that once a certain level of prosperity has been established, the next generation looks for something else. So for the next generation, satisfaction requires a different definition, a greater quality of life in material terms, a greater quality of family life, and a greater quality of self-actualization. This is why the Renewal Cycle just keeps on turning, even at a national level.

Lessons from the Salarymen

As the previous section illustrates, Japan is currently dealing with a different global environment than it was in the latter half of the twentieth century with fundamental changes in the business, political, social, and technological arenas. The move from the era of administered competition to the era of open competition has fueled much of this change. Democracy continues to evolve, adapt, and become more entrenched in Japan. Citizen movements are growing; traditional political parties are starting to break down. The long-ruling Liberal Democratic Party (LDP) is increasingly forced to the margins as more independent governors are elected. A famous pair of comedians—Aoshima and Yokoyama—are now mayors of the two largest cities. Internet-based democracy is nascent.

Trade unions are in decline, along with a big growth in individualism that has many manifestations: growth of consumerism, a breakdown of the traditional family structure, an increase in feminism, and the divorce rate. There is even significant growth in the diversity of Japanese society—a breakdown in homogeneity, an increase in emigration (touts in the famed Japanese bar district Roppongi are now Nigerian, not Japanese).

The education system is growing more open and flexible, with centralized curricula falling out of favor. Volunteerism is rising, along with social entrepreneurship. The lifetime employment system—never as universal as we in the West tended to assume—is now clearly dying, accompanied by the loss of certainty, perquisites, and identity.

Japan has also been changed by technology. The country is now a sea of video games, computers, instant messaging, and camera phones. In many ways Japan would be lost without its technological conveniences. Japan is enormously changed from the country of 100 years ago.

All of this creates many implications for competitiveness. As the individual becomes the focal point for organizational analysis, that has huge implications for corporations. Now that the national purpose of rebuilding the country has been achieved, it is time for a new national purpose. That means companies have to synthesize their own sense of moral purpose more than ever before. They can no longer rely on the national challenge as their corporate challenge. So a whole new set of employment relationships is coming into play, as the "iron triangle"—bureaucrats, big companies, and unions—fades in influence and power.

The Japanese are known for having a long-term sense of time, but now they have to pay more attention to more immediate matters. Shorter-term profitability is paramount. This shift will have huge implications for Japanese business, and those who adapt will reap the rewards. That's what this book is all about. How do companies renew themselves? How do they adapt? And what methods and mindsets can we learn from bushido that create more successful Cycles of Renewal?

THEORY OR REALITY?

In Chapter 3, we touched briefly on results from our survey, which among other things found that Japanese, more than anyone else, see warlords as their role models. The survey covered a much broader range of topics though, and in the sections that follow you'll be seeing a lot more data from this source. At this point, it's useful to understand where those data came from.

In late August 2004, and then again in January 2005, we surveyed nearly 1,300 Japanese and a similar number of American managers on their attitudes toward change, the future, business success, etc. We wanted to see how these two groups differed in their attitudes and reported behaviors. The surveys in the United States and in Japan were conducted at almost the same time; both were administered on the Internet. As this was an opt-in survey, we don't know what the response rates were, but given some narrow criteria we had about career track and employment experience, we were very pleased to see such a large number of respondents on both sides of the Pacific.

Our samples are not nationally representative of the Japanese or American adult population; that was not our desire or intent. Even using the most stringent criteria, about the closest anyone can get is 95 percent certainty that the results are close to what they'd be if the entire adult population had been surveyed. What we wanted was a diverse sample of working adult professionals who had experience being an employee, managing others, living in an organizational culture, and dealing with the demands of business. We are confident we got just that.

For our Japanese survey, we used a leading Japanese market research firm with 620,000 total panel members who receive points that can be exchanged for merchandise as compensation for their responses to Web-based surveys. We selected an online sample of working professionals between the ages of 25 and 55. An e-mail was sent requesting their response to a survey concerning work, life, and management issues. The survey was in the field, allowing respondents to answer the questions, for five days.

The average respondent was 39 years old and the majority were male (60 percent). And among the Japanese executives and managers (59 percent of respondents), a quarter were women, a small triumph in the traditionally male-dominated Japanese workforce. As expected, the respondents were well-educated. Some 78 percent had at least partial college or graduate training. The majority were white-collar professionals working in a broad range of industries from retail to forestry. The largest Japanese industry sectors represented were high-tech electronics (19 percent) and financial services (21 percent).

In the United States, we worked with a premier market research firm with over 2 million households in their panel of participants. Panelists earned incentives for the surveys they completed—some earned points redeemable for merchandise or gift certificates and sweepstake offers. The panel was strictly managed to limit the number of studies and themes surveyed throughout the year. An e-mail request to respond to the survey was sent to qualified panelists. This survey was in the field for seven days.

As with the Japanese sample, our U.S. sample of working adults aged 25 to 55 had an average age of 39 years. The majority were male (56 percent) but among the 40 percent of respondents who were managers and executives, 31 percent were female. Respondents were highly educated, with 64 percent having at least some college experience and 25 percent earning advanced degrees. They also represented a wide range of industries from pharmaceuticals and biotech to hospitality and travel, with the largest percentage of respondents coming from the healthcare (11 percent), education and training (11 percent), and electronics and high-tech (10 percent) sectors.

Modern Day Samurai

Based on this survey, we created a measure we call Modern Day Samurai (MDS). It is a composite based on agreement with the following four statements from the questionnaire:

- I am proud of my national culture.
- Military-like strategy and tactics are effective in modern business.
- Businesses should avoid appearing weak at all costs.
- A soldier's (the word *samurai* was used in the Japanese survey) example of loyalty, commitment, dedication, and effort is a good way to get business done.

Those respondents expressing the strongest agreement with most or all of these four statements were termed our Modern Day Samurai, as they exhibited the strongest characteristics of samurai-like thought compared to the population at large. Willingness to go along with the general ethos expressed by these four statements implies, to our mind, an extreme pride in one's cultural origins combined with a soldier's love for tactics, strength, and loyalty to achieve victory on the battlefield of business. We wager these are the people that chief executive officers (CEOs) would most like to have on their side in times of crisis.

We found it interesting that so many Americans are Modern Day Samurai, about the same percentage as in Japan. The data show that while you find MDS in the executive, managerial, and nonmanagerial ranks, they actually are mostly executives in the United States and mostly at lower professional levels in Japan. This raises some interesting implications. We believe that if companies want to revive themselves and have the tools in place to keep the revival moving forward, they need to develop more Modern Day Samurai within all of their ranks. It would appear Americans need to push this Modern Day Samurai spirit down the ladder in their organizations. Conversely, the Japanese need to push it up.

These differences in organizational demographics of the Modern Day Samurai beg an even more important question: What will this mean for the future? If this spirit is an age effect in both countries, then Japan will continue to have troubles with renewal as top executives naturally lose their bushido mindset as they mature into leadership positions. Meanwhile, American leaders will continue to be great change agents, but will be opposed by the less-than-samurai who dominate the ranks of U.S. middle management.

On the other hand, if what we see in these variables is a generational effect, then Japanese will see more of their leaders as well as their middle managers become samurai-like revival masters, and America will see the opposite. This could be a reason to expect a tremendous competitive shift between Japan and the United States in the coming decades.

CAN ANYONE LEARN FROM JAPAN?

> "The Japanese spirit!" say the journalists. "The Japanese spirit!" say the pickpockets. The Japanese spirit has crossed the ocean in a single bound. In England, lectures are given on the Japanese spirit. In Germany, they stage dramatic spectacles on the Japanese spirit.... Now if you ask, "Well, what exactly is this Japanese spirit?" they say in reply they've gone five or six paces, one can hear them clearing their throats with an hrrmph.... Is the Japanese spirit triangular, or is it quadrangular? As the name indicates, the Japanese spirit is a spirit. And since it is a spirit it is always blurry and fuzzy.
>
> —Natsume Soseki,
> *Wagahai wa neko de aru* (1905)[9]

There was a time that everything about Japan seemed odd and very exotic. Actually, it was for a very long time. Westerners have been enamored of Japanese society throughout the entire twentieth century. Well, there was that decade in the middle of the century where *enamored* was probably not the word, but even during World War II, there was an unfathomable quality to Japan that made the nation intriguing to the West.

In this book, we're embarking on an exploration of the things that Japanese and Westerners alike can learn from the Japanese approach to renewal and change. Quite frankly, this exploration will probably not interest you much—if you believe that the Japanese are so unique that their approaches can't translate to your situation. But if you look closely, you will find that there is a surprising amount of common ground. The most obvious connection is the obviously global nature of most business. We believe that the parallels make it not only worthwhile but compelling that we Westerners don't simply dismiss Japan as different. In an era when renewal is truly a survival issue for so many firms, it is clearly worthwhile to understand and learn from the culture that epitomizes the renewal mindset. Not surprisingly, some of the best examples of renewal-in-action come from Japanese companies. But we have also found important examples that come from Western firms as well. And from all of these examples, you'll learn that a samurai mindset may be exactly what you need in your company—no matter the nationality of your corporation.

For the most part, in this book we will look at the positive aspects of samurai thinking and show how those elements can actually help an organization to revive itself. But Newton's third law reminds us that, at least in physics, "for every action, there is an equal and opposite reaction." Bushido seems subject to this law as well, so we cannot neglect an exploration of the dark side that shadows every aspect of bushido that we will explore. For instance, on balance, we believe that bringing out the warrior in your organization and in your employees can be a really good thing. But, obviously, if you take it too far, and your people believe in the warrior ethic to the point that they begin to commit the corporate equivalent of war crimes, you may have pushed too far. Each of the elements we discuss can become the basis for some really negative behaviors. If the dark sides of a combination of these variables are strung together, the outcome could be disastrous. So we'll point out the pitfalls along the way. Our strong belief, however, is that the emphasis belongs much more on the light side. The gains you can achieve for your corporation by applying the Way of the Samurai far outstrip the risks.

ABOUT FACE

When we decided to write this book, we knew things were changing again in Japan. But we were startled to find just how much the old Japanese Management System has begun to break down, giving way now to some exciting and dramatic changes. Although the changes themselves were apparent fairly quickly, to understand them—to find out why they *had* occurred—we ultimately had to look beneath the surface.

The answer largely comes from where Japan currently finds itself in the Renewal Cycle. Faced with the catalytic events of the early 1990s (slow growth and the land-price bust), Japan moved through the Gaming part of the cycle, where organizations and the people in those organizations desperately try to hold on to some semblance of the old system. As Japan's economy moved into the Framing phase, the need for change became pretty clear to the average Japanese. And in any renewal process, it is that realization that allows for complete rethinking—in this case, the complete revamping of business attitudes and beliefs that is currently under way in Japan.

By contrast, over the last decade, business in the United States has become more routinized and bureaucratic than ever. As we sit in the Taming square of the Renewal Cycle, our focus is on more cost-cutting, more efficiency, more profits. Most American organizations haven't started to think about renewal yet, because everyone still believes increased profitability is possible from current products and services. In many ways, this explains why in the last few years in American business life we found troves of analysts, journalists, and politicians repeating, "everything's going to be fine, everything's going to be fine," each in their own way. It's eerie how similar this period is to the late 1980s in Japan—even the stock market charts from these two periods markedly resemble each other.

What We Thought We Knew

During the 1980s, when most of the Western books on Japanese business systems were published, everyone came to believe a lot of maxims about basic differences between Japan and the West. Things such as:

- Japanese are more loyal to their companies.
- Japanese are good at operational efficiency, but don't care much about strategy.
- Americans look for entrepreneurial opportunities more than the Japanese.
- Japanese prefer to stay in Japan (except for short vacations abroad in groups led by Japanese tour guides).
- Japanese love hierarchy and tradition.
- Japanese venerate their corporate leaders and completely support them.
- Japanese are content with being cogs—they don't aspire to lead their organizations.
- Japanese revere their elders and try to avoid social change.

What We Learned

Sometime within the last two decades, as both the U.S. and Japanese economies moved around the Renewal Cycle, these two business cultures seem to have traded places. Results from our August 2004 and January 2005 surveys of Japanese and American business attitudes (presented in Table 5-1) show how drastically things have changed. The Japanese now have attitudes much closer to what American beliefs were in the 1980s. On the other hand, American responses are much more like those expected from the "typical" Japanese of the 1980s.

TABLE 5-1

WHAT WE THOUGHT WE KNEW ABOUT JAPANESE BUSINESS (BUT WERE WE WRONG!)

	JAPAN	UNITED STATES
MYTHS ABOUT JAPANESE BUSINESS THINKING:	PERCENTAGE OF JAPANESE WHO AGREED WITH THESE STATEMENTS:	PERCENTAGE OF AMERICANS WHO AGREED WITH THESE STATEMENTS:
"Japanese are more loyal to their companies."		
I really care about the fate of the organization I work for.	70%	87%
I would support and protect my company in the face of hostile business conditions.	61%	86%
"Japanese are good at operational efficiency, but don't care much about strategy"		
Companies should lower costs and add efficiencies (versus being unique and acting different).	24%	46%
Companies should achieve operational excellence (versus making the best strategic choices).	33%	48%
"Americans look for entrepreneurial opportunities more than the Japanese"		
It is shameful for companies to make products in other countries to save money.	27%	59%
I am interested in launching a new business as an entrepreneur.	61%	48%
"Japanese prefer to stay in Japan."		
I would like to live in a culture for a while that is unfamiliar to me.	65%	58%
People who've lived in more than one culture have an advantage.	85%	80%

(Continued)

TABLE 5-1 (*CONTD.*)

	JAPAN	UNITED STATES
MYTHS ABOUT JAPANESE BUSINESS THINKING:	PERCENTAGE OF JAPANESE WHO AGREED WITH THESE STATEMENTS:	PERCENTAGE OF AMERICANS WHO AGREED WITH THESE STATEMENTS:
"Japanese love hierarchy and tradition."		
Companies should use wisdom and traditional values (versus adopting systems and practices from the rest of the world).	38%	57%
Workers should show respect for my country's traditions.	42%	83%
"Japanese venerate their corporate leaders and completely support them."		
Leadership in my company makes me enthusiastic about the future.	28%	59%
It is important for company leaders to be respected and appreciated by other leaders in the company.	83%	92%
"Japanese are content with being cogs—they don't aspire to lead their organizations."		
I consider myself a team player at work.	61%	94%
I would prefer to be in charge of my own organization.	53%	41%
"Japanese revere their elders and try to avoid social change"		
I feel like I'm part of a revolution at my organization.	67%	42%
I wish my organization felt more youthful.	64%	43%

These responses reflect a real spirit of renewal in Japan. Most Japanese are not pleased with the current direction of their organization, or their leaders. Most want to see some significant change, but also believe they can be a positive force to create such change. In these ways, modern Japanese samurai are acting less like traditional samurai, who followed the master's orders. Instead, they are acting like *ronin* (masterless samurai). They expect to take individual responsibility for their own futures, and are ready to make it happen. They have confidence and faith in their own ability to change business and society for the good.

CONCLUSION

In the previous chapters we've provided you with the necessary context to begin understanding how bushido will influence Japan's next moves in the Cycle of Renewal.

You know a little more about the history of the samurai and their journey from protectors of royalty to leaders of the country. You also know how samurai went from ultimate warriors to bored city dwellers to successful businessmen. And you have learned how their business ethic morphed from a military warrior ethos in World War II to the life force behind the corporate powerhouses of the 1970s and 1980s.

But how do the specific elements of bushido—the way of the sword and the pen—fit into Japan today? More importantly, what can we learn from these examples? How will the attitudes of *ronin* lead Japan to once again take on the world with their competitive model? We'll address these questions, beginning first with a discussion of the most basic tool the samurai uses to defend his place in the world—his sword.

NOTES

1. Sheldon Richm an, "The Consequences of World War II," November 1991, http://www.fff.org/freedom/1191c.asp.
2. Walter LaFeber, "The Unmasterable Past: The Limits of Japan's Postwar Transformation," *Foreign Affairs*, July/August 1999.
3. Toyota Motor Corporation, *Toyota: A History of the First 50 Years*. Toyota City: Dai Nippon Printing Co., Ltd, 1988.
4. Yukiyasu Togo and William Wartman, Against All Odds: The Story of the Toyota Motor Corporation and the Family that Created It. New York: St. Martin's Press, 1993.
5. John Nathan, *Sony: The Private Life*, New York: Houghton Mifflin Company, 1999.
6. Ibid.

7. Tim Clark, *Japan Entrepreneur Report*, October 2003, http://www.japanentrepreneur.com/200310.html.
8. Sanrio Company Profile, http://www.sanrio.co.jp/english/about_s/profile/profile.html.
9. Quoted in Peter N. Dale, *The Myth of Japanese Uniqueness*, New York: St. Martin's Press, 1986 (Introduction).

PART TWO

The Sword

CHAPTER
6

Sword-Wielding

Although the word *samurai* has many defining features, for most of us, *samurai* conjures up a sword-wielding fighter. But how could understanding samurai warrior mindsets and methods help corporations with renewal? One of the first places to look for answers is in the act of swordplay itself, known as *kenjutsu* and later, *kendo*. How these ancient arts influence the samurai spirit is key to understanding how bushido can influence corporate success today and into the future.

SWORDPLAY IN JAPAN

Each Japanese samurai was allowed two swords, compared to only one for regular citizens. (That fact alone tells us that swords were awfully important in establishing status and social order in feudal Japan.) The sword became a nearly sacred item very early in the history of the samurai. In fact, there is evidence that as early as the year 3 B.C., the sword was used as an offering to the gods. Swords "were said to possess the three critical holy elements of purity, rarity, and value."[1] Over time, this most important weapon became synonymous with the samurai. It remains their most potent symbol.

The samurai developed a philosophy to go along with this weapon, originally known as *kenjutsu* (the art of the sword). *Kenjutsu* focused on how to defeat others through swordplay, and was quite useful during the time when samurai were charged with fighting and winning actual battles. *Kenjutsu* emphasized technique as well as offensive and defensive strategies and stances. *Kenjutsu* was at its heart a practical discipline.

The Three Styles of *Kenjutsu*

Kenjutsu, the art of fighting with a steel sword, had three major styles. *Katori shinto ryu* was created around 1400 by Choisai Ienao. This style, the oldest of the three, "stresses mobility and variety in body movements, cuts, blocks, and tactics [through] a complex series of actions and counter-actions."[2] In *katori shinto ryu*, complexity and a diverse array of maneuvers are the keys to success—making the samurai effective in any position or situation.

The second style, *itto ryu*, was created in the 1500s by Ito Ittosai Kaghisa. This remains one of the most studied styles of swordsmanship, as it emphasizes beating your opponent with one stroke. In *itto ryu*, "cuts are direct and forceful. Blocks and parries are simple and require a minimum amount of energy and movement. Body movements are generally straight and linear."[3] Ito developed this style after being attacked by an unknown assailant and unconsciously cut his enemy in half with one slice. The sport of kendo grew directly out of this style of *kenjutsu*. Kendo, played with a wooden rather than a steel sword, remains popular in schools and sports clubs to this day in Japan. Its defined set of rules, scoring procedures, and acceptable targets, make it very similar to the sport of fencing in the West. Today, kendo is as much about improving oneself, both mentally and spiritually, as it is about the art of swordplay.

Finally, we have *yagyu shinkage ryu*, developed in the 1500s by Yagyu Muneyoshi. This style of swordplay is a more defensive one; it involves "battling and enticing the opponent to strike...there are twisting, turning, and evasive body movements and study in this style requires a certain amount of physical agility."[4] This style is the most mentally demanding, as it focuses mainly on outwitting one's opponent rather than defeating him with brute force.

Samurai versus Knight

Who would win in an even fight—a samurai or a medieval knight? Well, maybe it's not a terribly important question for anyone you know—at least on the literal level. But there are those who worry a lot about such things. We know the samurai chose to wield their swords in three different ways—through extreme mobility, a singular stroke, or through cunning. Knights did not necessarily develop discrete battle philosophies, but rather used their swords in combination with several other tools—namely, with armor and shields.

Speaking specifically to the knight's use of a sword, it was most effective as a thrusting instrument. Dual edges on most knights' swords gave a greater range of motion, allowing for back-edge and reverse cuts. Mainly, swords of this type "were made for hacking, shearing cuts delivered primarily from the elbow and shoulder and employing wide passing steps."[5] Actions used more energy and were fast and whirling, with an idea toward defeating the enemy by weakening him or breaking through his armor. While the knight's swordplay method may have been all about power, there was little chance of defeating an enemy with one stroke or even outwitting an opponent—the only viable option for victory would have been brute force.

Whereas knights were effective in Europe, they were eventually outmoded by faster foes. Their brute-force method was only really powerful up close. Samurai were no match for gunpowder or archers either, but in a close fight, samurai still possessed several different tools they could use. While we will obviously never know for sure who would prevail in such a fictional contest, it is safe to say samurai possessed a flexibility that knights did not. Therefore knights wore armor to better protect themselves against more agile foes.

If we are going to use the samurai metaphor to think about modern business practice, the implications are quite clear: to get your people in top mental condition, they need to have more than just brute force at their disposal. They need to have access to all three of the *kenjutsu* styles—brains, agility, and swiftness. At different times, employees will need to be able to rotate and pivot around new competitive challenges, or jump with lightning-fast speed to eliminate new threats. There are times in the revival plan of any organization when plain brute strength—basic blocking and tackling (to badly mix a sports metaphor with another from medieval swordplay)—can be exactly what is needed. But the point is that having more than one method of operating is important in renewal. As a leader of a company that needs to change, you'd probably like your people to be so versatile, so brilliant that your competitors are dumbfounded by their stealthy, swift, samurai-like moves.

FENCING YOUR COMPETITORS

The evolutionary path from the heavy-handed knightly form of European swordplay into the relatively delicate modern sport of fencing may not be obvious at first. But the key to winning the game (or to staying alive in a real swordfight) is understanding the competition's weakness and using it to one's advantage. Consequently, fencing, like kendo and all three forms of *kenjutsu*, is as much a game of the mind as it is of the body. One of the authors of this book (Mark Fuller) lettered in fencing in college—and naturally has an affinity for and understanding of the mindset of the sword warrior. His coach, Edo Marion, was a four-time Olympic medalist and coach of the U.S. Olympic team. Edo emphasized there were three physical elements that made a swordsman great: legs, hands, and timing. He would say to Mark, "Your legs are made of cement—why can't you move faster? Your handwork is not so bad; we can do something with that. But your timing is your real strength. You can win with that."

The point of Edo's advice was that physical strength and speed are important—very important. But don't underestimate the advantage you can gain by understanding your competitors. That is what timing is really all about: understanding competitors. While most modern sports are played out in minutes or hours, fencing is all about milliseconds. The fencer who can sense a competitor's feint or parry can respond appropriately without being drawn into a "fatal" move. But it is all about anticipating the moves and the responses of the competitor *before* any action has taken place.

TURNAROUND AT NISSAN

Timing is particularly important when it comes to understanding and beating competitors in business as well. When Carlos Ghosn took over as head of Nissan in 1999, he found an organization that had forgotten its sense of timing and competitiveness—it had lost its *kenjutsu* skills, as it were. He had much to accomplish in order to bring the company back into a competitive position. And he succeeded by instilling in Nissan's people a fight they had forgotten they had.

Ghosn was called "the destroyer"[6] by many inside and outside Nissan, as many feared what he might do, both as an outsider and as a Westerner. But overriding all of that was a sense that something dramatic needed to be done if Nissan was going to survive. "There was a lack of urgency, declining market share, unprofitability, debt and [no] long-term plan—and everyone was always finding excuses."[7]

Those who worked with Ghosn found his sometimes autocratic style to be just what the company needed. Early in his tenure, Ghosn figured out what Nissan needed to do—shake up the industry with cars that would be on the cutting edge of style and design. One press report described Ghosn's revolution within Nissan as part of a "vanguard of change…sweeping many of the country's big companies. His approach, or something like it, is more Japanese than many Japanese managers would like to think."[8]

Ghosn's plan was to focus on a goal and stick to it—cut costs (even though that meant layoffs and shifts in purchasing, almost anathema to Japan), slash debt, divest nonperforming assets, and improve the product mix. Even though implementing this plan involved sacrificing a lot of sacred cows, Ghosn was determined. "One thing that Ghosn brought to the party was a clear focus on our priorities and a clear plan by which to execute those priorities. He has not wavered from day one,"[9] said Jed Connelly, Nissan North America's senior vice president of sales and marketing.

Even though he offended some within the company with his management style, others did not find Ghosn so terrible. Yukio Kitahora, a senior vice president, said his relationship changed with the head office when Ghosn arrived. Kitahora "was never able to approach Nissan's previous management with ideas or observations but that such access is now routine."[10] Ghosn improved information flow and openness throughout the company, contradicting the stereotype that a company that prided itself on militaristic tactics would overemphasize top-down management.

Ghosn's efforts have paid off not only in spurring Nissan's revival but also by raising his standing within Japan itself. Nissan has overtaken Honda as the number two company in the Japanese domestic market and boasts the largest operating margins (11.1 percent) of any auto manufacturer in the world. Six-month earnings for the company recently topped $2.4 billion, and they now have a stable of hits including the Altima sedan, the Micra subcompact, and a redesigned 350Z. And Ghosn was recently named one of the top four men Japanese women wanted as a potential good father for their children. He was even asked if he would consider running for prime minister, a quite unusual sentiment for any foreigner in Japan.

Ghosn refuses to take all the credit for Nissan's turnaround, but he did think people inside the company had lost their way and needed someone to show them what they were capable of. "The Japanese have done this in the past," he said, meaning turned their fate around. "Why? Because you have this capacity that when people like the vision, they're going to do better. When it comes to executing a vision, they're second to none."[11] There is no reason to think this ability is limited to Japanese, however.

In Ghosn's tenure at Nissan, we can see a company that had forgotten what it was capable of. Ghosn reinvigorated the organization through new ideas and thinking, but in an orderly fashion. By putting employees and management in touch with their inner samurai, Ghosn was able to give Nissan renewed dynamism. He encouraged these corporate samurai to perform deftly, skillfully, and with a careful eye on the competition. Thanks to these efforts, Nissan's market share continues to rise, and its reputation continues to improve.

But it was not only Nissan that has benefited from Ghosn's wake-up call. It seems that there has been a revolution of sorts, a return to Japan's natural innovative, creative, scrappy tendencies. These had been lost, as the Japanese Management System of salaryman seniority systems and lifetime employment became an important part of business in Japan. But as we have seen, these systems were relatively new, post–World War II innovations in Japan.[12] Before that, there was bushido. And it really never left. Whenever there is a need to adapt or face a catalytic event in Japan, there has always been bushido. And using bushido principles, Ghosn may have delivered to Japanese big business a direction (and a model) for the next Renewal Cycle.

THAT WARRIOR SPIRIT

But what kind of employee is capable of learning the wide variety of *ken-jutsu* fighting styles? In our survey, we found a particular breed that seemed more "battle ready" than most. These employees were less likely to be upset by life's unpredictability, more willing to accept a heavy workload, more able to thrive under pressure and despite continuous change. In our survey, these battle-ready employees were almost *twice as likely* as others to fit in the Modern Day Samurai (MDS) category we described in Chapter 5.

Unsurprisingly, both Japanese and American MDS think of themselves as warriors far more often than their fellow non-MDS—about two-thirds of the time compared to only a quarter of the time in Japan (and a third of the time in the United States for nonsamurai).

What does this tell us—hire nationalistic, bellicose types who have a militaristic philosophy of life? No, not really. But it is good to know certain people will fight for your company when you need it—these are the ones who will strengthen your organization when your company is most in need of some extra power. If you go to work every day believing you and the people around you are special and you endeavor to make it true through your actions at work, wouldn't you want your colleagues to feel and act the same way?

THE DARK SIDE OF THE SWORD

There can be a dark side to the fighting spirit, however, which may appear as an overreliance on one method in particular, or a belief that your company has become invulnerable. Many companies have succumbed to the belief that what they're doing is perfect and always will be, or that market forces can't possibly catch up. Guess what? They will. Companies who rely on what they see as their traditional strengths may not be looking hard enough for a new method of "swordplay" that could cut them down in their prime.

Don't Get Caught Napping

On balance, Matsushita has done much better financially than Sony over the last few years. But it has lost a couple of major battles. CEO Kunio Nakamura has devoted a lot of his time to making sure that a single method of swordplay doesn't keep Matsushita from anticipating and responding appropriately to the marketplace. This was a lesson learned only after Sony's Wega flat-screen televisions took the market by storm, leaving Matsushita's traditional offerings in the dust. In an effort to learn how this setback happened, Nakamura asked his lead television developer why they hadn't developed a flat-screen to combat Sony and was told that flat-screens make "the middle part of the picture look sunken in." In effect, the development engineer was deaf to the voice of the market, choosing to rely on technological measures instead. Seeing the danger in overreliance on one approach, Nakamura vowed at that point to make sure both marketers and engineers contribute to product planning.[13]

As Matsushita's experience and the earlier example of Nissan prior to Ghosn's arrival illustrate, companies that become entrenched can miss market opportunities worth billions. To avoid this fate, companies should constantly be practicing new maneuvers. They should learn and exercise all available methods of swordplay at their disposal in order to stay both strong *and* smart. Management should shake things up by running the occasional war game or practice drill on what a competitor might do next. Ghosn himself agrees: "The biggest danger for Nissan is to get complacent."[14]

Good warriors try to anticipate what will happen next. So it's also important to keep your people versatile and to look for opportunities to bring different perspectives together. Scenarios that help teams practice reacting to a wide range of possibilities not only foster agility but also highlight potential vulnerabilities associated with overreliance on a single perspective or expertise. The time you spend planning out what others may do is time well spent. Sure, 99 of the 100 potential scenarios may never become reality, but the one that does will be one for which your people are ready.

Don't Lose Spirit

Companies need to ensure that their employees never lose their warrior spirit. And they must be certain to school them in the various arts of *kenjutsu*: swiftness, agility, flexibility, and outwitting their opponents.

Sharp Corporation is a good example of a company that has managed to be a flexible and quick-witted warrior in overcoming its relatively small size to claim many victories in corporate battles in Japan and abroad. In the past, Sharp sometimes has felt like the ugly stepsister to Sony and Matsushita. Sharp made a similar product line of electronics but traditionally without the name-brand cache. But all of that has changed in the last few years as Sharp has become the darling of investors and consumers.

Sharp has always invested a higher percentage of sales into research and development than its rivals. Whereas Matsushita puts about 6 percent of sales into research, Sharp spends 9 percent. But because Sharp has always been so much smaller than its *kieretsu*-tied rivals, it learned early that the investment had to be much more targeted and competitive. They have adopted a "contrarian R&D strategy" in which the corporation puts money into emerging technologies not yet proven. It even invests in technologies not even demanded by the marketplace.

This is the strategy that led them into solar power—where they now control 25 percent of the global market for solar cells. And it also led them to license liquid crystal display (LCD) technology from RCA in the 1960s. Sharp put LCDs into calculators in the 1970s and 1980s and built quite a cash cow for itself. But even during a major downturn in LCD screen demand in the late 1990s, CEO Katsuhiko Machida insisted that Sharp continue to invest in the development of the LCD television screens that are so popular today. By 2003, Sharp claimed 35 percent of the global market for LCD TVs. And those television sales have been largely responsible for Lehman Brothers naming Sharp as the most profitable electronics maker in the world for the last five years.

CONCLUSION

In leading your corporate warriors, make sure they are as well prepared as you would want to be before you yourself would venture onto the battlefield. Have them practice their techniques on each other before a big project or the next product cycle. Encourage them to think like warriors and adopt strategies for winning that anticipate competition and prepare them for innovation and opportunity.

NOTES

1. John Yumoto, *The Samurai Sword: A Handbook*, Tokyo: Charles E. Tuttle, 1958.
2. Risuke Otake, *The Deity and the Sword – Katori Shinto-ryu Vol. 1*, Tokyo: Japan Publications Trading Company, 1977.
3. Ibid.
4. Ibid.
5. http://www.thearma.org/essays/knightvs.htm.
6. Yumiko Ono, "Nissan's New Chief Gets a Full Hibachi Grilling," *Wall Street Journal* (Eastern edition), New York, June 21, 2000, A.18.
7. David Ibison, "Reinventing the Japanese way of doing business: Interview with Carlos Ghosn, Nissan Motor: The president of the Japanese motor group has taken it 'from the emergency room to the recovery room' by rewarding talent and drive,"*Financial Times* (London, England), July 23, 2001.
8. Ibid.
9. Norman S. Mayersohn, "Nissan's U-turn to profits," *The Chief Executive* (U.S.)., Montvale, N.J., January 1, 2002.
10. Ibison, op. cit.
11. "Carlos Ghosn: What Japan Needs Is a Vision: The Nissan turnaround ace talks about the pace of reform," *Business Week*, New York: Dec. 16, 2002, Issue 3812, p. 22.
12. John C. Beck and Martha N. Beck, *The Change of a Lifetime.* (Honolulu) University of Hawaii Press, 1994.
13. Benjamin Fulford, "The Tortoise Jumps the Hare," *Forbes*, Feb. 2, 2004, p. 56.
14. "Ghosn says Nissan turnaround shows potential of Japan," *Kyodo News*, Feb. 13, 2004.

CHAPTER 7

HIERARCHICAL

As we mentioned in the last chapter, the sword is the most enduring symbol of the samurai and of bushido in Japan. But the next most defining characteristic is probably the position that the samurai held in feudal Japanese society. During their heyday, the samurai occupied the top rung of the social ladder. In 1586, Toyotomi Hideyoshi created a law codifying samurai status as permanent and heritable. As a result, the samurai stayed on top for about 300 years.

UPPER CLASS

Even before the official codification, however, the place of the samurai at the top of the social ladder in Japan had been clear to everyone. As mentioned in Chapter 3, samurai were above farmers, artisans, and merchants (in that order), and in some parts of the country were the only class permitted to kill without justification. Japan took its notion of four main social classes from China. The bottom three classes were the same in both countries, but in China the top distinction went to scholars and government officials—not warriors.

In many societies, if you are in the upper class, you really don't understand the need to "look up" to anything. But in Japan, because of the fine-grained nature of hierarchy, even the samurai were programmed from birth to respect those of a higher rank. And unless you were the emperor or the shogun, there was always someone of higher rank. The daimyo looked to the shogun, the bannermen looked to the daimyo, the lower samurai looked to the bannermen, and so on. The shogun and daimyo conferred land, power, status, and an annual rice stipend on the samurai as payment for their services. You'll remember that the word *samurai* is derived from the word *saburo*, the classical Japanese verb meaning "to serve."

It's said that samurai were unequaled as warriors; yet for all of their power, they never questioned the judgment or strategy of their leaders. On the battlefield, a samurai would sacrifice everything for his daimyo, even his life.

Yet even the basic samurai were not created equal. There were distinctions within the samurai class, resulting in levels and sublevels, according to the rank and prestige of each samurai's daimyo, or lack thereof. The *ronin*, known as "masterless samurai," were usually a rank below the regular samurai, as they had either given up or been forced out of their landed positions. And it is interesting that the samurai with no one to look up to or link into were actually the lowliest of all the samurai. Once you were out of the hierarchy in feudal Japan, you were no longer nearly as important as if you were well connected.

WE LOVE A GOOD HIERARCHY

What was going on in Japanese feudal society with regard to hierarchy was probably no different than what happens in most societies. Most of us, even in the United States, have a pretty good sense of where we fit in the social stratum, despite our lip service to a classless society. And whether we admit it or not, human beings have a natural tendency to look up. Any group of humans establishes a pecking order before long—an alpha takes control and the rest of the group takes its cues from him or her. Occasionally, a challenge is made to the order, and control can be wrested away, peacefully or otherwise.

Socialization has tamed the assumption of power—with elections and due process largely replacing duels as means of settling disputes. But different societies still possess varying degrees of this hierarchy impulse. The Japanese have a reputation for being particularly hierarchy sensitive. Two of the classic studies on Japanese society describe vertical (as opposed to horizontal) relations as the basis for Japanese social order. Chie Nakane's book *Japanese Society*[1] suggests the whole social nexus in Japan is up-down rather than side to side. This same theme is echoed in Doi's *The Anatomy of Dependence*.[2]

Our survey also suggests that a tendency toward hierarchy is still alive and well in Japan. Nearly two-thirds of Japanese agreed with the statement

"Compared with other people, leaders are better at understanding what should be done to fix problems"—as opposed to just over half of Americans. And among our Modern Day Samurai in Japan, the numbers were dramatic—over 70 percent were willing to defer to leaders when the time called for it.

Whether acting on explicit instructions from their bosses or not, Modern Day Samurai nevertheless seem to constantly be looking above themselves for signals of what management wants. With this potential synchronization already in place, changes are much easier to implement when called for, as everyone is already in agreement. No politics, no begging for buy-in—just a nod of the head and it's done.

In our survey, we found that, by a 3-to-1 ratio, Japanese managers who are comfortable with change prefer to be responsible for decisions in their work group. But Japanese who are *not* comfortable with change prefer to be responsible only about half the time. Japanese who aren't bothered by change are more comfortable taking the lead role on a project. But there are still a sizable number of Japanese who admit their discomfort with change and will not take the lead under any circumstances.

Americans, on the other hand, say they want to be responsible for their group's decisions more often, especially men, who claim this right 80 percent of the time—a room full of wannabe leaders potentially run amok. In contrast, only 7 out of 10 Japanese men and just over half of Japanese women want the same. So Americans seem much more willing to take the lead in any given situation—regardless of the appropriateness of such a move. This leads to the classic dilemma where there are too many bosses and not enough subordinates to do the work.

But with respect to age, younger employees in Japan are less willing to take control over decision making than their older counterparts are. More Japanese professionals over 35 want to be responsible for decisions than those under 35. In the United States, equal percentages (about 3 to 1) of younger and older professionals want to take charge.

In these data, we see a pattern emerge. In both Western and Japanese cultures, those comfortable with change (typically older men with the accumulated wisdom of longer experience) tend to want to take charge. The difference is that Japanese managers also seem to have self-sorted into groups that know their tolerance for being on the edge of change and those that don't. Americans, on the other hand, prefer to be responsible for decisions no matter what their comfort level with change—indicating a sort of blind faith that to be in charge is inherently good, no matter what one's actual ability.

THE DEATH OF HIERARCHY

These attitudes are no surprise. In the West, the last 30 years of corporate theory have focused on breaking down hierarchies wherever they stood. This was a reaction to the ossified silo-based structures built up during the headier growth-oriented days of the 1950s and 1960s. These corporate structures were filled with Organization Men who knew their place and strove to climb the ladder one rung at a time. In fact, good management was all about hierarchy. Much of the management "science" of the 1930s to the 1970s was about structuring the right kind of hierarchy (through concepts like "span of control" and "linking pins"), for the most effective deployment of human resources.

When economies were struggling in the 1970s, managers and employees alike called for a completely new model. Hierarchies were suddenly evil and needed to be broken down immediately to make the organization leaner and more responsive. By the 1990s, the business classic *Reengineering the Corporation* by Michael Hammer and James Champy made explicit the need to eliminate wasteful layers of management and business processes that had outlived their usefulness.[3] Unfortunately for some, companies often took that to mean destroying huge cohorts in the naïve hope that fewer people could do the same tasks more efficiently.

Sometimes it worked. But often it resulted in increased fear, loathing, and mistrust among the company's managers for those at the top who blindly foisted new restructuring initiatives on their departments without regard for the consequences. Upper management often didn't care—they simply needed to report to those above them that they had reengineered their departments.

All that change ignored what we talked about at the beginning of the chapter—human's natural tendency to look up to see what others above him or her in the social chain are doing. For all the talk about striking out on one's own and blazing a new trail, rarely do people have the courage to do so in real life, especially when what's on the line is a steady income to cover the mortgage and tuition...as well as a place in the professional world.

A 1998 Accenture study highlighted the positive effects of hierarchy in the globalization of businesses. Those corporations that had the best returns calculated by economic value added (EVA) were the companies that had more power concentrated at the center by the chief executive officer (CEO) or a small group of people concentrated around the CEO. The more decentralized the companies, the less financially successful they were. This certainly runs counter to much of the organizational behavior studies over the last 20 years.

And in truth, we in the West respect hierarchy more than we may admit. No matter what the books say about flat organizations, all of us are loath to change unless we get a clear signal from above to do so. And if a trusted leader says we must now move as an organization, and he or she can find a way to convince everyone that change needs to happen for the company to survive, people will gladly follow. A study in *Management Science* found statistical evidence that "hierarchical managers are necessary to actively enforce routine, even after the routine has been assimilated, and to introduce innovation, even in this unique setting of perfect incentives."[4] We want, need, and crave direction. That doesn't mean building layer upon layer of process—it just means getting your people's inner samurai to accept management directives.

The Japanese tendency, then, to look above themselves for answers and direction is not necessarily a bad thing, especially for a company trying to revive. In fact, it can be the most productive solution possible. And when business enters a crisis phase, hierarchy rises from important to paramount. Companies rarely get through a crisis without a strong leader. Usually, that leader cannot be the same person who led the company into crisis in the first place—a completely new leader is needed to wash away associations with the old regime.

LEADERSHIP IN ACTION

Take the example of Japanese department store giant Daiei. Executive Takashi Hirayama attempted to lead two different revolutions at Daiei. His first revival project, which was started in 1983 when he was a division director in Osaka,[5] was called the "V-revolution," so named for Hirayama's attempt to improve sales in a "V" pattern—a sharp rise up again after an equally sharp drop. At the time, Daiei was facing a loss of 6.5 billion yen—a fierce challenge for any manager.

Hirayama's goal was to make the revival project easy for everyone to understand. One of the plans was called the "3-4-5 *sakusen* (3-4-5 strategy)." The "3" meant all stores should achieve a 30 percent reduction of inventory. "4" referred to a 40 percent reduction in lost merchandise, and "5" meant a 50 percent reduction of merchandise marked down for clearance. With this simple catchphrase and precise set of goals, Hirayama easily spread the plan throughout the whole organization, even to part-time employees.[6]

After this time, Hirayama played a very important role in Daiei's revival by helping to reinvigorate their Yunido grocery store subsidiary. Hirayama would personally visit Yunido stores, talking frankly to store managers while trying to establish a common feeling with employees.[7] Hirayama was shocked at first to see unmotivated employees and stores that had never been remodeled. He proclaimed, "people, goods, capital are said to be three important resources in management, however, those three do not stand in line. Goods and capital come after good people."

In order to raise employees' motivation, Hirayama frequently visited stores on little or no notice. One store manager panicked one day to see Hirayama making a surprise visit, and unfortunately presented Hirayama with an unkempt store. The store manager apologized profusely saying, "If I knew you were coming, we would have cleaned up beforehand." But instead of being angry, Hirayama said, "I'm sorry for assigning you such an old and dirty store," taking full responsibility for the condition of the enterprise. For this management style, Hirayama drew lots of fans both inside and outside the company. In 1988, a year after Hirayama came to Yunido, the company returned to profitability, and in 1990, Yunido showed the highest increase in revenue among the top 10 supermarket chains in Japan.[8]

Unfortunately, due to internal politics, Hirayama was forced to leave Daiei temporarily. But thanks to an internal scandal and the resignation of his political enemies, he was brought back in 2001 to attempt his second revolution, this time at the highest levels of the company. Immediately, Hirayama launched the "*Genki* 500 *Sakusen*" or "Fight 500 Strategies" to improve company sales, the 500 indicating the amount (in hundreds of millions of yen) by which he wanted to increase revenue.[9] Hirayama wanted to infuse the company with a fighting spirit, from top to bottom.[10] Through the Fight 500 Strategies, Hirayama wanted to rebuild a corporate culture where everyone would take an active role in their work.

This time Hirayama's second attempt did not last long. Unfortunately, Daiei was already too deep in debt and caught in a maze of preferential agreements with suppliers to sell particular brands of merchandise. Thus, Daiei did not have the flexibility in product mix or financial leverage to effectively compete in the retail environment. Hirayama's methods were not enough to turn Daiei around, and he was forced to leave in 2003.

Even though Hirayama met with mixed success, the powerful role of hierarchy still applies. In both situations, he was able to pull his company out of a desperate situation (at least temporarily) through strong leadership at the top and direct forceful contact with workers and managers. The fact that he could not succeed the second time because of preexisting conditions shows that sometimes superior forces overwhelm even the best samurai.

In the Hirayama example and in countless other examples in the United States and Japan (Idei at Sony, Gerstner at IBM, Barnevik at ABB, and Welch at GE), we see a leader establish a strong directive, and those below follow or find themselves pushed out of the way. The corporate culture is unified, singularized, and propelled forward simultaneously. Ideas were not subject to consensus, committee, or focus group—our own best instincts tell us success is never found in these places. By relying on efficiency and "flatness" to deliver improved performance, companies easily lose sight of exactly *what* they're supposed to be making efficient in the first place. Or they're so busy perfecting a good idea from five years ago that they don't notice the new ideas that their competitors are working on. This is classic Taming behavior. The danger of focusing only on the status quo is obvious, but there is also a danger that leaders will push their employees out of their comfort zones and directly into Framing before they're ready. By skipping the Gaming phase of the cycle, they not only miss the opportunity to pass the vision on to their employees but they increase the anxiety level to no apparent good end. Hirayama, Welch, and Gerstner all took steps to make sure employees were constantly on their toes, but productively so.

A CHANGE IN THE AIR?

Although some of our survey results fit with our preconceived expectations about attitudes toward hierarchy, other results were actually opposite the accepted wisdom about how Japanese and American societies work. There is evidence that both Japanese and Americans are starting to think about hierarchy in surprising ways. For example, 25 percent of Americans agree with the statement "People should not criticize those in authority, even when they think they are wrong." Meanwhile only 15 percent of the Japanese surveyed would agree not to criticize authority. Can it possibly be true that the supposedly meek Japanese are more willing to speak out against authority figures than supposedly brash Americans?

Japanese people also feel less strongly than Americans do, by about 10 percentage points, that company leaders should be respected and appreciated by other workers in the company. And only about 1 out of 4 Japanese feel their company's leadership makes them enthusiastic about the future—compared with more than 3 out of 5 Americans. Given the amount of downsizing and corporate restructuring Americans have faced over the past few years, we have to wonder just what these Americans are telling themselves to still be so enamored of their companies.

Japan seems to be more skeptical of its leaders these days, and rightly so. They've been wandering in an economic wilderness for some time now, and have only started to emerge from it. But we think Japan's current attitudes about leadership are actually healthier than the American tendency to refrain from questioning and to believe unfailingly in one's leaders. Nevertheless, the survey results surprised us because the stereotypical view is that Japan's group society is unfailingly orderly, while Americans like to question authority to the point of absurdity.

These different attitudes are likely to lead to very different outcomes. Perhaps the questioning attitude among the Japanese comes from a more realistic idea of the capabilities of their leaders. If they do not build their leaders up as infallible heroes, or wish for an unfailing knight to come along and save the day, they may be better prepared and more willing to take an active role in the Renewal Cycle. By contrast, Americans seem to always be "holding out for a hero"—in both politics and business, to make everything OK. This, in turn, limits their adaptability. In this case, it appears that the Japanese have done a better job of balancing the need for hierarchy with the respect for humanity's fallibility.

PRIDE GOES BEFORE A FALL

Of course, in any hierarchy, there can be a temptation to abuse the power that comes with being at the top. Megalomaniacal managers have often thrown good money after bad in ill-fated ventures that were doomed to fail. How do you know whether you're really leading your people down the right path, or taking them down a destructive one?

To help prevent taking a seriously wrong turn, make sure that you as the leader are never cut off from information from the outside. Good daimyo always want to listen to their samurai's field reports, so they can identify the need for redirection and take swift action. Being a leader doesn't mean being omnipotent. You still need the help of those around you and below you to effectively manage. You can do that by establishing trust with the samurai on your staff, promising, "If you fight hard on my behalf, I will lead you to the best (most winnable) battles."

Second, be clear with your people about what you mean by success and failure. If goals are clearly laid out, reachable, and relatively short term—"we will take *that* hill by noon tomorrow"—your people will be much more enthused and willing to go forth on your behalf. Keeping the number of goals to a manageable number doesn't hurt either.

Finally, follow through on your vision. One of the more interesting findings in *The Attention Economy* (which, like this book, was co-authored by John Beck) was that subordinates not only know what their leaders are paying attention to but they also tend to pay attention to the same issues.[11] This book showed that employees were accurate 80 percent of the time in judging where their boss's attention was, and paid attention to the same thing about 70 percent of the time (that missing 10 percent is where employees' own agendas come into play). So if you, as a leader, want your people to pay attention to a particular subject, just give it more of your own attention. Be clear about what you want done, but also follow your own example by paying attention to what you've directed others to do.

CONCLUSION

The notion of hierarchy is somewhat in flux, but some things hold true—we do need some hierarchy in our lives. Despite all the books out there that tell us everyone is now a free agent and that flat organizations rule supreme, hierarchy can still be very valuable. Smart leaders and smart organizations will use this knowledge to their advantage by developing a healthy hierarchy to deal with these new conditions.

Smart organizations will develop good samurai who are attuned to what their leaders want and are ready to execute those wishes on a moment's notice. At the same time, however, these organizations will not want unthinking drones within their ranks, nor will they want leaders abusing their positions of power. They will make sure their people still have a healthy skepticism for ideas presented to them, so they can push and poke concepts until they really make sense. And leaders need to make sure they are doing right by their people by collecting information, being clear about goals, and following through on their vision.

NOTES

1. Chie Nakane, *Japanese Society*, Berkeley, Calif.: University of California Press, 1970.

2. Takeo Doi, *The Anatomy of Dependence*, Tokyo: Kodansha International, 1971.

3. Michael Hammer and James Champy, *Reengineering the Corporation*, New York: HarperBusiness, 2001.

4. Anne Marie Knott, "The Dynamic Value of Hierarchy," *Management Science*, 00251909, March 2001, Vol. 47, Issue 3.

5. Takashi Hiromatsu, Shinichiro Kaneda, Ayako Hirono, and Takahiro Hosoda Tokushu, "Kuchita soshiki no soseihou—Tachiagaru Daiei," *Nikkei Business*, Nikkei Business Publications, Inc., Tokyo: March 26, 2001, p. 36.

6. Ibid., p. 38.

7. Ibid., p. 36.

8. Ibid., p. 38.

9. Ibid.

10. Ibid., p. 39.

11. Thomas H. Davenport and John C. Beck, *The Attention Economy: Understanding the New Currency of Business*, Boston: Harvard Business School Press, 2002.

CHAPTER 8

LOYAL

Before the Tokugawa period, samurai as we have come to know them really didn't exist. Warriors of that era were loyal to a particular warlord as long as it was convenient. But as soon as that warlord ceased to be successful, the samurai moved on. That is a pretty common human behavior. Why stay on a sinking ship if there is another perfectly good ship floating by?

This "looking out for number one" is clearly evident in the sixteenth century story of samurai Akechi Mitsuhide. In 1582, daimyo Oda Nobunaga (who was at the time consolidating power and turning into an uber-lord in eastern Japan) ordered one of his loyalists, Mitsuhide, to assemble his troops and march to the west to attack another daimyo. Without getting too involved in the details, Mitsuhide instead betrayed Oda, killing him and his heir to take over as shogun. Crime doesn't pay in this instance, however. After his treachery, Mitsuhide survived as shogun for a mere 13 days before being killed in battle.

DYING TO DIE

After centuries of such behavior, the loyalty of the samurai slowly became institutionalized. When we think back to movies we've seen about samurai, we think of loyalty to a stable lord in a stable environment, as evidenced by oaths, sometimes even sealed with contracts written with the samurai's own blood, which were then burned with the ashes dissolved in liquid and ingested (ick).

Most famous is the story of the 47 Ronin, immortalized in drama and film, and one of Japan's best-known legends. Author Kyoko Hirano said about this story, "whenever a film studio fell into financial distress, it would produce a film based on this story, for a guaranteed hit."[1] After their daimyo was killed, the 47 Ronin not only avenged his killer, but were then forced to sacrifice themselves in the classic *seppuku* ritual. Now that's loyalty!

Loyalty is one of those basics that seems to have survived in every incarnation of bushido. Regardless of when it was first implemented among samurai, if you're trying to revive an organization, loyalty is not just a key concept—it's a strategic asset. You need everyone in agreement and committed to you in order to effectively implement your plan. Perhaps because of the samurai influence, Japanese prefer loyalty and commitment as a basis for reward more than Americans. Although a majority favor rewarding individual performance in both countries, loyalty is more acceptable in Japan. Americans favor this practice fewer than 1 out of 5 times—meritocracy reigns supreme.

Our corporate samurai also have something to say about loyalty. The Modern Day Samurai in our survey reported that they were much quicker to defend their companies in the face of hostility. Four out of five Japanese MDS and 19 out of 20 American MDS say they would defend their company in the face of hostility or adverse business conditions. Fewer than half of the nonsamurai in Japan and approximately 3 out of 4 nonsamurai in the United States say the same.

So even though many of your people will be loyal to your company in a crisis, there will still be those who will flee in the face of danger. Even though they may be a minority, it is important to identify them in advance of any actual danger—the price will be too high once the danger is already upon you. Since a healthy housecleaning can be an important part of renewal, you need to sort out who wants to stay and who wants to go. This is essential to starting any organization's renewal plan.

THERE'S SOMETHING ABOUT SHINSEI

Take the case of Shinsei Bank in Japan. The new CEO, Masamoto Yashiro, wanted to implement a more Westernized management style to save the bank from certain ruin. This included introducing a more performance-based system for personnel, changing the relationship between bank branches and their customers, and hiring new managers, even foreigners, to replenish the staid corporate culture that had been in place.

Yashiro's efforts met with resistance at first. Employees who would not adhere to the new practices were let go, enough people to fill four of the bank's twenty floors. But this was an important step. As for any reform to succeed, Yashiro would first have to clear out resistance.

In implementing the performance-based system, Yashiro took steps to make sure high performers were rewarded with much higher salaries than their counterparts—something unusual in Japanese companies. He also drastically shifted authority over personnel issues from the human resources (HR) division into each individual business unit.[2]

Yashiro's plan was to tighten the bank's relationships to the conglomerates, to make the bank more responsive to their needs instead of trying to dictate the terms of the relationship. This, too, was unpopular at first, but he knew it had to be done. "The bank-and-customer relationship has to be changed, from traditional total reliance on banks to support[ing the company] when the management is at fault," he said at the time.[3]

Finally, Yashiro put new blood into the organization to replace those who had been unwilling to go along with new reforms. When it was over, 45 percent of employees working for Shinsei Bank were new, and had no memory of the painful old days.[4] Yashiro also brought in managers from outside Japan—from India and the United States—to give the old traditional culture some balance.[5]

Yashiro also instituted a telephone meeting every two weeks at 8 a.m. between the head office and branch offices where everyone participated. In the meeting, management would explain its business decisions and new services to the branch, and vice versa. Additionally, participants could ask any question they wanted of Yashiro. Thanks in part to these efforts, Yashiro was able to reform the company. Said one new managing director, "I feel speed in Shinsei's business that I have never experienced" before.[6] As a result, financial performance rose to JPY 66.4 billion in net income as of 2003.[7]

Contrast that with Enron, or with victims of the recent crash, which ultimately could not be "renewed." When their number came up, they simply died. Why? Well, besides the obvious financial difficulties, organizations like Enron cultivated little in terms of loyalty. Employees were taught to look out for number one—and they did. "It was a tremendous pressure cooker," said one senior trader about life at Enron. "You ended up with a bunch of people trying to shoot for number one. And you can't get there by being a nice guy and doing what you're told. You had to be a superstar, and that's what everybody tried to be."[8]

When trouble came, many employees left without looking back. As financial troubles mounted for Enron in 2002, attrition started to hit the rate of one employee quitting per business hour. "We are losing our most talented employees," said Daniel Leff, chairman and chief executive officer of Enron Energy Services, the executive charged with overseeing the continuing liquidation of Enron's energy-trading portfolio. "Everyone in the entire organization feels the taint that comes from the collapse...and many people are just looking to get down the road."[9] Enron had clearly never built up a reservoir of goodwill among its employees, and could not marshal them when a crisis hit.

THE LOYALTY MINDSET

Loyalty may appear to be more prevalent across an organization that is in the Taming stage—people are making money, everyone seems to be doing well, and organizational cohesion is at a high. But when the catalytic event comes, you quickly see who was truly loyal and who was just looking to ride the company's good fortune to the top. The good news is that once that sorting out has occurred, you at least know that the people who are still around after the catalytic event are really committed to the organization.

How can you try to build such loyalty in advance of a crisis? We have several guidelines. It seems that smaller companies are a lot better at keeping employees happy, which in turn, keeps customers happy. In one survey, when workers were asked to complete the sentence, "Around here, customers are...," it turned out that "72% of people working for firms with fewer than 50 employees said something positive. At companies with 1,000 or more employees, just 37% did.[10] What can you do if your firm is already over 1,000 people, as we imagine many of yours are? Make sure directives from the top are clearly communicated with a minimum of interference from middle levels. This doesn't mean you need to get rid of the middle levels, as those parts of an organization often play an important role in keeping a company running smoothly. But getting your middle levels to be *conductors* of the company's message, rather than an interference, will go a long way toward removing the disconnect between employees in large firms and customers.

Leaders must project a particular mix of characteristics to incur loyalty from subordinates. "Leaders must be believable, competent and enthusiastic" while simultaneously expressing "competence, caring, fairness, candor and authenticity."[11] It is said that you can't trust the message if you don't trust the messenger, so keep that in mind as you communicate with those below you.

One other thing you can do is make sure to properly train your people to keep them ready for the challenges ahead. "Training and development is critical in terms of employees feeling good about working for their organization," said Marc Drizin, a vice president at Walker Information and director of a study on the topic. "But I think most CEOs—and to a lesser extent, other managers—look at training and development as a cost."[12] That is unfortunate, because loyalty isn't born overnight; it's developed over a matter of years as employer and employees engage in a series of mutually beneficial transactions. Showing you're committed to your people and to helping them expand their skill sets is one of the most powerful ways to lower turnover.

Not surprisingly, there is also evidence that loyalty translates into increased employee retention. Think about it—who would you rather have working under you? Someone who stuck with you through the tough times or someone who quit the first opportunity they got? Companies and managers often choose the former, as studies show employees who stayed put during the lean times are often looked at more favorably when times at the company get better. A study by the U.S. Department of Labor showed that during the recent recession, "the number of short-tenured managers and executives falling victim to job cuts rose by 50 percent in 2001, while those who have expressed loyalty to organizations are being retained."[13] In other words, a sort of "first in, last out" philosophy.

There's no question the lifetime employment system has ceased to exist in both the United States and Japan, with younger workers more likely to hop around than any other working generation who have come before. In fact, U.S. Department of Labor data also show college graduates held an average of 11.7 jobs between the ages of 18 and 34![14] This means managers will have an even harder time retaining truly talented samurai to charge with them into battle. How you tackle this challenge through the directives you set and the vision you lay out will be of paramount importance to keeping your best people and having their talents show through to customers.

Unthinking Warriors

Of course, with unquestioning loyalty comes a darker side. What happens if the boss tells employees to never question directives, no matter how harebrained? You run the risk of turning the organization into a bunch of automatons that can't make an independent decision ever. Japan's salaryman culture was described as just that loyal. In fact, the Japanese loved to describe employees in large corporations as *kintaro ame*. *Kintaro ame* is a round rod of hard candy with an image of a boy, Kintaro, running through the entire candy. Wherever you slice the rod, the smiling face of Kintaro is exactly the same. No matter which salaryman you look at, they were basically the same. They were all trained in exactly the same ways. They were brought up in the organization to think in very similar ways. And they were encouraged to never *ever* question those in authority.

No smart executive wants an army of unthinking robots doing his or her unquestioned bidding—except a few mad geniuses we see occasionally at the movies. You want your people to think through problems and come up with solutions to match. Part of loyalty is being true to yourself and what you see as best for your organization at the same time. If the boss has prescribed a program, give it a careful once-over before proceeding—don't just automatically accept what is given to you. Likewise, if you're in charge, make sure to solicit honest opinions from those around you—not just hollow affirmations of what you think you already know.

Given Japan's history of loyalty, hierarchy, and face-saving, you'd expect the average Japanese professional to fall into this category of "unthinking warrior" pretty easily. But contrary to what one might believe, our survey results actually showed that Americans were more likely to have these attitudes than Japanese. On a wide variety of questions, Americans were found to agree more than Japanese about the importance of loyalty, of not criticizing superiors, and of the fear of losing acceptance. On some questions the differences were small; on others, they were quite significant—but in all cases, they were enough to make us think something interesting is happening in both countries that we hadn't expected.

The biggest differences were in regard to the statement that a "soldier's loyalty, commitment, dedication and effort [is] a good way to get business done." About 18 percent more Americans agreed with this statement than Japanese. Perhaps this is not surprising, as the military had been a discredited and toothless organization in Japan since the end of World War II. But how many media stories had we been fed about Japanese workers' loyalty and commitment to their organizations? Americans are supposed to be free agents, yet they are much more willing to sign up for a military model in the workplace.

Two more survey statements really highlighted an important difference in the philosophy of the two countries. Nearly all Americans agreed that "When you need to correct someone, you should communicate it in some way to avoid embarrassing them," but only about 5 out of 6 Japanese felt the same. Also as we mentioned previously, a quarter of Americans said "People should not criticize those in authority, even when they think they are wrong," while only 15 percent of Japanese did. So Americans find themselves more worried about saving face and criticizing higher-ups than Japanese do.

On two other survey statements, "It is important for company leaders to be respected and appreciated by company employees" and "When I disagree with a supervisor, I am concerned about losing his or her acceptance," American agreement barely edged out Japanese agreement.

And finally, when we asked Americans and Japanese directly about loyalty, the answers were astonishing. On the statement "I consider loyalty very important," 94 percent of American respondents answered affirmatively. Only 61 percent of Japanese reported that loyalty was very important to them. On the statement "Loyalty is the most important virtue in life"—not just "very important" but "most important"—76 percent of Americans still believed this statement. But only 35 percent of Japanese felt this way. Even more telling to any sociologist is a simple fact: these attitudes about loyalty differ very little from age group to age group. Across the board, Japanese report that they don't believe loyalty is nearly as important as Americans seem to believe it is.

If you've ever read much theory about Japanese management in the past, you know these data are pretty shocking. It is hard to believe that the Japanese are answering questions this way. But if you begin to understand where both societies are in terms of the Renewal Cycle, it becomes clearer. The U.S. economy is for the most part still in the Taming stage of the cycle. The Japanese have already faced the catalytic event and are moving on to looking at what is next. At times like this, most organizations, most societies, and most individuals who are going through the Renewal Cycle want to ring out the old and ring in the new. The answers that Japanese and Americans are giving on this survey relate directly to where they are in the cycle right now. Japanese respondents are expressing a need to distance themselves from the overwhelming societal norm of loyalty in order to accomplish the work of the Renewal Cycle. Similarly, Americans are avowing deep loyalties as they Claim and Tame their business worlds.

Factional Strife

Another area that leaders of organizations have to be careful about in instilling loyalty to the company is that sometimes loyal people are so focused on protecting their turf, their boss, or their budget, they forget about the largest mission at hand—creating value for the company. You should be heartened when people fight for those things which are near and dear to them, but only to a point. After all, once a decision is made, it's fairly common for toes to be stepped on.

Keeping people in the loop and involved in the process is important, but make sure everyone knows where the limits are when they fight for a pet project or favorite employee. Let them know you respect their wishes and will do everything reasonable to make the final call—but sometimes, loyalty asks too much of a corporation.

For example, in the spring of 2003, Mitsui Chemicals and Sumitomo Chemical canceled the proposed merger plan they had expected to implement in October of that year. For more than two years, each company had tried to reach an agreement, but nothing had worked. Outstanding issues ranged from disagreements over financial details to overseas operations and accounting procedures. In the beginning of 2003, Sumitomo Chemical made an announcement about a planned chemical complex in Singapore that caught Mitsui off guard and substantially changed the assumptions for the merger. But it was more than just numbers and spreadsheets—employees of each firm had been conditioned to think of the other firm as a competitor, and thus were dragging their feet toward reaching an agreement. The two companies were clearly not communicating, and any hope of synergy from merging the two firms was quickly disappearing. The merger was called off.[15]

Japanese steel companies NKK and Kawasaki Steel also tried to merge two separate corporate cultures through a joint venture, but over the years Japanese steel companies have been bred to be very independent. The two companies had very different corporate cultures—NKK is more laid back; Kawasaki is more aggressive. However, this time the joint venture went forward only because the top two executives for each firm had strong emotional ties to the idea and insisted on it.[16]

CONCLUSION

We can see real benefits to inspiring loyalty within organizations, modeled on the samurai who went selflessly into battle on behalf of their daimyo. But the samurai did not blindly charge ahead without giving their actions serious thought—they wouldn't have been samurai for long if they'd done that!

Loyalty is an excellent tool that can be used to help eliminate uninspired people from a corporation, or inspire people to persevere when the going gets tough. It will help you decide which employees are really committed to your organization and which have their minds elsewhere. But be careful: loyalty can turn your people into mindless drones or fierce backstabbers. Some actions committed in the name of loyalty can actually help weaken your organization from within. Instead, encourage a healthy yet intellectually curious approach to running the organization. Doing so will help you ward off attacks even in the worst of times.

NOTES

1. Kyoko Hirano, Mr. Smith Goes to Tokyo: Japanese Cinema under the American Occupation 1945–1952, Washington, D.C.: Smithsonian Institute Press, 1992.

2. Tsunefumi Matsumoto, "Jinzai Ikusei no susume Vol.10—Seika shugi wo hashira tosuru jinjiseido kaikaku de kiseki no fukkatsu wo togeta Shinsei Ginkou," Nikkei BP. Nikkei Business Publications, Inc. Tokyo: April 15, 2004. http://nikkeibp.jp/wcs/leaf/CID/onair/jp/jp_print/302082.

3. Phred Dvorak, "The Trials of a Reformed Japanese Bank—A Restructured Shinsei Has Boosted Its Profit But Drawn Public Ire," Wall Street Journal, New York: March 27, 2001, p. A.14.

4. Tsunefumi Matsumoto, op. cit.

5. Takashi Hiromatsu and Syunichi Tamura, "Tokushu: Dame Ginkou no Soseihou—Shinsei Yashiro magic ni manabe," Nikkei Business. Nikkei Business Publications, Inc., Tokyo: June 25, 2001, p. 28.

6. Ibid., p. 29.

7. "Shinsei Bank Performance Highlights," Shinsei Bank Home Page, Sept. 8, 2004. http://www.shinseibank.com/investors/en/ir/performance/index.html.

8. Alexei Barrionuevo, "Jobless in a Flash, Enron's Ex-Employees Are Stunned, Bitter, Ashamed," Wall Street Journal, New York: Dec. 11, 2001, p. B.1.

9. Mitchell Pacelle, "Questioning the Books: Enron Employees Are Quitting at Nearly a 90% Rate for 2002," Wall Street Journal, New York: April 17, 2002, p. C.15.

10. Anne Fisher, "A Happy Staff Equals Happy Customers," Fortune, July 12, 2004, Vol. 150, Issue 1, p. 52.

11. Robert D. Costigan, Richard C. Insinga, Grazyna Kranas, Vladimir A. Kureshov, Selim S. Ilter, "Predictors of Employee Trust of Their CEO: A Three-country Study," Journal of Managerial Issues; Summer 2004, Vol. 16, Issue 2, p. 197.

12. John McClenahen, "Headed for the Exits," *Industry Week/IW*, 00390895, Nov. 2003, Vol. 252, Issue 11.

13. John Challenger, "Short-term staff face the axe, while loyalty pays off," Canadian HR Reporter, Toronto: Feb. 25, 2002,Vol. 15, Issue 4, p. 4.

14. Ibid.

15. Yurko Sotozono and Momoko Kugawa, "Jiji Choryu: Tougou hiritsu mondai ha hyouzan no ikkaku—Mitsui Sumitomo Kagaku wo tsubushita Pandra no hako," Nikkei Business, Nikkei Business Publications, Inc., Tokyo: April 7, 2003. p. 9.

16. Tsuneaki Saitou, "Case study: JFE Steel—Ibunka tokashi tetsuno kizuna," Nikkei Business. Nikkei Business Publications, Inc. Tokyo: April 21, 2001, pp. 54, 58.

CHAPTER 9

EUDEMONIC

The hierarchical structure of Japanese society made the feudal relationship between lord and commoner very clear. Farmers and fishermen produced the food that kept samurai, daimyo, and shogun alive. In exchange for turning over their bounty, farmers and fishermen received great respect and protection. After all, without them, even nobles would starve.

PROTECTORS OF THE COMMON FOLK

So it is no surprise that even though the samurai were above these other classes in terms of social order, they were still expected to respect them. According to the samurai codes, they were charged with the stable functioning of society. "Warriors are functionaries who are supposed to punish criminals disrupting society, and bring security to the members of the other three classes," stated the code. "Therefore…as a warrior you should not abuse or mistreat the other three classes."[1] Even though, without a doubt, samurai frequently failed to live up to these ideals throughout history, this was still the ideal to be met.

One of the most archetypical stories of samurai coming to the aid of the "lower classes" is found in the classic Japanese film *Shichinin no samurai* (*The Seven Samurai*). Based on an ancient anecdote, director Akira Kurosawa told a tale of seven fierce warriors drawn to protect a small town from rampaging bandits for no reason greater than "honor" itself. The samurai are not promised much payment or glory in return for risking their lives on behalf of the hapless villagers. Yet the samurai undertake the challenge anyway. Why? "For the adventure of it all, of course," according to essayist

David Ehrenstein. "These men have seen many battles, but only in this one will they be truly able to test themselves. There's no reward, and the odds against their winning are a good 100 to 1—and that's exactly why they want to stay and fight."[2]

UESUGI YOZAN

The story of samurai Uesugi Yozan brings this protection theme into harmony with some important business lessons. In the mid-eighteenth century, Yozan was adopted into the daimyo house of Yonezawa. He was around the age of 17. Yonezawa was one of the relatively larger fiefdoms within Japan at the time, yielding an annual rice production of about 150,000 bushels. Even so, it had been mismanaged to the point of insolvency.

As the story goes, on one chilly autumn day, Yozan was warming his hands on a piece of charcoal, which was about to burn out. By blowing on it, he revived it, and had an inspiration. He called all his subjects before him and said, "As I saw with my own eyes the poverty of my people, I was just about to lose all hope when I became aware that the piece of charcoal in my hand-warmer was about to go out. As I blew lightly on the charcoal it began to glow again. I wondered whether I could rekindle the same sort of flame in the heart of my domain and the hearts of my people and restore them to better conditions. The prospect fills me with hope."[3] Through new policies of thrift, promotion of local industry, and increased development of available farmland, Yozan eventually brought the fiefdom back to economic health. This became a well-told story about the importance of saving and hard work, and was repeated through the generations.

SAMURAI PATERNALISM

Paternalism can't be ignored, even in today's modern business environment in Japan. In the Japanese corporate culture, leaders are usually carefully cultivated to rise up through the ranks, sometimes taking as long as 35 years to reach the pinnacle. Over time, the leader is inculcated in the ways and cultures of the company. Since they used to be at the bottom themselves, they know what the lower-level workers are going through, and will be more likely to protect them—rather than laying off entire divisions, looking to cash in on a quick merger.

Japanese employees expect this kind of behavior from their leaders. And the communities around these firms almost demand it. Foreign firms have been relegated to second-class status in Japan partly because reputedly they did not treat their employees the way Japanese wanted to be treated. Japanese imagined U.S. corporate leaders as money-grubbing hatchet men who valued profits much more than they valued the lives of their employees and associated families. In some cases, that characterization was close to the truth. Meanwhile, large Japanese corporations were not accustomed to letting employees go. For one thing, companies had been growing at such breakneck speed since the 1950s that very few Japanese leaders could remember the last time that the company had suffered from anything but a lack of qualified employees. There had simply been very little need for layoffs.

In the mid-1980s, Motorola bought a semiconductor plant in rural Aizu-Wakamatsu. The U.S. corporation sent an engineer named Rick Younts from Texas to run the new shop. The acquisition was, at the time, the largest merger of a U.S. and Japanese company in history. And Younts, the new general manager, had never really set foot outside the United States before in his life. Those who heard about Younts's case figured he was probably doomed to failure—he didn't speak Japanese, didn't really understand the culture, and you can't get much more "typically American" than a Texan. There was little hope to begin with, and what little there was disappeared completely when the semiconductor industry found itself in a terrible recession in 1985.

But things soon got strange. Both Younts's Japanese and American employees worked hard to convince him of one simple fact—if Motorola laid off Japanese employees less than a year after they had acquired the semiconductor plant, they would have a tough time hiring any of the better class of engineers in the country *ever again*. City officials begged and pleaded with Younts to follow Japanese paternalistic attitudes and try to keep his people employed no matter what. Younts listened, and though he may not have understood Japan, he did understand the semiconductor division at Motorola headquarters, whose influence he used to keep the plant open and staffed.

In the end, Younts's natural willingness to try to understand Japanese culture, the hard-driving lobbying on the part of the Japanese, and Younts's high-level contacts back in the United States combined to create a strange situation that employees in other parts of the world couldn't understand. While entire semiconductor plants in the United States and the United Kingdom were shuttered, not one employee in Aizu-Wakamatsu lost his or her job.

Even though only two of three semiconductor lines were running for short periods of time and many employees were only working one-half or one-quarter time, Younts kept them inside Motorola. When employees weren't expected to be at the factory, they were encouraged to do volunteer work in the community. They painted schools and civic buildings, mowed lawns and swept streets—all the while wearing their Nippon Motorola T-shirts. Everyone in town knew who was helping to pay for a beautiful town even though salaries were depressed and expendable income was much lower than it had been a year earlier. And when regular line workers did show up at the office they were assigned to "quality circles." They discussed how to improve their jobs, they learned how to repair the semiconductor equipment, or they took classes in semiconductor design. Can you imagine any firm in the United States paying for high-school–graduate line workers to take classes in semiconductor design because it would make them better, smarter employees when the market came back?

The downturn was longer than anyone had imagined. It lasted almost 18 months. But when demand returned, it did so with a fury. And Nippon Motorola was in the enviable position of being one of the most respected companies in Japan—not just the most respected among non-Japanese firms, but the most respected by Japanese firms such as Sony, Fujitsu, Hitachi, Toyota, among others. Motorola had proved that it could do samurai-like paternalism with the best of Japanese firms. In the process, the company earned the respect of the business press, government leaders, and the attention of prospective employees from the best universities in the country.

IT ROLLS DOWNHILL

Think about what might have happened if Motorola had taken the usual approach to downturns. It was often said during the 1980s in the United States that "costs wore a blue collar." It has been common for American firms to begin trimming fat at the bottom of the corporation.

But it is not just that layoffs start at the bottom in the West. It is also that blame finds its way to the lowest levels of the organization with fair regularity. Partly this is consistent with the Western philosophy to push responsibility down the hierarchy—empowering divisions and managers to make decisions. This empowerment is good for the leaders at the top in a couple of ways. First, it leaves CEOs free to go on CNBC's *Squawk Box*, engage in other high-profile partying, and other forms of image building and fund raising. But perhaps more importantly, it keeps top leaders out of harm's way, because they weren't the ones who made questionable decisions in the first place. For example, during the recent rash of corporate scandals, it was rare to see a CEO take complete, direct, and immediate responsibility for his behavior or for poor company performance. We could go on and on about the usual suspects, but you know all their names by now anyway.

One of the more striking findings of our survey of Japanese and American professionals was the difference between the two countries on the question: "If a company leader discovers improper work practices, who is responsible?" U.S. respondents overwhelmingly (69 percent) responded, "The worker who committed the improper acts." Another 13 percent said, "the supervisor"; 10 percent said, "senior leaders and management," and finally 8 percent responded, "the worker's group or team."

Now look at how those responses differ from the Japanese. On the same question—"If a company leader discovers improper work practices, who is responsible?"—the Japanese gave the same number one response as Americans, but only 41 percent of Japanese responded that the worker is responsible. Meanwhile, 31 percent of Japanese believe that "senior leaders and management" should be responsible for the wrongdoing (compared to 10 percent of Americans who responded the same way). And those answering "work group" (14 percent) and "supervisor" (15 percent) were comparable to—but slightly higher than—the U.S. sample.

THE BUCK STOPS THERE

Indeed, decision making has also been decentralized over the years in Japan, but even at the national level it is still always clear who is ultimately responsible for group fortunes. Even when there is a case of failure to accept responsibility, it becomes clear through behavior what has transpired. Case in point: Japan's surrender during World War II. At the end of the war, not only did Hirohito renounce his divinity but it became clear to all Japanese that he was not "in charge" because the emperor did not take the blame for the war. He allowed himself to appear to have been a puppet—to have been duped by the generals. No real "god on earth" could allow this to happen. The emperor took a fall from grace in an attempt to save himself and the ongoing legitimacy of the throne.

The differing attitudes toward responsibility that we uncovered in our survey bear themselves out in another way. Large majorities of employees agree with the statement "Company leaders should drive danger or attack away from their company." But nearly half of Japanese employees say someone in a position of power is responsible for improper work practices. Less than a quarter of Americans agree. Americans are much quicker to put the blame on the workers themselves or on their teammates. Japanese tend to blame supervisors or company leaders for setting the tone. The responsibility of top leaders in Japan is great. In question after question on our survey we found Japanese (in comparison with Americans) had serious reservations about their corporate leaders' abilities to unify, protect, or even care about the people in the organization.

This difference in attitude is striking. There seems to be much more agreement among Japanese workers that companies are more than just collections of autonomous individuals. They are comprised of people bound together by a higher purpose. When that higher purpose is compromised, it is up to people in a position of power to step in and put a stop to it—for the benefit of everyone. These attitudes increase cohesion felt by those in a company. And leaders have to lead the charge in protecting the organization.

The Case of Toyota

Take Toyota Motor Corporation. As North American auto manufacturers issue routine announcements about cutting back production because of overcapacity, Toyota continues to ramp up its activity, planning new investments all over the world. In fact, "Over the next two years Toyota plans to invest well over $1 billion in new production facilities in North America alone, including $800 million on a Texas plant to build a new Tundra pickup truck."[4] Because of its success, Toyota is now the number two global car company, just recently outpacing Ford. Throughout its expansion, Toyota has continually increased head count in Japan, even as Japanese labor costs rose to become some of the most expensive on earth.

But Toyota is determined to avoid what it calls "big company disease," even as it grows to more than a quarter of a million workers worldwide. "Maintaining a competitive and challenging spirit is the key to keeping a company vigorous," said Fujio Cho, president of Toyota. He "defined 'big company disease' as what happens when management and workers carry out their duties slowly and repeat inefficient processes." Toyota aims to protect its workers from complacency just as the samurai protected their wards from evil forces. In a recent interview, Cho said keeping his people continually challenged was part of the key to success. "I think putting my people in competitive situations and encouraging them to continuously challenge themselves to grow is the best way."[5]

But Toyota does not demand this high performance from its people without giving something back in return. As large companies all over the world pull back on their pension and health coverage commitments, Toyota has held the line. At one plant in Texas, considered representative of Toyota's benefit level, "in addition to health, dental and vision plans, employees also receive a pension plan, life insurance and a 401(k), according to Toyota officials. Other perks include free work clothes, an on-site day care and a discount on a Toyota vehicle."[6]

Toyota also encourages team leaders to protect team members by closely watching everything they do on the assembly line. All team members are "interchangeable"—they each know each other's jobs and can alternate jobs at will wherever they are needed. In addition, if a problem arises, all team members will have a say in how to solve it because each is intimately involved with the aspects of each others' work. This forms a closer relationship overall among team members than mere co-workers have. Management techniques such as these have been copied the world over by Toyota's rivals.

The Case of Toray

Another example of protection in action is Toray Industries, a Japanese manufacturer of synthetic fibers. Even though Toray has faced sluggish business conditions because of import pressures, they still have managed to preserve some job security for their employees. Toray's philosophy was to guarantee a secure employment for as many employees as possible. The idea is that by leaders doing everything within their power to keep employees from worrying about their job security, this actually improves employees' performance...which of course actually increases both returns and job security.

When Toray faces tough times, instead of forcing painful layoffs that carry large transaction costs, the employees are instead transferred to a separate entity called a "*Shokusan Kaisha* (Encouragement Company)." At the *Shokusan Kaisha*, most workers work on light-duty jobs with hardly any shift work and without having to switch jobs. These workers stay in this position until they either retire, or business conditions improve enough to have them return to full status. In exchange for this transfer, these workers' annual income decreases about 20 percent and they receive a severance package. The benefits package is more or less equal to the decrease in salary, so employees don't really notice a change in compensation. The *Shokusan Kaisha* functions as a sort of graceful exit for workers, allowing them to have a greater transition period between their regular job and the prospect of having to find another one.

The company has been running *Shokusan Kaisha* since the 1970s, with great success—Toray currently has 10 *Shokusan Kaisha* operating nationwide. With the *Shokusan Kaisha* in place, Toray has decreased its main head count by about 2,000 employees over the past five years. Toray also offers this option to factory workers who have reached an early retirement age at around 55. Workers are free to turn down the offer, but most accept.[7]

The Case of SAS

SAS Institute, a software firm based in North Carolina, was tempted with the bright lights of the stock market boom during the heady times of the late 1990s. SAS resisted that lure and has managed to avoid the bust cycle that went with it. If SAS had gone that route, under the current circumstances, they would now likely be "forced by investors and Wall Street over the past three years to slash costs to prop up the stock price. Its campus would be a much drearier place after waves of layoffs and lost perks."[8]

Instead of laying off thousands like so many other high-tech companies, "SAS has gone on a hiring spree, increasing staff by 6 percent in 2001, 8.5 percent in 2002 and 3 percent in 2003."[9] SAS credits its ability to keep expanding in part to its decision to avoid the siren call of investment bankers. "There was a lot of talent on the street out there,"[10] willing to work cheaply in the job environment, says firm CEO Dr. Jim Goodnight. Without the pressure of quarterly reports and earnings estimates, Goodnight could let profitability take a short-term hit while he built a stable long-term enterprise.

Goodnight says SAS has endeavored to keep its employees happy and protected from the economic storm prevailing over the past few years. Studies have shown that the company saved upward of $70 million a year because of low turnover. "You can pay that money to employees in the form of benefits, or you can pay headhunters and corporate trainers to fund the revolving door of people coming in and out. To me, it's a no-brainer," says Goodnight.[11]

Goodnight argues that he runs his company this way because of a new paradigm emerging among white-collar professionals. Companies must take care of their employees better because what employees do on the job is no longer physical, but mental. Stressed-out organisms do not always make the best decisions, and management should recognize that and work to reduce stress in employees' lives. To look at keeping "employees motivated, loyal, and doing their best work as merely an expense and not an investment is, I think, a little shortsighted,"[12] says Goodnight. Jim Davis, an SAS senior vice president, agrees. "We are firm believers that happy employees equal happy customers. If you disrupt that balance, you run the risk of disrupting [y]our whole business model."[13]

All three of these companies have deliberately fought against the pattern of letting market forces play havoc with employees' livelihoods and fortunes. And each company has, in its own way, had great success through a rejection of that trend. The argument can be made that by convincing employees that if they contribute to the bottom line and work as hard as they can, the company will not leave them in the lurch. Even if doing so is not conducive to maintaining the highest possible stock price of the moment, the strategy should keep your company around for a long time to come—especially if a crisis hits.

DARK SIDE OF PROTECTION

But what about the dark side of protection? Paternalism or overprotection can stifle independence and render an employee incapable of making his or her own decisions. How can you know when shielding workers from harsh realities, supposedly for their own good, may lead to long-term damage? All managers want to have their people's best interests at heart—they want happy and productive workers, which in turn lead to a productive organization. But your employees can't be sheltered forever. They need to be able to change and grow in their careers and their lives. And a well-coddled employee may not be the one most likely to work really hard and perform at top levels.

Japanese in our survey report that their organizations are "too complacent" (46 percent of Japanese versus 38 percent of Americans) and are much less "eager to accept new ways of thinking" than the Americans (38.5 percent of Japanese versus 58 percent of Americans).

Studies have shown that humans can perform well up to a certain point of stress, and then after that point, they begin to break down. The figure is often represented as a "human function curve." With too little stress, humans don't perform as well because they see nothing at stake. But with too much at stake, humans perform worse with each additional stressor.

And let's not forget the fact that paternalism is just plain expensive. It is arguable that in the long term, there may be cost and productivity advantages to protecting your employees. They'll be knowledgeable about the company, more loyal, and more willing to be flexible than if your company is in the habit of cutting them loose at the first signs of trouble. But in the short term keeping employees on the payroll to "mow the lawn" and "paint public buildings" isn't exactly the quickest path to great-looking quarterly financials.

FIND THE HAPPY MEDIUM

There are plenty of signs that the systems that encourage the worst abuses of a paternal society are already breaking down in Japan as the legal system is being beefed up. In 2004, 68 new law schools opened in the country. Japan hopes to boost its number of lawyers from 23,000 to 50,000 by 2018.[14]

Many Westerners have seen the relative lack of lawyers in Japan as a very positive thing. In the United States, there are over 1 million lawyers—1 lawyer for every 300 people. In Japan, the ratio has been 1 lawyer for every 12,000 people.

This lack of lawyers in Japan has been accepted for many years because of the central role of the government in controlling business activity. With more deregulation, globalization, and individualization of the society, however, more lawsuits are being filed (up 140 percent since 1990), and the need for lawyers is naturally increasing. Japanese companies are suing non-Japanese firms for intellectual property infringement. Individuals, such as former Toshiba employee-inventor Fujio Masaoka, are suing their employers for loss of intellectual property profits.

Japan will never approach the lawyer headcount of the United States in the near future. This may be a good thing, given that the cost of tort litigation alone is $230 billion in the United States (or 2 percent of GDP). It is not surprising that almost everyone (even the attorneys themselves) agrees we have too many lawyers in the United States.[15]

CONCLUSION

There is still a sense in Japanese culture that political and business organizations do have the best interests of their citizens and employees at heart. But there is some change afoot—a balance is being struck. Bosses and their companies will continue to look out for their people, but individuals are taking more of a role in protecting themselves and their own rights. No longer will samurai bureaucrats be totally responsible for the well-being of the populace. But, on the other hand, leaders who give their people a sense of well-being and safety will get more productivity and more attention from their employees.

Your people are looking to you for guidance—that's only natural. If you're the boss, they want to know what's on your mind. You can't coddle your people and tell them everything's going to be fine forever. But neither should you expect them to take personal responsibility for every single swing in market forces. You need a clear strategy, and you need to be clear that your strategy will be followed through, even if circumstances change.

Start by being completely honest with your people about what the situation is—tell them to be ready to face changes and a new reality if need be. But follow that up with a clear statement about what protections you are willing to provide in exchange for meeting clearly outlined goals. Doing so will leave no questions unanswered about what each party expects from the other. Finally, follow up relatively frequently on their progress using the predefined metrics you agreed to earlier. This will make for a consistent pattern of behavior for both them and you, that each party can examine as evidence that each is living up to his or her side of the bargain. No one's asking you to babysit your employees, as was done in the past. But your people will be a lot more ready to follow you through thick and thin, if they know you won't abandon them the first chance you get.

NOTES

1. Thomas Cleary, Code of the Samurai: A Modern Translation of the Bushido Shoshinshu of Taira Shigesuke, Boston: Tuttle Publishing, 1999, p. 46.
2. http://www.criterionco.com/asp/release.asp?id=2&eid=24§ion=essay.
3. http://www.rk-world.org/ftp/invisible030.html.
4. Tom Holland, "Toyota Triumphant," *Far Eastern Economic Review* (Hong Kong), Vol. 167, Issue 32, Aug. 12, 2004, p. 36.
5. Hiroshi Hirai, "Toyota boss: Competitive spirit key to success," The Daily Yomiuri (Tokyo), Oct. 27, 2003 (Monday), p. 8.
6. Greg Jefferson, "At Toyota, the employees work for their pay; The income and benefits are great, but so are the mental and physical demands of the job," San Antonio Express-News (Texas), June 22, 2003 (Sunday), p. 1A.

7. Toshihiro Abe, "Case Study: Toray—Gijutsu no atsumi de muketsu no V-ji," Nikkei Business, Nikkei Business Publications, Inc., Tokyo: March 22, 2004. p. 64.
8. Kevin Maney, "SAS Workers Won When Greed Lost," USA Today, April 21, 2004.
9. Ibid.
10. Ibid.
11. Jennifer Schu, "Even in hard times, SAS keeps it culture intact," Workforce, Costa Mesa, Vol. 80, Issue 10, Oct. 2001, p. 21.
12. Ibid.
13. Kevin Maney, "SAS Workers Won When Greed Lost," op. cit.
14. "Japan Grooms New Lawyers," Wall Street Journal, April 13, 2004, p. A18.
15. "The revolution comes home," The Economist, Jan. 15, 2005, p. 25.

CHAPTER 10

YOUTHFUL

With no modern antibiotics and poor medical care in general, the average life span in Japan during the samurai era was short by today's standards. Even children in the Meiji era, under the constant care of the best medical practitioners of their time, often didn't make it to adulthood. The average life span stayed under 45 years even as late as 1930,[1] and samurai didn't often live much longer, even given their lofty status.

YOUNG AT HEART

In modern times, popular media dwell abnormally on the young—rarely does a movie or TV show focus mainly on anyone over age 50. But in looking at samurai, this obsession with youth is probably warranted, particularly for the warrior aspects of bushido. The obvious advantages to being younger—more limber, quicker reflexes, and a greater ability to heal quickly and completely—made being a samurai a young man's game. Samurai were trained in the ways and codes of bushido as early as age 14, when they received their samurai name. A samurai, much like an athlete, would be expected to peak in his 20s in terms of performance on the battlefield before succumbing to the ravages of time.

But ironically, many of the writings we refer to for understanding samurai behaviors and thinking were actually the musings of relatively elderly *bushi*—who had made it through the battlefield and could now reflect on their past experiences. They were the only ones who had the patience and willingness to sit around and write—and the ones who felt they had enough wisdom to write something important.

It is much the same in business. Business does not seem to respect the twenty-something much, except as a consumer. (As former twenty-somethings ourselves, we can remember an impatience with having to wait our turn. Now that we're a little wiser, we, of course, think the twenty-somethings of today should wait to take over until after we've retired.) But you rarely see tomes on business coming from newly minted MBA graduates. There's a good reason for that. They're much too busy worrying about how to make their mark in the world and survive the battlefield of business. If they succeed at that, they'll have plenty of time to write their share of tomes later.

Fortunately, there's a way to handle this dichotomy. We think the best businesses harness the natural energy that comes from their twenty-something employees. Maybe they don't put them in charge—but they do find a way to get their passionate and philosophical younger workers to the top. The reason is, for the most part, renewal and revival come naturally to the young. Even though younger folks don't have as much wisdom, per se, they also don't have as many prejudices about trying new things. The era of the new, new thing, especially in the United States, was driven by young people who didn't know the *right way* to do things—they just did them. Sometimes it worked and sometimes it didn't, but trying and failing didn't hurt very much.

YOUTH AND RENEWAL

Think back to the dot-com era. Younger managers developed business models that were new and untried—and many went bust almost as soon as the ink dried on the initial public offering (IPO). Yet despite all the carnage, some of these ventures were very successful. It only took U.S. e-commerce exactly *one* year longer than Forrester predicted in 1999, during the outrageous predictions made in the middle of "e-phoria," to reach $95 billion in annual revenue.[2] Amazon now sells billions of dollars worth of merchandise every quarter. eBay and Yahoo overcame drastic stock plunges to build successful businesses and brands. And Google, king of the late-to-the-party dot-coms—and started by two graduate students with no claim to business expertise—now has a market cap rivaling Ford and General Motors.

Likewise in Japan, the dot-com companies that were successful were largely driven by the relatively young. In fact, many successful start-up companies of the last decade have been comprised of mostly young people. Joi Ito, the founder and chief executive officer (CEO) of Japanese venture capital firm Neoteny Co., is one of the most dynamic and visible figures to emerge from Japan's youth revolution. He can claim responsibility for the country's second largest portal, Infoseek Japan, as well as Rakuten, Japan's largest online shopping site. You can read all about this interesting character's exploits at his daily blog, joi.ito.com.

Uniqlo

Another important figure in Japan's new breed of leaders is Genichi Tamatsuka of clothing retailer Uniqlo, a vibrant retailer with an average employee age of just 29.3 years. Tamatsuka became president and chief operating officer (COO) a mere four years after he started working at Uniqlo, and he was only 40 years old when he was promoted to this position—practically unheard of for someone his age. In fact, Tamatsuka was the first company president in his 40s among all companies in the First Section of the Tokyo Stock Exchange. Tamatsuka's youth provided a positive influence on the company, according to one executive, who said, "Since he became President, we came to have a lively exchange of views about management because we are in the same generation."[3]

Tamatsuka believed in making Uniqlo quick and responsive. He expects all employees to keep a high sense of urgency, self-abnegation, and self-innovation. The company provides its people with robust human resource development to maintain this spirit. Under Tamatsuka's system, the boss takes full responsibility for employee morale and performance. Only supervisors who have a strong passion to encourage their subordinates can advance to the next level.[4]

"When I talk about strengthening our selling power, I firmly believe that our store managers should be able to respond to minute customer demands and should be as independent-minded as possible," explains Tamatsuka. "We will continue to offer training and incentives to accelerate the acquisition of these skills. We will continue to focus our corporate efforts on how to improve the sales skills of individual stores, optimize the very close links between production sites and final stores, minimize any production hiccups and present our customers with the most up-to-date new products in the most timely fashion."

Tamatsuka hasn't forgotten how he got to the top, and he has made it possible for others to rise quickly if they show they have the talent. One rising star inside the company is 33-year-old Makoto Hayashi, who started his career at Uniqlo as an entry-level staffer and later led Uniqlo's efforts into China. Hayashi is president of Uniqlo China, and the retailer now has six stores open in Shanghai, with more planned.

Uniqlo's motto is to be "a modern Japanese company that inspires the world to dress casual." Similar to how companies such as The Gap shook the American retailing environment away from department stores in the 1980s and 1990s, Uniqlo keeps prices low, quality high, and fashions current, which keeps shoppers happy. "It's cheap, and the quality's pretty good," says Takuro Suzuki, 19, a Waseda University student brandishing three pairs of socks bought for about $8."[5]

Uniqlo has led a casual wear revolution in Japan, opening 500 stores over the last two decades alone. The company has "made basic staple fashion items acceptable to a highly brand conscious consumer group and has been credited with, among other things, 'turning fleece into fashion.'"[6] Even though consumer spending took quite a hit during the 1990s, Uniqlo bucked that trend by pricing themselves below popular retailers and department stores, but still offering a popular product.

The company keeps it simple by offering a limited set of colors, no logos, no visible labels, and a store layout based on the "pile 'em high, sell 'em cheap" approach. By becoming one of the first clothing retailers to outsource completely from China, the company has "subverted the traditional Japanese retail business model by retaining manufacturing, distributing, selling and marketing under one roof."[7] Under Uniqlo's merit-based sales system, called the "Super Star *Tencho Seido* (Super Star Store Manager System)," each store manager has substantial independence from headquarters. Their profit-sharing system encourages managers to operate their stores at maximum profitability.

Sony

Even some of Japan's most staid conglomerates have had to rediscover their inner child to achieve a new success. Through the 1970s and 1980s, Sony had grown from a simple maker of telecommunications equipment to a major keiretsu with its hand in everything from cosmetics to insurance. Many inside the company were worried that Sony would lose its way.

But in 1979, Sony began to shift toward the personal entertainment business in a way that would change the world. Its revolutionary products such as the Walkman and CD player (co-developed with Philips) changed how people interact with music, taking the relationship to a truly personal level (and making family vacations suddenly endurable for all). Sony's capture of the personal electronics market in the 1980s and early 1990s revitalized what some considered to be a graying company.

Sony would make a successful shift in the mid-1990s as well, redefining the notion of "play" for millions of global teens. Company leaders Ohga

Norio and Idei Nobuyuki issued forth a new challenge to Sony—to build on what their predecessors had started. "With advances in digital technology, we have a new era coming upon us," said Idei in 1996. "It is my assignment to encourage the continued development of many exciting products. In the area of our software operations [such as motion pictures and music], we must pursue the many opportunities available."[8]

Key among these moves was the birth of the Sony Computer Entertainment division. The head of this division was Ken Kutaragi, who came up with the ingenious answer—the Sony PlayStation. This little device and its next version, the PS2, would go on to sell over 100 million units in total worldwide, and sales show no signs of slowing down. Sony looks to maintain its dominance with the announcement of the next generation PS3 for early 2006.

Yet even with this near overnight success, Kutaragi faced skepticism from within Sony. After PlayStation launched in 1994, says Kutaragi, "many in Sony looked down on us because we were in games."[9] But because of the product's amazing success, Kutaragi finally appears to be winning people over and making a name for himself as a potential future leader of Sony. Others in the company "used to say I was merely lucky with the PlayStation," says Kutaragi. "But now they're realizing it was no easy thing to create an $8 billion business from scratch."[10]

Sony now receives more than one-quarter of its revenue from the various entertainment sectors—including games, music, and motion pictures. These revenue sources are outpacing growth in electronics, and are the future of the company. Sony adeptly positioned itself to take advantage of how people spend their leisure time by creating new products in the entertainment area. From that success Sony is now positioned to expand its revenue streams by moving beyond just manufacturing.

THE CULTURE OF PLAY

Uniqlo and Sony provide two examples of how companies took cues from a younger generation—in both clothing and entertainment—to decide how to move into the future. But how do companies manage to keep themselves young?

A large part of the renewal process centers on how people deal with the concept of "play" in business. Of course, business is not just a game—there's real money at stake. But in many ways, business and sports have a lot in common, besides merchandising of jerseys and bobbleheads. Business is a competition; an industry has "players." Revenues, earnings, profits, and stock prices keep score—and if the team isn't doing well, a new manager or coach is brought in.

What do our modern-day samurai think about sports and business? Three out of four modern-day samurai in both Japan and the United States believe that sports can teach valuable lessons about business. Only three out of five nonsamurai agree.

In Japan, formal sports and business are forever intertwined. The national baseball leagues all have teams sponsored by corporations—the Softbank Hawks, the Nippon Ham Fighters, and the Yomiuri Giants, just to name a few. Japan's companies have even adopted American football through their "X-League," where teams like Fuji Xerox, IBM Japan, Fujitsu, and Nissan all compete for gridiron glory. Games are complete with cheerleaders, pop anthems, and chants of "DE-FENSE," just like any NFL stadium on a fall Sunday.

Corporations' history in sports goes back a long way. As early as the 1930s, corporate sports turned into something of a paternalistic relationship between boss and worker. "Sporting activities and facilities became part of a range of services provided by companies, through which they were able to exercise control over their workers' life outside the work place."[11] Pioneers in the corporate sports arena included Yawata Steel, Mitsubishi, the National Railways, and the Municipal Administration of Tokyo, who "successfully reconstructed their employees' free-time practices and the institutions that supervised their conduct even during time-off."[12]

Also important in the equation of play are video games. In fact, one could write a whole book about video games and their effect on workers' attitudes.[13] Naturally, one would assume Japanese have more experience growing up with computer games, given that the heavy hitters of the early video game industry were all Japanese. The differences between Japan and the United States on this score are indeed substantial. Three out of four Japanese said they had moderate or heavy game experience growing up, compared to only 65 percent of Americans. But we found an even bigger difference in the "over 35" segment—Japanese over 35 had experience playing games far more (65 percent) than Americans (less than 50 percent).

YOUTHFUL RENEWAL

But it is not just in play that youthfulness is an important component of samurai-spirit-based renewal. A youthful culture is almost always able to push for revolution in an industry or in a corporation in ways that an older, more conservative culture would avoid. In Uniqlo, a group of 60-something executives would arguably be less interested in shaking things up—either because they already bought in to the industry culture, or because they just don't want to take the risks necessary to change things completely. Youthful thinking of modern-day samurai may be the secret ingredient in turning around a corporation or an industry in desperate need of renewal. At Sony, it is interesting to note that Idei was not next in line when the board picked him to be CEO. In fact, he was really quite far down the list in terms of age and seniority. He vaulted ahead of the others and was able to revive the culture of the firm in the process.

But this kind of youthfulness is something that is lacking in many companies in Japan—and in the United States to a lesser degree. Our survey showed that most Japanese (64 percent versus 43 percent of Americans) reported that they wished their organization "felt more youthful" even though a minority of the respondents agreed with the statement "My organization feels old and ailing" (42 percent of Japanese versus 30 percent of Americans). Maybe the desire for youthfulness is the first step in allowing Japanese firms to transform themselves from an overreliance on seniority systems to an organizational and leadership model that allows "younger" corporate samurai to make decisions and direct competitive strategies.

THE DARK SIDE OF YOUTH

We have already alluded to many of the limitations of youth: inexperience, foolishness, brazenness, lack of confidence, etc. When you think of it…it really *is* a long list. And for every one of these qualities, there is a good reason not to encourage your company to be "youthful"—it will be too quick to make mistakes, it will not learn from failure, it will make commitments that leave the company overextended. Youth will also only have at most one round of experience with the Renewal Cycle. Face it, there's a reason why CEOs are usually older—they've been around and seen enough that boards can trust them to have at least some experience with anything that has gone wrong. They've also been around long enough to have "earned" a shot at the top. And although it may be embarrassing to admit, one of the many reasons we don't let twenty-somethings run major corporations is because it just offends our sensibilities.

So any strategy that tries to use the young (or at least youthful) parts of an organization to shake up the rest of the group will face a natural skepticism. The opinions and advice of relative youngsters are naturally discounted when compared to the old and the wise. If you want to create the opportunities for such youthful renewal in your corporation, you must constantly fight against the natural human tendency to ignore people with less experience. We're not suggesting, however, that wisdom and experience should be ignored. In fact, we think both should be given careful consideration—but that is exactly our point. Listen to the young and the inexperienced just as carefully as you do to the wise, and you may quickly facilitate your company's path to revival.

CONCLUSION

Whether it's traditional sports or the more modern video game variety, the notion of "play" can have a large impact on your business. To stay young, you've got to think young—and play young. Games keep our minds agile, encouraging us to think of new strategies, react quickly to the competition, or just keep things loose around the office after a big project has finished. Modern-day samurai know games can teach us a lot about ourselves as human beings.

So try to resist all efforts to let old, experienced ways of thinking have their run at the top. Don't give the youngsters the keys to the place just yet, but try and tap their thinking whenever possible. If you at least listen to what they are thinking, you'll maybe glean some intelligence that your competitors are overlooking. Having your ears to the ground and being open to young thinking is half a measure better than refusing it completely. You just may find the next Joi Ito within your ranks.

NOTES

1. Complete Life Tables for Japan 2000, Japanese Ministry of Health, Labour and Welfare.
2. "The E-Biz Surprise," a *Business Week* special report, May 12, 2003.
3. Tatsuo Yamakawa, "Hito Retsuden: Datsu Charisma ni idomu 40sai," *Nikkei Business*, Nikkei Business Publications, Inc., Tokyo: Jan. 6, 2003, p. 82.

4. Ryosuke Harada, Henshucho Interview: Hanten kousei no ki ha jyukushita, *Nikkei Business*, Nikkei Business Publications, Inc., Tokyo: April 5, 2004, p.71.

5. Clay Chandler and Akiko Kashiwagi, "Japan Becomes the Land of the Falling Price; Nation Divided on Deflation's Impact," *The Washington Post*, Washington, D.C.: April 11, 2001, p. A.01.

6. Just-Style.com, http://www.just-style.com/store/products_detail.asp?art=24134&lk=sup.

7. Ibid.

8. http://www.asiaweek.com/asiaweek/96/0216/biz2.html.

9. http://www.businessweek.com/magazine/content/03_02/b3815615.htm.

10. Ibid.

11. http://www.opensys.ro/rjjs/manzenreiter/4.html.

12. Ibid.

13. John C. Beck and Mitchell Wade, *Got Game*, Boston: Harvard Business School Press, 2004.

PART THREE

The Pen

CHAPTER 11

PHILOSOPHICAL

Anyone trying to lead a renewal has to be at least a bit of a philosopher. Successfully leading change certainly demands action. But it also demands thought—thought powerful enough to change how others think. After all, change means different behavior. You won't get sustained, significantly different behavior without first changing mindset. And changing mindset is, obviously, what philosophy is all about.

When you think of philosophy, swordplay may not be the first thing that comes to mind. But the *bushi* would surprise you. Though mostly thought of as warriors, samurai valued philosophy just as much. To them, the "art of the pen" was exactly equal to the art of the sword.

PEN IS EQUAL TO THE SWORD

Samurai were literally "masters of the pen"—they were the only ones allowed to use the more complex and higher-status Chinese writing system to express their thoughts. Women were outright forbidden from doing so, leaving them out of affairs of state and other high-level pronouncements. Most nonsamurai were uneducated in these arts as well. Thus samurai kept a stranglehold on the "important" missives of the day, which allowed them to claim the mantle of philosophy for their own.

Samurai thus became change agents through their dominance of philosophy, using their knowledge of the written word to connect society with an established and proven set of behaviors. This is not unique in history. American revolutionaries, for example, called on the Bible to justify many of their beliefs about liberty and their unpatriotic behavior of declaring independence. In a more recent era, Ronald Reagan managed a similar feat. He was unyielding in his opposition to communism—almost a throwback in modern political thought—and explicitly founded that opposition on first principles. In other words, he adopted, championed, and acted on a philosophy. His obstinate nature—and the political support that his explicit, steadfast use of philosophy gave him—is given credit for successfully staring down that system in Russia and Eastern Europe.

Japan's change agents have often used philosophy in much the same way. At the start of the Edo era, Tokugawa Ieyasu called on Confucian beliefs (along with real military might and a war-weary nation) to convince potential competitors to submit to a "natural order" of society. The Meiji restorers used an almost unknown ancient imperial system to keep samurai families in power even after the omnipotence of the shogun was clearly called into question by Commodore Perry and those on the American black ships.

Within your organization, change agents must arm themselves with a suitable philosophy that can make change happen. Our survey found that modern-day samurai believe, more than nonsamurai do, that their "company's business philosophy brings meaning to their life." Nearly 50 percent of Japanese and American modern-day samurai believe this, versus about 25 percent of Japanese nonsamurai and about 33 percent of American nonsamurai. Nearly all modern-day samurai in both countries also say they believe it is important for company leaders to appear strong and resolute even during times of uncertainty. Projecting confidence is important to your samurai, and they won't follow you unless you lead. With the right philosophy—one they will believe in, one you believe in, and one you can hold to as stubbornly as President Reagan—you can become that kind of leader.

PHILOSOPHER SAMURAI

But how did samurai originally create themselves as philosopher-leaders? During the Tokugawa period, peace and prosperity reigned. In the urban centers of Japan—notably Kyoto, Osaka, and Tokyo—there was an increasing demand for an education. Samurai weren't finding as many battles to fight those days, so the growing government bureaucracy held great promise of employment. Schools flourished. These thriving cities became the place to go for a quality education. And with education came the life of the mind—philosophy.

Samurai came to concentrate on two schools of philosophical thought—metaphysics and ethics. The Shushigaku school of thought "analyzed reality in terms of the dynamic between 'configuration' or 'principle' (ri) and 'material energy' or 'vital force' (ki)"[1] in nature. This was an early attempt to give some structure and meaning to the universe, and through knowledge of the universe, samurai could stand to gain some peace of mind about their place in it. These new philosophers took a renewed interest in science and nature. Westerners were only allowed in the country for a short period, but during that era a curiosity-invoking smattering of Western science was absorbed.

Philosophers developed complex systems for categorizing the phenomena of nature. Although their efforts did not approach the levels of complexity being developed by Western scientists of the same time period, the Japanese retained a healthy interest in how nature worked. Over time, philosophy would focus more on the *ki* than the *ri*, as both medicine and martial arts practitioners tried to quantify these natural energies and forces and use them in the real world. These practices would make Japan well suited to advance quickly when Western science and learning came around again during the Meiji Restoration.

In the field of ethics, a school of thought emerged that concentrated on ancient learning—the study of the classics of Confucianism, especially the Chinese roots of the belief system. For these thinkers the "goal was to clarify traditional Confucian social philosophy so that it could become the basis for Japanese society."[2] Ancient learning practitioners emphasized virtue and character as part of a complete human being. Some philosophers added to this a mix of warrior values such as loyalty, service, and honor, as well as discipline and a regimented lifestyle. Out of this combination came much of what we now call the original samurai code.

CORPORATE PHILOSOPHIES

Establishing a philosophy works best early in the Renewal Cycle, as more people are open to new thinking and ideas. In fact, sometimes a new—or even revised—philosophy is the key to getting people through the very complex and difficult process of revival. What is the philosophy that should drive the corporation? For most entrepreneurial organizations, the philosophies of the founder naturally become the philosophy of the organization.

But in a more established organization—one where the old philosophies are outmoded or stale, one that has experienced a catalytic event and feels the need to renew itself—new philosophies are developed in the Gaming and Framing stages of the Renewal Cycle. Companies in these situations should ask all the questions they possibly can. What is our mission? Why are we doing what we're doing? What is the larger goal? How do we believe the world should work? How do we make our organization and our lives as happy and productive as possible? Your philosophy must connect with how people actually work, or you may confuse your employees. And philosophies unrelated to the actual moral character of the leaders who profess them become objects of derision—at both the philosophy and the leader. Worse yet, of course, they ultimately create mistrust rather than loyalty and enthusiasm.

To succeed, a philosophy must be clear. Establishing that clarity in your organization can be tough. Large companies are made up of thousands of individuals, all working toward small personal goals. What ties them together, besides a paycheck with a company logo on it, is the company's philosophy. That philosophy is a combination of moral purpose, corporate mission, and the organization's vision. Later we'll deal with moral purpose in more depth, but for now we'll look at the philosophy behind the mission and vision of the organization.

MISSION STATEMENTS

Spending a lot of time and effort developing mission or vision statements for an organization always seemed to us like a bit of a waste. We'd sat in too many top executive or board meetings where dozens of highly paid people spent hours arguing over where to place a comma or insert a modifier. It felt pretty pointless and seemed a poor use of perfectly good brain cells. What good could all this time spent wordsmithing possibly do?

The answer may seem like "not much" at first. But as it turns out, top executives regularly report that mission and vision statements are among the most important management tools at their disposal.[3] Once we started thinking about this, it made perfect sense—on a variety of levels. With a clear vision statement, chief executive officers (CEOs) and other top corporate leaders can communicate clearly their firm's direction. Each person can then develop a "tag line" to use when talking to others about the company's direction. This process also brings the most influential people in the firm together to create one singular vision and direction. The process of creating the careful wording of mission statements may seem picayune to outside observers, but really serves as a forum for resolving major disagreements among top stakeholders. By working together on a mission statement, this top group can claim a major victory in having everyone on the leadership team agree to one "destination" for the company. There is sufficient benefit in that alone to justify the effort spent on developing and refining mission statements.

But a well-worded and conceptually clear corporate mission statement actually has much more to offer and can have an enormous impact on the entire organization. We live in an "attention economy" where concepts are communicated in very short, pithy sound bites—statements that are easy to remember and naturally hold our attention. And here's where mission statements usually go off track. The statement we envision is crisp and clear. What we actually produce is more often several wordy, jargon-filled paragraphs about the direction of the company. Many employees can't understand what the words even mean, much less use them as a handy compass to navigate through their workdays and -weeks. While a wordy statement may be necessary to encompass all the subtleties that a board of directors envisions for its company, the real challenge is how to disseminate that vision to the rest of the organization...or even to remember it yourself, without prompting. This is where a well-placed slogan can be most effective—teaching both employees and customers what you are really trying to do.

SLOGANS

Our samurai philosophers appear to have figured this out long before we in the West did. It's not that Americans didn't understand how slogans worked—there just wasn't as much meaning for the common people packed into phrases like "Tippecanoe and Tyler Too." (Bonus points for everyone who knew this was the election slogan of William Henry Harrison touting his victory over Native Americans at the battle of Tippecanoe and the fact that his vice presidential running mate happened to be named Tyler.)

The Japanese have always loved a good shorthand way to communicate complicated philosophies. Creating these shorthand messages always fell to the social group responsible for writing and philosophy. During World War II, the Japanese military drilled the concept of "sacrifice life" into their recruits. As Japan was modernizing, the phrase "Civilization and Enlightenment" was used to encourage western education. "Asia for the Asians" was a rationale for driving European colonial governments out of the region. But one of the best known Japanese slogans was "*fukoku kyohei.*" This slogan dates back to the Meiji Restoration and was the battle cry of modernization. By themselves, these words meant nothing—a contraction of Japanese characters that mean basically "wealth" "country" "strong" "weapon." The four Kanji characters taken together came to assume the imperative form and can be translated to "enrich the country and strengthen the military."

Coca Cola

Companies like Coca Cola fundamentally understand the power of slogans packed with meaning, using slogans to motivate employees and attract customers throughout its history. "It's the real thing" was a slogan that appeared first in 1942 as the company was attempting to corner military business during World War II. Coke was rewarded on June 29, 1943, when General Dwight Eisenhower ordered 3 million bottles of Coca Cola sent to allies in Northern Africa, and by the end of World War II, the military had imbibed an estimated 5 billion bottles.[4] "The Real Thing" slogan reappeared in the 1970s and 1980s as Coke battled endlessly with Pepsi for market share and attention. The slogan told employees that their company and their product were "for real." At the same time, the same four words told consumers that this product was better than anything else out there. When "I'd like to buy the world a Coke" was launched in the early 1970s, not only did it make sense in the political and social climate that consumers were caught up in, but it also jibed with Coca Cola's buying up of international bottlers and expansion outside the United States to maintain growth and profitability—a story employees, executives, and investors could relate to.

Coke wasn't the only company to twist philosophy into simple and memorable phrases communicating their internal and external strategy. Disney infused a creative spirit within its employees and motivated fun-seeking buyers with the slogan "We create happiness." Apple Computers encouraged its employees to not just think—like their cultural opposites at IBM—but to "think different." Ford emphasized quality by saying it was "Job One." Even the U.S. government got into the act, with the U.S. Army saying, "Be all you can be," and later, to appeal to individualists, "An Army of One." These organizations knew that slogans were important, and put a lot of time and effort into developing them. Remember, slogans can't be technically clear and complete; they are more like poetry than like prose. Slogans are just shorthand for the philosophy of the organization. But as the samurai (both modern and historical) discovered, if you get that shorthand right, then the slogan becomes a powerful and accessible communications tool that can accelerate the change process.

But make no mistake: your philosophy needs to be about a lot more than how you communicate, or even what you communicate. It should be about who you are, and what your organization needs to become, at the deepest level. Take a look at the heart behind one successful, very nuts-and-bolts company.

Kyocera

Japan's Kyocera has been successful for over 40 years. Founded by Kazuo Inamori in 1959, Kyocera branched out from ceramics to electronics, film, and optical equipment. The company now also does a brisk business in telecommunications and finance as well. Obviously, this is a company that makes its numbers. But that market strength rests on a strong philosophical tradition. This ideological bent has helped them succeed in both good times and bad. Inamori explained how early adversities did not stand in the way of implementing his vision. "When I founded Kyocera, I didn't have sufficient funding, let alone decent facilities or equipment. However, I was fortunate enough to have associates with whom I felt a spiritual bond. We shared every joy and pain, just like a family. I therefore decided to run this company with faith in the human spirit. The human spirit is said to be easily changed. Yet, when a deep sense of trust exists, I have found that there is nothing stronger or more reliable than our spiritual ties. Today, this faith in the human spirit forms the very heart of Kyocera."[5]

Inamori-isms

Inamori says his philosophy was influenced heavily by Takamori Saigo, who played a significant role in the Meiji Restoration. Inamori has even distilled his philosophy down to 12 "principles," easily learned by management and new employees at Kyocera. Together, these principles are known as "Inamori-isms." Inamori-isms have become the main focus for all Kyocera employees, largely thanks to the work of new chairman Kensuke Ito, who said, "when our Kyocera philosophies get weakened, it's a time when the fate of the company ends."[6]

The 12 main Inamori-isms are nothing more than concise statements that get to the heart of what he wants from employees:

1. Set objectives that are fair yet reach for a higher standard.
2. Set specific goals and always share them with employees.
3. Hold a strong but stable desire to succeed.
4. Make your efforts second to none.

5. Maximize sales, and minimize costs. Profit will come through your efforts.
6. Good pricing is essential for good management.
7. Good management depends on strong willpower.
8. Keep an unwavering fighting spirit.
9. Get the bit between your teeth—do not be cowardly.
10. Always work creatively.
11. Have compassion for others, and be honest.
12. Always think positively; have hopes, dreams, and a good heart.

Clearly, these are practical statements about how to act. Yet compare them to most of what you hear and read in many large organizations. They are short. (Simplicity is key. Because these statements are not complex, they are easy for employees to commit to memory.) They are simple. They sound like a person speaking—and speaking from experience. And they leave things out that any committee would say should be in there. They almost resemble poetry rather than any traditional corporate speak. And even though they are practical and focused on results, they clearly reflect the view of the human spirit articulated by the founder.

Think Like an Amoeba?

Kyocera philosophy also stresses something called *amoeba management.* Built on the premise that all employees are equal partners in the company—just like a group of samurai recruited to defend on behalf of a *daimyo*—amoeba management organized the company into small units focused on particular products or processes. Amoeba units were given relative autonomy to do what they thought was right for the company as a whole. They were allowed to look for vendors either internally or externally, for instance, and to negotiate their own prices. "They were created whenever employees felt the need for them. Thus, amoebas had the flexibility to be formed, expanded, divided and disbanded. Amoebas were relatively unstructured, although some contained teams working for special projects or tasks, such as cost reduction, special process studies, quality improvement or implementation of new process technologies."[7] Managers supervised amoebas to ensure they received the necessary materials and support. Other than that, amoebas were left mostly on their own to make decisions. Having already drilled in the various Inamori-isms, Kyocera didn't have to worry about amoebas spinning out of control and subverting larger goals.

The philosophy of Inamori has clearly had a major impact at Kyocera. According to press reports, "before beginning work in the morning, employees read short passages" from a collection of his sayings. The sayings have been translated into several languages—including Portuguese, English, Spanish, even Chinese—to get Inamori's message out to all Kyocera employees. People at Kyocera sometimes even "discuss the meaning of the passage for up to 10 minutes before beginning the workday."[8]

The market has noticed Kyocera's approach, which has kept costs down and employee morale high. "This strong philosophy is quite unique among Japanese companies," said an analyst with Merrill Lynch. "It keeps their employees happy enough to allow the company to pay salaries 20 percent lower than comparable companies."[9] And Kyocera's performance has been impressive—doubling its revenue over the past decade while increasing headcount by over 6,000 during the past three years.

DARK SIDES OF PHILOSOPHY

There is a downside, of course, to reliance on philosophy. Some philosophies are not flexible enough to change with circumstances. As a result, people get left behind. This can happen especially after a catalytic event, where the old philosophy just doesn't fit the new circumstances. But people will be reluctant to change, especially after the old philosophy has worked for so long. Sears had a philosophy of "protecting the assets" of the company. That may have been a fine philosophy when Sears was on top of the retail game in the United States, unchallenged by companies like Wal-Mart. But by the 1990s, that philosophy was totally outmoded. The problem was, the employees couldn't get that ideology out of their system. It took at least a decade (some would argue much longer) to begin to rid the firm of that way of thinking. In the meantime, the company lost valuable, irretrievable ground to the competitors, ultimately becoming an acquisition target for a competitor that once would not have been viewed as being in the same league.

Other people may resist the entire idea of a philosophy in the first place—they may think it's too touchy-feely and take refuge in the certainty of numbers and data. Tell your people to resist this urge—your customer is not a number. Each customer is a human being, with feelings, values, hopes, dreams, and fears. Even if your department doesn't face the customer on an everyday basis, you are affecting those who do. Everyone in the organization needs to be equally aware of what the corporate philosophy is and how to implement it.

CONCLUSION

Philosophical underpinnings came to form the basis of what samurai life would be like during much of the Edo era. Likewise, they have formed the basis for how many successful modern companies represent themselves. Of course, each company's approach will differ, and depending on your stage in the Renewal Cycle, you'll be answering different kinds of questions about your philosophy.

In Chapter 17, we'll address the issue of Moral Purpose. We find that really great companies are able to advance corporate philosophies in ways that both explain the purpose of the corporation and give the organization's goals a weightiness that borders on the metaphysical. A great philosophy is the first step in the process of mastering both pen and sword. So ask yourself—how well has your company communicated its vision? Is it just lip service, or is it lived and breathed every day within the company walls? If the answers are positive, then you're in a lucky minority. But if not, your samurai may be at risk of drifting off because you haven't told them just how important their mission is.

NOTES

1. Thomas P. Kasulis, "Japanese philosophy." In E. Craig (Ed.), *Routledge Encyclopedia of Philosophy*. London: Routledge, 1998. Retrieved Sept. 29, 2004, from http://www.rep.routledge.com/article/G100SECT6.
2. Ibid.
3. Ten years of results of a Bain and Company survey of top executives on the most popular and effective management tools shows that mission and vision statements are at or near the top of the list year in, year out.
4. "Coca-Cola and World War II," http://members.lycos.co.uk/thomassheils/war.htm.

5. "Message from the Chairman Emeritus and Director," Kyocera Home Page. Oct. 3, 2004. http://global.kyocera.com/company/rinen.html.
6. Haruhiko Miyahigashi, "Tokushu: Inamori-ism ha fumetsu ka—Kyocera seicho no genkai ni idomu," *Nikkei Business*. Nikkei Business Publications, Inc., Tokyo: Sept. 27, 2004, pp. 38, 39.
7. Robin Cooper, "Kyocera Corp.: The Amoeba Management System," *Harvard Business Review*, August 1, 1994, p. 1.
8. Thomas Crampton, "Kyocera Chief Leaves Imprint On His Empire," *International Herald Tribune*, Monday, May 28, 2001.
9. Ibid.

CHAPTER 12

SPIRITED

As we saw in the last chapter, samurai evolved over time from pure warriors to thinkers and philosophers. Throughout their history, the samurai have also had a spiritual quality. The notion of the *Yamato Damashii* (Yamato Spirit) was always associated with the samurai, and it was this esprit de corps of their mission that gave purpose to their lives. Yes, samurai served their particular daimyo. But in doing so, they also served the essence of Japan and the beliefs that came to be such an important part of that society.

SPIRIT OF HARD WORK

The spirit of samurai service is wrapped up in the quality of their works. Much like St. Paul's admonition in the Bible to couple faith with good works, samurai were expected to serve others without caring about reputation or credit. One famous samurai, Dogen, was quoted as saying, "A truly righteous man does good deeds without letting his beneficiary know of his deeds. He does good deeds freely and does not expect that in the future someone will recognize his deeds. In treating all sentient beings, he must not discriminate between those who are close to him and those who are scarcely known to him."[1]

RYOMA SAKAMOTO

The living embodiment of this spirit for many Japanese is the famous samurai Ryoma Sakamoto. As we will see in Part Four, Sakamoto is one of the most popular samurai role models for Japanese businesspeople today. He is best known for his role in toppling Japan's feudal government in 1867. When Admiral Perry's ships arrived, Sakamoto was a mere student—but seeing their arrival aroused great feelings inside him. He felt Japan had every right to be as successful as the nation that sent those ships. Thus he was determined to steer Japan on a course toward modernity. Throughout the turbulent 1860s, Sakamoto worked to overthrow the existing government, resulting in his assassination. But his goals—equality and freedom with a clear vision of a better future for Japan—truly lived on.

Sakamoto still holds a sacred place in the hearts of many Japanese today. He has been lionized by corporate and political leaders alike. His likeness has appeared in advertising for products as far flung as accounting software and insurance. Sony's employees have a Ryoma Sakamoto Research Club, and Masayoshi Son, a billionaire and head of Japanese tech giant Softbank Corp., once led a pilgrimage of entrepreneurs to Sakamoto's grave in Kyoto. "He was just so cool," said Mr. Son. "I wanted to live a life like that, put my life at stake for something."[2] Sakamoto's efforts to modernize Japan are revered to this day by Japanese eager to believe in a strong leadership that seems to be lacking now.

A PASSION FOR WORK

As we've discussed, the values considered most important for a samurai were respect, honor, and valor. We find similar results in our survey. Modern Day Samurai in both Japan and the United States agree more with the statement "I prefer to work hard with maximum effort" than they do with the sentiment "I prefer to work enough to get the job done" (by about 16 points in Japan and 7 points in America). Samurai in both countries like to go hard at their tasks—and prefer to surround themselves with those equally willing to work as hard as they do.

It's no surprise that modern-day samurai in both countries are also more likely to say that they "really care about the organization they work for" than nonsamurai are. When the chips are down, corporate samurai in your organization will put company first because they believe in its mission. No motivational speeches or gimmicks are needed with these workers—they believe the fate of the organization rests on their efforts. (And in the end, of course, it does.) A devoted team of samurai like these could be like Sakamoto in your company—dedicated to taking your company to a higher level.

Modern-day samurai are also more likely to believe "A military soldier's example of loyalty, commitment, dedication, and effort is a good way to get business done" and that because of their country's spirit, they are different from other countries around the world. Though this cult of exceptionalism may make some squirm at first, it needn't be something to fear. Many strong companies attribute much of their success to a robust culture, part of which is believing they are different. Think of Southwest Airlines, which has managed to avoid most of the labor strife affecting its competitors.

Given the survey responses that we've already mentioned in this chapter, we began looking for other indicators of "work passion." It's not an easy thing to measure, but it is important. To that end, we created a composite variable composed of three variables that we thought were good proxies for work passion: (1) At work, I do what I do best everyday; (2) I am optimistic about my future; and (3) I care about my organization. On this work passion variable, Modern Day Samurai in both the United States and Japan score much higher than the nonsamurai. Sixty-six percent of the Japanese MDS and 61 percent of the American MDS scored high on this measure.

These results show clearly that modern-day samurai tend to be more passionate and forceful about their jobs and their mission at work. Modern-day samurai are also people who prefer to work hard all the time. At the very least, this means they will respond if you push them. They also tend to be more accepting of military methods to get things done inside organizations, and believe they are truly unique in the world. What this all boils down to is that MDS put more spirit into and draw greater sustenance from the work they are doing.

These beliefs have several implications. You don't have to fear taking these warriors to the limit, because that's how they enjoy working. Not only that, they'll be completely loyal to your organization when you need them the most. Also, you can push them in ways you may not be able to with more sensitive employees. You can also play up to their sense of uniqueness, giving them special missions that others in the organization aren't able to handle. Odds are you know exactly who we're talking about inside your own organization.

SPIRIT IN THE COMPANY

Over the years, companies have often attempted to inspire their employees and their customers by connecting the deepest elements of the human spirit with the everyday tasks people need to accomplish to keep everything running properly. It can be awfully hard to connect the deepest thoughts of the cosmos to filling out one's expense reports, yet successful companies find that right combination of words to let employees believe they are playing a role, no matter how small, in something larger than life.

For example, during the dot-com boom, many companies promised we were building a better world. Microsoft asked us "Where do you want to go today?" and lately they have started talking about "your potential [and] our passion." Cadence Software asked, "How big can you dream?" But it wasn't just the dot-coms that figured out spirit: DuPont talked about the "miracle of science." Fujitsu said, "the possibilities are infinite." Philips wanted to "make things better."

Matsushita is one Japanese company with a strong corporate spirit that guides its people to this day. Its original corporate philosophy was outlined by founder Konosuke Matsushita in 1929, who said "Recognizing our responsibilities as industrialists, we will devote ourselves to the progress and development of society and the well-being of people through our business activities, thereby enhancing the quality of life throughout the world." After its founder's death in 1989, Matsushita established an on-site museum so employees can view how the company came to be the industrial giant of today. Over 25,000 people from around the world visit it annually.

What those visitors see is how Matsushita grew, partly by tending carefully to the company's spirit. Matsushita's "morning meeting" was noteworthy for how it brought company principles directly to employees. The seven principles, which stress the employee's contribution to society, attendance to team spirit and cooperation, as well as a sense of humility and gratitude, are not only repeated at the start of each workday but also sustained through conversations with supervisors and customers.

Matsushita was a pioneer in bringing this kind of ethic to the workforce. He also openly discussed profitability, which was unusual for Japan at the time. But these were revolutionary concepts needed to bring Japan out of its post–World War II slump and give employees a new mission in life. Matsushita's efforts along these lines helped transform Japan into the economic powerhouse we know it as today, achieving the founder's goal of developing a company which made "goods people could afford, [it was] not about developing the economy and technology to protect Japan from Western powers."[3]

OTHER SPIRITS

Companies in Japan have a special method of infusing their employees with a unique spirit. January 4 is thought of as a special day in the working life of Japanese—it is the first work day of the New Year. On this day, all employees are typically required to attend Shinto shrines for a ritual called *kaisha sampai*, or literally, "corporate worship." Whereas such a ceremony would be thought of as ludicrous in the West, not to mention an invasion of privacy, Japanese employees are often eager to rededicate themselves to the corporate mission after a long holiday. The January 4 trip is one of many events throughout the year that serve to "inculcate the concept of the community, the idea that each person is a member of a group and must act with the group in mind."[4] Said one bank branch chief of the ritual, "It just feels right, to start a new year, that we all come here together."[5] Staffers even receive small gifts to commemorate the occasion—one newspaper's employees got, among other things, a wooden paddle with the inscription, "A rising destiny for the honorable members of The Washington Post Co."

Toyota has long been known for its meticulous attention to worker pride. Even when building factories in the United States, Toyota transferred its rigorous and quite Japanese sense of work ethic and company spirit to American workers—who may have been selected for their own work ethic. At one plant in Kentucky, workers trained with Japanese-style motivational techniques, including "inspirational messages and warm-up exercises." On one typical morning, "even when the siren sounded for a 10-minute coffee break, many workers continued working for a minute or two while others gathered into small groups for further cheerleading sessions on safety and hard work."[6] Toyota now produces more than 1.3 million vehicles annually in its American plants, with more expansion planned in the future.

But it is not only big companies who can instill a sense of spirit. One Japanese entrepreneur has sparked a small cooking revolution inside Japan thanks to his love of Dutch ovens. According to Hitoshi Kikuchi, the self-described missionary of the Dutch oven in Japan, "Dutch ovens provide food for the Japanese spirit in these days of economic gloom and a sense of community for Japanese who are weary of the excesses of Japanese consumerism."[7]

Kikuchi is a representative in Japan for one of the last family-owned Dutch oven manufacturers in the world, based in the United States. Kikuchi quit his life as an advertising executive to follow his passion for Dutch oven cooking—and his goal is nothing short of evangelism for the product. "I want people to understand what Dutch ovens are all about," he says. So far, he has sold over 10,000 Dutch ovens in Japan and made many successful converts along the way.

These examples show that spirit can sometimes transcend culture—*if* what's at stake is something people really care about. Small things can make a big difference in creating a long-lasting and profitable organization.

Simple acts help, like bringing employees together once in awhile to remind them they're part of a team, or to instill the company spirit and mission in new hires, or even to find a product or service, no matter how small, that your people really care about. This is how spirit can be built every day in your organization where you might not have thought it possible.

THE DARK SPIRIT

But there can also be a dark side to all this spirited behavior. We've all seen that fine but important line between enthusiasm and zealotry, along with the terrible costs of crossing it. And we've also seen how damaging even the right spirit can be when it is directed toward less than honorable ends. We have seen the power of a belief, and the latitude it brings for hierarchy and military methods. Without casting aspersions, perhaps the people at Enron were a bit too spirited to recognize where their actions crossed over from getting the best deal for their company to outright fraud and abuse. No one can doubt the "spirit" of several corporate moguls who wanted to see their companies do well—but at what cost? Even though your truest believers can often be huge assets for the organization, there are clearly scenarios where they become not only liabilities but also potentially the fatal flaw. How to avoid that?

Obviously, the answer is balance. But balance with what? The two most important factors are integrity and measurable action. Spirit cannot and should not overrule regulatory measures or ethical boundaries. One way you can make sure you don't have a potential lawsuit or investigation on your hands is by making sure you direct company spirit within a reasonably accepted legal and ethical framework. What is spirit worth, after all, without integrity?

Spirit is no substitute for having a good product, service, or process in place, either. If all you have is spirit, you may have some success some of the time; if all you have is great product (and no spirit), you'll have success most of the time. But if you can manage to get both, you will succeed all of the time. In other words, without the Sword of skillful action, even the eloquent Pen of spirit has no power.

CONCLUSION

As we know from the history books, samurai valued their station with great solemnity. Their work was considered their legacy and gift to the society at large. Over time, this message has infiltrated into some corporate landscapes both inside and outside of Japan. But is it in yours? If you died tomorrow, would your people start an "appreciation society" on your behalf? If your company went out of business, would your customers mourn its passing? Have you brought your people together to demonstrate how they're part of something special? Our survey shows that you have people inside your organization waiting to respond to messages from you—what are you doing about it?

A powerful spirit can be the best thing ever to happen to an organization—the lack of one can be its undoing. Taking a "spiritual inventory" at your firm can help you find out who on your staff is ready to respond when you need it most.

NOTES

1. David Lu, *Sources of Japanese History*, New York: McGraw Hill, p. 134.
2. Yumiko Ono and Robert A. Guth, "Samurai Fever: Celebrated in History, Ryoma Moves Japan—Tech Moguls Idolize Him, Comics Spread His Fame; A Symbol of Modernity," *Wall Street Journal* (Eastern edition), New York: June 14, 2000, p. A.1.
3. Harvard Business School Case, "Matsushita Electric Industrial in 1987," No. 9-388-144.
4. T. R. Reid, "Corporate Worship Day; In Japan, Getting the Company Spirit;" *The Washington Post*, Washington, D.C.: Jan. 5, 1994, p. d.01.
5. Ibid.
6. Fred Hiatt, "Americans Shift into Toyota Gear; Catching the Company Spirit Precedes Kentucky Plant Debut," *The Washington Post*, Washington, D.C.: March 13, 1988, p. a.29.
7. Bill Spindle, "Hitoshi Kikuchi Followed His Heart to the Lone Prairie—There, Around the Campfire, He Found Nourishment for the Japanese Spirit," *Wall Street Journal* (Eastern edition). New York: June 4, 1998, p. A.1.

CHAPTER 13

CONSERVATIVE

GUARDIANS OF THE CULTURE

The original samurai had an interesting relationship with cultural change. They were supposed to make sure that the basic tenets of society were protected…yet they also adapted over the years. Their main efforts were aimed at instilling cultural norms in successive generations and making sure the basic culture didn't change even when behaviors did. Ceremonies were a large part of this, including the famous tea ceremony, handed down by older Japanese to the young since the 1500s.

Called the *cha no yu*, the tea ceremony took place in a special room, called a *chashitsu*. Samurai would leave their swords at the door, with the last to enter closing the door behind him. A scroll would be displayed with a philosophical saying tied to the mood of the season, which guests would take a moment to acknowledge before seating themselves. The host would enter and be thanked by guests who would then be served a light meal to liven the palette—often some fruit or dessert accompanied by sake. The guests would then leave the room while the host prepared two kinds of tea—*koicha*, a more formal and bitter tea, drunk from a common bowl. Then, *usucha*, a more informal tea, was served in individual bowls. Throughout the ceremony, the atmosphere was calm and tranquil, with the goal being to have the ceremony cause participants to "become oblivious of all worldly woes and worries."[1]

During the Edo era, samurai believed that while the world may change, their duty was to protect Japan by standing hard and fast against this change, through cultural treasures such as the tea ceremony. Samurai Uesugi Kenshin was adamant about his role in society, saying, "You may not be in the wrong to think that the world is always subject to change, but the warrior must not entertain this way of thinking, for his fate is always determined." And Yamamoto Tsunetomo stressed paying heed to what those who had come before had learned, saying, "We learn about the sayings and deeds of the men of old in order to entrust ourselves to their wisdom and prevent selfishness. When we throw off our own bias, follow the sayings of the ancients, and confer with other people, matters should go well and without mishap."

Do these attitudes belie a refusal to bow to new cultural pressures? Or are they merely a recognition that such changes should not be entered into lightly? Once the Edo era ended, samurai who never changed were thrown out as relics. But those who could successfully adapt became businessmen and politicians. The important thing was not change itself, but rather, the ability to judge external events correctly and act accordingly.

You want your people to stay the course, pay attention, and otherwise display the kind of steadfast focus needed to run a successful business today. Naturally, though, you also want them ready to handle any situation that arises. Again, it's a question of balance...and one that should tip a little toward flexibility. We'll get into the dangers of overconfidence a little later, but suffice it to say you'd rather have people who are not *afraid* to cope with cultural changes. Modern-day samurai in both countries are a fine example. They have an interesting relationship with change. On the whole, they believe they and their companies are well suited to make changes in both their personal lives and their company's activities. They also believe in actively taking charge of a situation. Perhaps this is because of overconfidence on their part, or perhaps modern-day samurai really are better at managing change than their nonsamurai counterparts. Either way, isn't it the attitude you want?

Modern-day samurai in both countries claimed that it was easier for them to change their behavior to suit different people and situations. In Japan, about 3 out of 5 said so; in America, the number rose to 4 out of 5. Samurai also claimed it was easier for their companies to change to accommodate different business and market conditions—in Japan, 2 out of 5 and in the United States, 3 out of 5. In all cases, samurai agreed more often than nonsamurai. For whatever reason, be it self-image or proven reality, modern-day samurai are more likely to believe that they can exert control over situations. This is backed up by their answers to the statement "I often work to gain more control over the events around me." Both Japanese and American samurai agreed with this about 80 percent of the time, with nonsamurai agreeing by about 6 or 7 fewer percentage points.

ATTITUDES TOWARD CHANGE

Westerners often value change and newness for their own sake, and glorify or occasionally vilify (for example, Bill Gates who gets his fair share of both praise and condemnation) the individual to whom we attribute the change. We encourage people to use their imaginations and drive change from within. We remember the individuals who successfully drove large changes, rather than the many decisions, ideas, and actions on the part of those who actually made the changes materialize.

But in Japan, the group is still much more important than the individual not only in word but also in deed. Even when change does take place, it is not the pioneer or the maverick who is the instigator of this renewal. Instead, a model of change involving a clear group "turning point" has to be reached first before anything happens.

This can be true in the United States as well, to some extent. But change usually happens after one highly motivated person or small group of people spends enough time agitating for a new direction. Sooner or later, the movement for change either dies, is absorbed or co-opted into other movements, or sweeps forward convincing everyone of its merit. But in Japan, the movement for change *doesn't even exist* until a tipping point is reached. The individuals who initiated the ideas are not celebrated nearly as much as the entire group that made something important happen. In fact, sometimes the leaders of new ideas and change almost feel marginalized within a company after their recommended changes were implemented.

CHANGE IN BUSINESS

Some of the most important changes in Japanese political and business history have occurred when the reason for the change was to protect the status quo, such as trying to preserve a valued part of their way of life, rather than trying to take advantage of some big new opportunity on the horizon. In a place where stability and harmony are traditionally revered, dramatic change can take place only when these innovations are in the service of future stability. The current economic climate of Japan may be exactly the kind of environment that makes significant change acceptable. In other words, Japan may be more open to change than usual. In our survey, we found that Americans (64 percent) are more likely than the Japanese (55 percent) to agree with the statement "My organization places a premium on tradition." Again, this is quite different from the usual perception of the Japanese.

The top leaders of Japanese organizations are often those who have been best able to balance the weight of change against the weight of tradition. These leaders were expected to institute change even though they showed little outward propensity for it. Sony's Idei is an excellent example. In the beginning of his tenure, he stayed far away from corporate headquarters, making few changes and thus creating no enemies. Yet when Sony really needed change, he was free to do so because he had reserved his political capital for when change was truly necessary.

Banking Sector

Change has overwhelmed Japan's legendarily rigid banking sector in recent years. Banks were often cozy with underperforming clients, knowing that a rich network of connections could bail everyone out even if times went bad. This was called a "convoy system," where every player held a share in every other player, so that risks were hedged almost out of existence. You won't call me on my debts, and I won't call you on yours. After the land crash of 1989, banks were suddenly faced with an ocean of bad debt. Not surprisingly, few if any called in their clients to help deal with the situation, for fear of upsetting the natural order.

But this system couldn't last forever. In 1997, the bankruptcy of Sanyo started the ball rolling toward a consolidation in the banking sector. Since then, nearly all of Japan's major banks have realized the fundamental problem with the status quo, setting off a wave of mergers that continues even today. Old habits are being washed out of the system, unproductive branches are being shuttered, and a healthier banking system is slowly starting to emerge. "It's a different era," says Tadashi Umino, manager of investor relations for Nippon Credit Bank Ltd. "We're changing how we protect institutions and who we protect."[2]

It is interesting to note it took eight years—from the time of the crash to the bankruptcy of Sanyo—for Japan to react. But this is the essence of how societies deal with the change cycle and catalytic events. Japan's bankers did not have to face reality right away; they thought they just needed to wait it out and hope things would be better soon. But as companies sank deeper into debt, they ultimately hit the threshold beyond which they could no longer hang on to the status quo.

Nissan

The change process at Nissan was similar: the lead-in was long, but once the change was ignited, the results were dramatic. After years of stagnation, the company finally reached the point where to not change would be to die. In 1995, Nissan employed Japanese baseball legend Ichiro Suzuki to convey its new *Kawaranakya* slogan, which means roughly "Gotta Change." The new campaign spurred sales of the brand so well that it was called the "Ichiro effect." But regardless of the boost from Ichiro, Nissan recognized that its old strategy just wasn't working, and capitalized on the change theme to reinvigorate its brand. But Nissan didn't stop there. A few years later, Nissan spun its *Kawaranakya* slogan on its head with a new version by saying, *Kawaranakya mo Kawaranakya*. This meant Nissan's "change" slogan itself should also change! Through this, they conveyed to customers that it was not enough to merely repeat a slogan of change; one should also live that slogan through continued renewal. Nissan has finally turned itself around, reporting three straight years of profitability from 2001 onward after several years of losses. It is safe to say that if Nissan had not employed its strategy of change at the right time, it would be way behind in the marketplace today.

THE DARK SIDE OF CONSERVATIVISM

As we mentioned, making a change in your company's culture just for the sake of change is often the worst thing to do. Your people are suddenly thrown into a frenzy, knowing they must change but without any larger guiding reason to do so. Plans are drafted, meetings are held—everyone knows they must look like they are changing—but why? This kind of change effort can often be the most destructive, because it should be done the other way around. Provide the context necessary for everyone to anticipate the change by sharing the pieces of information that, strung together like a geometric proof, illustrate the importance and relevance of the change. Without this type of preparation to establish why change is needed and what will happen if change doesn't occur, you are likely to be faced with very jittery employees.

Similarly, a refusal to change your company because of a blind fealty to tradition can be just as dangerous. "We've always done it that way" or even "we tried that long ago and it didn't work" can be very poisonous statements. Nothing lasts forever, and long ago is not now. A very important and necessary change of culture might be right in front of you, but a refusal to see it for what it really is might already be dooming your company to oblivion.

CONCLUSION

Change is constant—we know that from the world around us. We can't control the timetable of how change comes or how much it will affect our lives. But what we can control is how we react. Remember, the modern-day samurai agreed with the statement "I often work to gain more control over the events around me." That's how samurai differ from others—they take action to ensure whatever change is coming integrates well into their goals. Modern-day samurai do this by tying the coming change into the already existing culture. Rarely do they scrap everything and start over from the beginning. Just like adding to an existing structure, they find a place where the new change will fit best, and plug it in.

Notice how the companies we mentioned here did not change themselves completely—they went about renewal carefully and conservatively. Nissan still makes cars; the banking sector is still one of the most traditional in the world. But both realized that something about what they had been doing had to change. The changes were well-managed—far from chaotic. The result in both cases was an amalgam of what needed to be done and the best aspects of what worked before.

Samurai managed to survive for 700 years and then, even after the Meiji, transform themselves into leaders of that new era. This was only possible because they managed change conservatively. They took the codes and principles they had been living under...and reworked them to fit a new paradigm. Mastering the art of change is not easy; yet modern-day samurai seem to have already done just that.

NOTES

1. Daisetz Suzuki, *Zen and Japanese Culture*, Princeton, NJ: Bollingen, 1970, pp. 276–277.

2. Bill Spindle and Jathon Sapsford, "Japan's Investors Fear a Game with New Rules—Tradition of Propping Up Weaker Market Players Is Beginning to Unravel," *Wall Street Journal*, New York: Nov. 10, 1997, p. 1.

CHAPTER 14

GROUNDED

TIED TO THE EARTH

Being Japanese involves many things—a language, an ethnicity, and a unique set of behaviors and beliefs. The historical insularity of the Japanese has left a lasting mark on all individuals born and raised there. For the Japanese, "all paths lead to Mt. Fuji" for most of their lives. Even for hardy city-dwellers, there is a strong pull back to the *furosato* or "hometown." Nearly everyone claims a *furusato* outside of Tokyo, and as jam-packed train stations can attest, everyone celebrates the August Obon holiday by returning to their homeland to commune with dead ancestors.

In Japan, ringing in the New Year is not about staying up all night to observe an artificial time meridian called midnight. Instead, Japanese climb the highest nearby mountain early in the morning of January 1 to catch the first glimpse of the New Year sun. The sun is paramount in Japan—it adorns Japan's standard. "The root of the sun" is the name given to Japan by China (as opposed to China's appellate for their own country: "the middle kingdom"). For six centuries now, Japanese have grown up knowing they were born in the "root of the sun." To be at the source of the sun which, in turn, is the source of life for the whole world, must color Japanese thinking for their entire lives.

Now think of Americans, who have long since severed ties to any geography outside the United States and often seek to separate from nature rather than commune with it. True, there is a small nature-loving segment of society (including the Sierra Club) in the United States, but it is vastly overwhelmed by ever bigger houses, cars, and amenities designed to eliminate any exposure to uncertainty or the elements. People visit national parks, but in recreational vehicles the size of Delaware. People flee north and south, escaping the harsh winters or the arid summer, depending on the time of year. Second and third homes abound, allowing people to pick and choose whatever climate they desire. Even though Americans are surrounded by nature, it is impossible to say they are *of* it.

Compare this to Japan where Shinto shrines celebrate nature with beautiful fauna and well-kept rock gardens in the middle of bustling cityscapes. Japanese place great value on nature and "place." Even a metropolis like Tokyo is surrounded by rice fields where individual plot owners plant and harvest their crops. Japanese also tend to have less central heating and air conditioning than in the West. Japanese also send gifts and postcards to their friends to mark the changing of the seasons.

The *bushi* also appreciated nature, filling their poetry, writings, and art with images of the natural world around them. Their philosophy of *Musashi* (in "The Book of Five Rings") was all about becoming one with the world of ground, water, fire, wind, and space (the void). Famed samurai poet Basho often spoke of nature in his haikus. Modern *manga* (Japanese comics) are full of powerful and wise animals that draw their cultural impact from Japan's animist history. And the Japanese themselves, perhaps more than members of any other modern society, emphasize the arts of gardening and flower arranging.

This identification with nature builds the expectation of cycles deep into the Japanese psyche. This means that there is a greater willingness in Japan to accept setbacks simply as part of life. These things are viewed as temporary and not necessarily as signs of a permanent downward trend. The lulls in natural cycles of growth are viewed as an excellent time to reflect on the past and improve on the future because of the lessons that have been learned. Compare that to the West, where we desperately seek consistent straight-line growth, thus undervaluing and eventually driving out of our lives the time needed to learn and reflect. Downtime, for any reason (even reflection and learning), is usually seen as a weakness, not as a vital part of any growth cycle.

A BELIEF IN NATURAL CYCLES

Modern-day samurai in the United States exhibit the Japanese values of respecting cycles and needing time for personal growth. By and large, they believe more than nonsamurai that "Life's hardships have made me into a better person." In Japan, 93 percent of samurai believe this versus two-thirds of nonsamurai. In America, 97 percent of modern-day samurai believe this versus 85 percent of nonsamurai. Samurai are also likely to believe that in life "good times follow bad." In Japan and the United States, about 4 out of 5 samurai believe this.

So there is a greater acceptance—in fact, near unanimity—among samurai that adversity is important, and that despite adversity, something better will always follow. This is a great trait for employees to have—as long as it doesn't turn into Panglossian behavior. You want your people to be tinged by adversity, but not wallowing in it happily, or without urgency. We have all looked back on our mistakes as valuable lessons for the future. What sort of decisions would a person make if he or she never had to question his or her own judgment and reasoning?

This natural belief in cyclicality—the ebb and flow of prosperity—makes Japanese more prepared to deal with adverse economic conditions. They are thriftier than their American counterparts. As Americans become overwhelmed by consumer and mortgage debt, Japanese have cut back on everyday luxuries so as to live within their means. They are spending less on their daily meals, going instead to cheap buffets and drinking lower-alcoholic-content beer. (Japanese beer is taxed according to alcoholic content, resulting in a severe discount for "near beers."[1]) In fact, Japanese have saved an average of ¥13 million per household (or about $120,000 at current exchange rates), obviously by saving money on more than just beer.[2] Their savings rate has long been higher than the United States. In 2000, the household savings rate as a percentage of disposable income in Japan was almost four times that of households in the United States (though in recent years the gap has narrowed).[3]

Your employees should always hold the belief that good times are on the way, especially if the company is in a particularly troubled period. If people feel things will never get better, it becomes a self-fulfilling prophecy. They will ultimately bail, and you may ultimately fail. But if you can help people believe that this too shall pass, and that with enough determination and gusto you can make it back to previous levels of fiscal health, you'll have better motivated employees who will give time and energy to the cause.

The emphasis on cyclical thinking also ties in nicely with a respect for nature. Throughout Japan's history, nature has been highly valued. Because it is a small country with a small, sensitive ecosystem, each individual's behavior makes an impact. After a brief period of environmental disregard that came with industrialization, Japan's companies have come roaring back to place environmental stewardship at the forefront of their missions.

The head of Canon, Fujio Mitarai, started to use the term *kyosei*, or symbiosis, in his discussion of Canon's corporate philosophy. Mitarai said "[Our] activity focuses on triple bottom lines: environment, society, and economy. Some companies work on one by one. However, we believe our environmental activities lead to profits, not costs."[4] Canon's Web site also backs up its *kyosei* philosophy, saying, "The world is undergoing a major transformation from a 'throwaway' to a 'recycling' society."[5]

SUCCESS AWAY FROM HOME

We have already discussed Nissan and the incredible work of Carlos Ghosn among Japanese employees, who bent Japanese social practices around to his way. For example, instead of bonding with his team by participating in the traditional after-work drinks, Ghosn prefers to have professional lunches, conducted entirely in English.[6]

But what about Japanese managers working away from the homeland? Estimates from the Japanese government put the number of Japanese living overseas at about 800,000, with a plurality of those inside the United States.[7] This is about double the 1980 levels, when only about 400,000 Japanese chose to leave the island. None of these numbers are surprising because Japanese corporate investment abroad has been booming. In the last decade, Merrill Lynch estimates that the share of Japanese manufacturing capacity outside of Japan rose from 8 to 45 percent.

For both economic and social reasons, there appears to be more acceptance inside Japan of leaving the country to find work. One branch manager of a personnel placement company said her business has skyrocketed in recent years. "Before, it was mostly women who were looking for jobs abroad, but the recent trend is for more men to be registering with us.... Working abroad independently was considered something unusual and unconventional in the past, but now it is not. For many people, it is just one of the alternatives they consider."[8]

In fact, overseas experience is now viewed as one of the best ways to advance one's career inside Japan. As Japanese companies expand, those trained in Western styles of thinking and managing are seeing their stock rise within the company. Toyota's Yoshi Inaba, the head of Toyota's USA operations, is being considered for the next CEO of the corporation because of "his global outlook and his ease with American culture." Inaba is known for his "un-Japanese" way of acting, which is respected by Toyota dealers, especially San Bernadino, California, dealer Cliff Cummings, who said, "Yoshi's the first Japanese who's ever hugged me."[9]

Our survey showed that Japanese (more than American respondents) are interested in living in a different culture. 65 percent of Japanese (versus 58 percent of Americans) say they'd like to "live in a different culture for a while." And interestingly, 72 percent of Japanese in their 30s agree with the statement. They seem to recognize the need for understanding what's going on in the rest of the world. However, in an interesting twist many more Americans (84 percent) say, "My country can learn a lot from Japan" than Japanese respondents say, "My country can learn a lot from the U.S." (69 percent). One explanation for these responses could be that while Americans believe they can learn a lot from other countries, many really don't want to move there to accomplish that learning. Although this is pretty consistent with the general stereotype about Americans, our results suggest that we may want to rethink our assumptions about Japanese insularity and national pride.

SUCCESS AT HOME

Among those Japanese who do move abroad, many eventually want to get back to the homeland. Said one placement staffer, "Family is extremely important to them and if they are made aware of the opportunities available back home and the salaries they could command, they may well be tempted to return."[10] So it seems, even as Japanese corporations expand their reach into the furthest corners of the globe, the pull to go home will always be a powerful one for Japanese employees. They may be more willing to go overseas than before and can even gain valuable experience and perspective by doing so. But the natural cycles of life usually lead them back to the land of their birth—where the root of the sun still holds sway.

In some industries, there is evidence that the return of labor-intensive business to "the homeland" is also a good thing for Japanese companies. In 2002, Kenwood Corporation decided to move production of its mini-disc players from Malaysia back to Yamagata Prefecture. As it turns out, this was a good move from a couple of perspectives. Because Japanese workers tend to stay around longer than their Malaysia counterparts, they can be trained to do more than the most simple assembly-line activities. Consequently, a Japanese Kenwood employee is able to quickly perform four or five installation steps whereas Malaysian workers only do one. On the Japanese assembly line, four Japanese employees do the work that 22 workers used to do. That means that the assembly facility can be 70 percent smaller and defect rates have also fallen by 80 percent since the move.[11]

And Kenwood is not alone in moving production back to Japan. Now companies like Canon, Sharp, Toray, Matsushita, and Nippon Steel have all announced plans to build major production facilities in Japan. In fact, Canon has announced that it will put 80 percent of its planned $7.2 billion for capital investment over the next three years into domestic facilities.[12] Corporate Japan seems to be finding a nice balance between its attachment to the homeland and its need to cut costs and find new markets by venturing abroad.

THE DARK SIDE OF NATIONALISM

Is there a downside to being too "attached to the land"? Maybe—if one never considered any other option. But as we see, an increasing number of Japanese are willing to try life outside their home country for a while. And though many millions of Americans also live abroad, we Americans have always been relatively nomadic compared to the Japanese. That the trend is narrowing shows that the Japanese are increasingly willing to put themselves on the world stage.

What's important is to be open to new cultures and new ways of thinking. You don't necessarily have to live in another country to do so—but how about learning another language? The percent of multilingual Japanese far outpaces that of multilingual Americans. Samurai of the Tokugawa period were isolationist by decree, but even so their education was in the Chinese language and early Western science. In the same way, curiosity about the world around them is a natural characteristic of any modern corporate samurai.

CONCLUSION

Remember what the modern-day samurai have to say about hardship—they believe wholeheartedly that experiencing some suffering (in whatever form it takes) can make one a better person. Life is full of ups and downs, it's true. And having a place to call home can make it all worthwhile. There is some value in knowing where you came from. But sometimes it seems we must journey far from home to really appreciate it—otherwise, what would we compare it to? Japanese appear to be taking on this challenge in greater numbers, venturing outside the home country more than ever before to gain valuable experience.

Can you say the same of your own career, or of your company? Are you really seeking out opportunities all around the globe? The best opportunities probably don't lie within these shores—they lie, somewhere out there, untapped and waiting to be discovered. Being able to let go of one's origins, confident in the notion that one can always return, can make you better prepared to explore what's out there. The most successful companies and people break down boundaries while never forgetting who they really are. It's something our samurai friends have mastered, and something about which we could learn a lesson or two.

NOTES

1. GE Consumer Finance Co. Ltd. http://www.gecfjapan.com/company/jijyou/ji_kozukai2004.html.
2. Japanese Ministry of Internal Affairs and Communications, Statistics Bureau, "Amount of Savings and Liabilities (Workers Households)," http://www.stat.go.jp/data/nenkan/pdf/z19-2.pdf.
3. http://www.findarticles.com/p/articles/mi_m4456/is_73/ai_105851463, OECD Economic Outlook.
4. Makoto Isomichi, Toshihiro Abe, and Daisuke Takimoto, "Tokushu: Sonkeisareru Kaisha—CSR ranking best 100 companies," *Nikkei Business*, Nikkei Business Publications, Inc., Tokyo: July 26, 2004, p. 49.
5. http://www.canon.com/environment/index.html.
6. Takao Tanaka, "Carlos Ghosn ryuu performance jutsu no kouyou," *Keieijuku*, Keieijuku Publications, Inc., Tokyo: Sept. 2003, p. 41.
7. http://www.ipss.go.jp/English/psj2003/PSJ2003.pdf.
8. Yoko Hani, "Jobs for life may be on the way out," *The Japan Times*, July 13, 2003, p. 4.
9. Norihiko Shirouzu, "U.S. Success Propels Toyota's Inaba—Sales Executive Returns to Japan as a Leading Contender for the Top Job,", *The Asian Wall Street Journal*, July 29, 2003, p. A7.
10. Calling all expat Japanese staff," *Asian Business*, Hong Kong: Vol. 37, Issue 5, May 2001, p. 62.
11. "Still made in Japan," *The Economist*, April 10, 2004, p. 58.
12. Ian Rowley, "So much for hollowing out," *Business Week*, Oct. 11, 2004, p. 64.

PART FOUR

RONIN

CHAPTER 15

UNCERTAIN

Modern Japanese have a reputation for being highly uncomfortable with uncertainty. After all, they've been surrounded by efforts to increase certainty for their entire lives. The Japanese education system follows a precise plan. Japanese managers ask exacting questions about minute points. Japanese factories allow virtually zero defects. And no idea or product ever seems to come out of Japan half-baked. But as the world moves faster and less predictably, uncertainty is becoming a larger and larger part of everyday life. How will the Japanese adapt?

Maybe better than their competitors might like. To assess the Japanese potential for dealing with uncertainty, we need to understand what they love about stability, and why. For our purposes, it all began in the Tokugawa period. *During that entire 250-year span, almost nothing changed throughout the entire society.* That's about the longest unbroken span of harmony of any civilization on Earth.

BEING COMFORTABLE WITH CHANGE

By contrast, when the samurai first emerged during the Warring States Period (the era before Tokugawa stability), they fought in a landscape of constantly changing alliances. Life was peppered with change and betrayal. The samurai were accustomed to uncertainty, not knowing who their master would be tomorrow, let alone next year. Many were the fabled *ronin*—masterless samurai who became roving mercenaries forced to serve the highest bidder. In most cases, these samurai did not become *ronin* by choice. Instead, circumstance determined their fate. The untimely demise of their warlord, a disinherited fief, or economic hardship abruptly lowered the samurai's allowance below subsistence levels. *Ronin* had to make their own way in life, without the accustomed protection of a particular warlord or the Bakufu. Sure, no one could take away their status; each samurai inherited that at birth. But every *ronin* had to figure out for himself how to make his way in the world. Each had to decide how best to use his sword and pen skills in the service of the other classes.

History tells us some *ronin* became robbers or town drunks. Others even became merchants, plummeting from the most respected class to the least respected...although improving their lifestyle and financial position significantly in the process. Because of this, it's not surprising that the term *ronin* has a somewhat pejorative meaning in modern Japan. (For example, it's applied to high school seniors who fail college entrance exams and go on to spend an extra year studying to pass the test.) Yet there is clearly, even in Japan, a positive side to the *ronin* image: the romance of being free of any clear-cut organizational affiliation or hierarchy. There is even a particular strain of modern Japanese literature and the arts which celebrates these unattached samurai who succeeded in the face of so much uncertainty. Modern Japanese culture reveres the character who can create a worthwhile life in a vacuum.

It is interesting that this romanticized view of the *ronin* emerges today when Japan is again facing deep uncertainties. For won't *ronin*-like business and government leaders be most valuable in this latest renewal cycle? After all, companies that want to remake themselves into something greater need to be relatively comfortable with uncertainty.

Clay Christensen's famous "Disruptive Technologies" thesis holds that in today's business world, change—not stability—is the norm.[1] Life is about flirtations and fluctuations, not stability and straight lines. Based on our survey results, this is exactly the kind of environment in which the Modern Day Samurai (MDS) should thrive. Both American and Japanese modern-day samurai felt more strongly that their cultures were able to change more quickly and easily than other cultures. Over half of all Japanese MDS felt this way, versus only 43 percent of nonsamurai. In America, the differences were about the same, although the absolute numbers were a bit higher—75 percent of American MDS felt their culture could easily change, versus about 66 percent of American nonsamurai.

CORPORATE RESPONSES TO UNCERTAINTY

Stepping back to look at the two cultures more broadly, we noticed some interesting differences in how each visualizes uncertainty...and how that shapes the kind of response they formulate. Over the years, Japanese have often expressed an almost obsessive distaste for uncertainty, which is perhaps why in our survey, Japanese respondents favored moving quickly to stifle any new potential threat. After all, in the swordplay of the samurai, there are multiple forms of uncertainty, but the most dominant one is the enemy. What move will he make? How will he respond to your moves? In today's metaphorical swordfights, Japanese worry overwhelmingly—much more than Americans—about market share. In other words, they want to know exactly how their enemy's performance compares to their own. This focus on competitors is clear when we asked which is more important for achieving business success: "creating strong alliances" or "winning competitive battles." Overwhelmingly, Japanese opted for "winning competitive battles" (63 percent) whereas American respondents chose "creating strong alliances" (74 percent).

SOCIAL RESPONSES TO UNCERTAINTY

Throughout history, Japanese have chosen to deal with uncertainty through a rigid form of social hierarchy. In the past, the public registration of all foreigners and *burakumin* (the caste of Japanese who were traditionally the butchers and leather workers) let everyone know who was who. Today's counterpart is the strict meritocracy, based on age and where one went to college that funnels new workers into modern Japanese corporations. To this day, all companies in Japan use a pretty similar hierarchy of titles, so that when you meet someone from another company and learn his or her title, you instantly know where they fit in the hierarchy. The twin principles of *nemawashi* (consultation with peers before a meeting; it literally means "to smooth around roots before planting") and *ringisho* (management by consensus throughout a department) ensure that disruptions and disagreements are kept to a minimum.

The ritual of passing out business cards (*meishi)*, is an intricate part of establishing this hierarchy. For example, the card bearer "should make sure that it is clean and neat; no dog-eared corners or smudges allowed. It should not have been kept in a breast pocket of a shirt where it may have become warm....Upon receiving a card, it is polite to read it, carefully noting once again the name and title."[2] While these rules are surely good manners in the West, they have not been formalized and ritualized to the degree they have in Japan. One can only imagine the horror on the part of Japanese managers who encounter someone producing a business card from the back pocket of a pair of faded jeans.

Just as formal corporate hierarchies eliminate uncertainty in identifying subordinates, peers, and superiors across companies and industries, the lifetime employment system in Japan has traditionally offered an additional way to minimize uncertainty. Japan was one of the first societies to merge human social structure with the life of the modern corporation. This blending reached such a depth that it eventually became common to identify oneself as "John Doe of Hitachi" in both business and nonbusiness settings. Although the guaranteed employment system is becoming less common, Japanese still think of themselves largely in terms of their work roles.

As an insular and relatively self-sufficient nation that could easily close itself off from the influx of both people and ideas, Japan was well-positioned to employ strict social and corporate hierarchies to eliminate uncertainty about an individual's role or place. This stands in sharp contrast to the American experience, which is one of searching, longing, and exploring. Even when long-term or even lifetime employment with one firm was more common here, we Americans idealized the idea of a Horatio Alger–type self-made man or woman. And even though a school- and class-based system of elites did exist, primarily on the East Coast, it started breaking down significantly during the social revolutions of the 1960s and 1970s. Not surprisingly, given the social trends, Silicon Valley, which created much of our economic momentum through the 1990s, was itself created by a collection of social misfits and college dropouts. Though many Americans do not necessarily like uncertainty around their place in the world, most have not gone to the extremes of stamping it out as the Japanese once did.

Untold amounts of process revolution came from Japan in attempts to be ever more precise. Quality control was nearly a religion at Japanese companies, who used their position to wring ever more advantage out of their production methods. Efficiency was a clear goal for most Japanese organizations during the country's economic ascension. For the most part, Americans sometimes tried to match the Japanese in these uncertainty reduction efforts, but also devoted a lot of time to playing the protectionism game to keep the Japanese from infiltrating their market position.

WHAT GOOD IS CERTAINTY ANYWAY?

But now the nature of uncertainty is changing as Japanese companies have mostly routinized the efficiency game and, instead, face a whole new set of external worries. Japan has realized, after much torment, that trying to control the future can be a fool's errand, and thus they must prepare themselves for whatever might come next.

As a result, the Japanese are now reporting that they are far more comfortable with uncertainty in their personal corporate life than Americans. Some 65 percent of Japanese professionals report being "comfortable with uncertainty in my job." Less than half (45 percent) of Americans claim a similar degree of comfort with uncertainty. Now this is not to say the people in either country like uncertainty. In fact, about three-quarters of both Japanese and American respondents report that a lack of clarity in their organization's strategic direction makes them "feel very uncomfortable." Even at the corporate level, though, slightly more Americans (78 percent) are uncomfortable than are their Japanese counterparts (74 percent).

Internal uncertainty in both Japan and the United States is now feeding on external uncertainties, such as globalization and the speed of decision making—and the pace of both continues to increase. These external factors increase stress on individuals, probably increasing the demand for internal certainty even as the supply drops. Sharper competition and ever faster decision cycles create high stakes and less room for error. Yet one of the things people would like to fall back on under such stress, one's certain place in the hierarchy, is also less stable. How the Japanese respond to this changing nature of uncertainty will make or break their performance in this next Renewal Cycle.

TRIUMPHING OVER ADVERSITY

If anyone is willing and able to deal with uncertainty in a business setting, it is those who embody *ronin*-like characteristics. And we can think of more than a few Japanese companies that fit that profile and have triumphed in the face of uncertainty. In fact, every company that existed before World

War II and still exists today qualifies as a *ronin* organization. Every one of these companies had to remake itself, to find its own way in a world that was abruptly and uncontrollably transformed.

Nidec

There are also many good recent examples of how Japanese companies have dealt with uncertainty. For example, Nidec makes the tiny spindle motors that power most computer hard drives, digital cameras, and other electronics. From humble beginnings—in a shack behind founder Shigenobu Nagamori's house—the company now employs 41,000 people in 15 countries. The market for such motors was not always self-evident. Nagamori started work on his tiny motor at another electronics firm. When his boss canceled this development effort, he quit in disgust—and took his prototype motor along. Japanese firms weren't buying, but after a three-month trek across the United States, he finally found a buyer in 3M. This relationship would form the stable foundation for later growth.

In a further demonstration of courage in the face of uncertainty, Nagamori decided to take Nidec public on the New York Stock Exchange mere weeks after the attacks of September 11, 2001—at a time when global financial markets were still reeling. "What happened was terrible, but I'm not one to waver. We need to raise funds overseas to further expand our business,"[3] he said at the time. His bet paid off, with the stock rising more than 50 percent over the first year of trading.

Nidec now controls about 70 percent of the global market for these motors, but it hasn't stopped developing. Its newest versions will increasingly be used in cars, especially hybrid fuel vehicles as they gain in popularity, which "require twice as many micromotors as today's automobiles."[4] Volvo and Peugeot have already signed contracts worth upward of $200 million in sales.

Nagamori's experience shows that being resolute in the face of uncertainty can pay off big. He exemplifies the type of *ronin* spirit that modern Japanese revere. Nidec's goal is to become "the Intel of micromotors." Driven by his *ronin*-like approach, it is well on its way.

Toto Limited

One might not expect uncertainty to be attached to the toilet industry. To most Americans, there's really no significant differentiation possible with the average toilet—thus the market would seem pretty stable. But Japanese toilet king Toto Limited, makers of toilets with a dazzling array of features designed by "1,500 engineers working to improve every facet of the excretory experience,"[5] sensed opportunity in the American market where no new player had dared enter for decades.

Kazuo Sako, the 44-year-old president of Toto USA, is responsible for this change in Toto's strategy. Despite controlling 60 percent of the Japanese market, shrinking demographic forces and a dearth of new construction slowed Toto's growth in that market to a crawl. Meanwhile, the American market had never been touched, thanks to U.S. indifference toward toilet preferences and a lack of appreciation for warmed toilet seats and gentle warm water jet sprays.

Toto found a willing clientele among contractors who liked not only the quality of the product but the margins each toilet brought in. A high-end client like George Schaeffer, CEO of a North Hollywood nail polish manufacturer, was convinced, buying a dozen of Toto's top-end model, the Neorest, for both his home and office. Schaeffer's enthusiasm for the benefits of the Toto product was almost evangelistic: "What do you do on a toilet? You read. Sit on this one. It'll change your life."[6]

Sako's move in the face of a seemingly nonexistent U.S. market has paid off. Toto USA, their American subsidiary, has now reached "$117 million in sales—a healthy slice of the estimated $820 million U.S. market and a 35 percent jump since 2002."[7]

Both Nagamori and Sako changed their respective markets by anticipating where change was going to take place well before it actually happened—perhaps ignoring more sound and realistic judgment—then moving themselves into position to strike early before more established players could react. They are proof that despite Japan's reputation for being ultra-cautious about risk, some modern Japanese *ronin* (those unfettered by tradition and stale ways of thinking) know how to take advantage of opportunities when they present themselves.

A BETTER TOMORROW

Right now, a new Japanese attitude is reflecting itself in optimism across political, consumer, and financial sectors. Prime Minister Junichiro Koizumi has been a steady presence at the helm since 2001, gaining the trust of the Japanese public and investors. Outside observers visiting Japan have noticed "a return of the old optimism and energy responsible for the technological miracles and economic strength that so astounded the world in the 1970s and 1980s."[8] Corporate debt levels are falling, and new development is rising. The Roppongi Hills complex in Tokyo is a shining example of the new passion for good living that has infused Tokyo of late with its futuristic feel.

The Japanese consumer is changing as well, taking a greater role in spurring economic growth. A recent study by the Hakuhodo Institute of Life and Living (HILL) suggests "men's desire to spend on 'family life' and 'recreation and leisure' showed the biggest gains."[9] It seems that Japanese men are transforming from the stereotype of the dogged and dependable salaryman to individuals who value and seek out the finer things in life, including relaxation and family. The work at HILL has even shifted its terminology when studying the Japanese consumer, from *shohisha* (people who consume) to *seikatsusha* (people with lives).

Even though Japan's economy has not fully pulled out of the doldrums, the average Japanese doesn't seem to be that worried about it. Spending on luxury goods has absolutely skyrocketed. "Our business in Japan is formidable," reports Gucci CEO Domenico De Sole. "The Japanese economy has been in really tough shape for a long time. But luxury products are just part of the national culture."[10]

Could a society so concerned about never deviating from the norm really be capable of spending millions on luxury purses and gadgets? If they were really nervous about the future, could entrepreneurs like Nagamori and Sako drive to capture new markets so forcefully? We don't think so; dealing with uncertainty like this simply requires a certain confidence. As we saw in the data, most Japanese prefer to act quickly in the face of a crisis, in order to mitigate any potential bad effects. That indicates tremendous confidence that they will be able to handle whatever change brings.

But while individual Japanese express higher levels of personal comfort with uncertainty in their jobs than Americans, they also believe that their organizations are less able to deal well with a changing world. Only 25 percent of Americans reported "my organization is disabled by uncertainty," but 37 percent of Japanese felt that way. So with yet another one of the traits of successful corporate strategy, we find Japanese at an individual level seemingly embracing renewal while expressing doubt that their companies are prepared to face the future appropriately. One of the challenges facing Japan in every single pen, sword, and *ronin* trait (the three major aspects of Japanese culture that we have explored in the three sections of this book) is embedding the emerging personal beliefs about renewal into a corporate culture that encourages the necessary changes.

THE DARK SIDE OF EMBRACING UNCERTAINTY

Yet despite strong fundamental forces in Japanese culture that have allowed individuals and firms to embrace uncertainty, there is substantial risk. One possible trouble spot is the absolute level of externally driven uncertainty. After all, there is only so much uncertainty the human brain, even the *ronin* brain, can take before shutting down. An even bigger fault line may be the gap between individual capacities to deal with an uncertain world, on the one hand, and company capabilities on the other. It's possible that even the more flexible *ronin*-style companies will have problems dealing with some of what uncertainty brings. We see that in the survey results discussed above, where participants doubt their firm's ability to respond. And we see it in the challenge posed by information flow through the corporation. One of the traditional ways of responding to uncertainty is to increase access to data. The whole notion of information technology (IT) is to democratize information and, therefore, decision making. The tools to manage IT continue to grow faster than anyone can track. Yet the Japanese ability to use these tools, in this way, faces severe cultural challenges. This idea that decisions can be empowered throughout the organization has yet to fully permeate the bureaucratic infrastructure of Japan. This is a significant risk Japan faces as it goes forward—will it have the courage to drive decision making down throughout the organization?

Currently, Japanese firms process information and make decisions in a very human-centric way. Even though it is nice to see the human element remain, in an increasingly complex world, the Japanese may face a disadvantage for not fully automating some decisions. For example, Japan has lagged in development and implementation of enterprise resource planning and customer relationship management software, ceding ground in this lucrative field to players such as Germany's SAP and America's Oracle and Microsoft. There's no reason why Japan should lag behind in this field, as they have one of the most advanced technological economies on Earth. Yet because of a basic mistrust of full-service industry automation (by contrast, was early to adopt full manufacturing automation), adoption of these technologies has been slower than one might expect. Japanese firms are also experimenting with replacing the ultra-certain seniority-based systems with performance-based systems. Though these new systems will create more instability, they will also create greater incentives to do well. As more powerful technologies come online in other advanced economies, they will certainly change the way many large corporations make decisions around the world. If the Japanese do not adapt, they may have more difficulty adjusting than companies in Western cultures.

Even if the Japanese learn to fully capitalize on high-level information processing systems, there is still a dilemma about how humans face uncertainties. From the ancient battlefield, Sun Tzu tells us that we must "attack where the enemy is not." To do that, you have to know where the enemy is. As the speed of battle increases, this means knowing what moves your competitors are making, almost before they make them. And that, of course, involves a certain amount of intuition, luck, and insight into human nature. In this regard, Japan's reliance on formal structures and hierarchies to simplify and rationalize the business world reduces its ability to cooperate and compete in situations where the same rules don't apply. The resistance to other nonhierarchical forms of conduct—not understanding why other cultures do not fully value the importance of corporate titles, for example—may be what ultimately prevents Japanese firms from gaining an advantage.

CONCLUSION

Like any nation, culture, company, or individual facing the uncertain future, Japan has a choice: adapt to reflect these new uncertainties, or attempt to ignore them. Historically, of course, Japan has sometimes chosen the latter, relying on its ability to isolate itself from the larger world. It may be tempting now for Japan to isolate itself once again. We don't think it will formally, consciously choose to do so. But the unconscious desire to do so, and decisions by some individuals or groups to try isolation, could easily determine how much adaptation occurs, and how quickly. We believe that observing how the modern-day *ronin* behave will provide a critical insight into Japan's direction as a society.

The inevitable information overload of the future will have to be dealt with. Firms will need to integrate their data and knowledge assets in ways never tried before in traditional Japanese hierarchies. This means everyone, from the lowest clerk to the CEO, should have access to whatever information will let him or her do his or her job better.

But more important is what those employees choose to do with that information. They will have to distinguish carefully between what they can control and what they cannot. This is where the role of the *ronin* is critical. *Ronin* will not try to control everything within their view—they know this is an impossible task. But what they can do is use available data to sharply improve their performance. *Ronin* will then be able to focus on the larger issues presented by the data, rather than trying to micromanage everything down to the last detail.

NOTES

1. Clayton M. Christensen, *The Innovator's Dilemma*. Cambridge, Mass: Harvard Business School Press, 1997.
2. http://www.netcentral.co.uk/satcure/meishi.htm.
3. Irene M. Kunii, "Outsize Earnings from Tiny Motors: Nagamori's 30 years of persistence have made Nidec a winner," *Business Week*, New York, Issue 3802, Oct. 7, 2002, p. 124.
4. Ibid.
5. Andrew Tilin and Mariko Mikami, "Heir to the Throne Flush with Success in Japan, Toto Ltd. next wants to conquer America with its wondrous high-tech toilets," *Business 2.0*, San Francisco, Aug. 2004, Vol. 5, Issue 7.
6. Ibid.
7. Ibid.
8. Caspar Weinberger, "Japan Works," *Forbes*, New York: Vol. 173, Issue 9, April 26, 2004, p. 33.
9. "Japan's Family Men Spur Consumption," *Far Eastern Economic Review*, Hong Kong: Vol. 167, Issue 37, Sept. 16, 2004, p. 8.
10. Deborah Ball, "Despite Downturn, Japanese Are Still Having Fits for Luxury Goods—European Manufacturers Now Depend on Japan for Sales: 'Part of the National Culture,'" *Wall Street Journal*, New York: April 24, 2001, p. B.1.

CHAPTER 16

KNOWLEDGEABLE

Over the past few decades, Japan seemed to build up a kind of knowledge advantage over the West. Western managers would often bow in awe upon visits to Japan, noting the productivity miracles as everyone inside these firms appeared to share the same information and plans. Yet despite its previous success, Japan seems to be entering a new phase of knowledge management—one that cannot help but fundamentally change its established behaviors. How Japan's Modern Day Samurai (and *Ronin*) respond will determine how Japan fares during this next Renewal Cycle.

JAPANESE KNOWLEDGE MANAGEMENT

The Japanese have often been touted as the perfect models of effective human-based knowledge systems. Their largely human-centric process of knowledge storage, back-up, retrieval, and distribution was mainly a creation and consequence of Japan's relatively uniform educational system. Organizational decision-making processes were built around a fuzzy logic accompanied by a homogeneous culture and language. A natural set of vertical hierarchical links formed within companies, along with an affinity for redundancy in personnel assignments, sped the integration of new talent. Automaton-like new recruits were simply absorbed into the larger company and culture. This increased their productivity, mitigated the bumps associated with people leaving the company, and (most important) ensured constant, almost automatic alignment across the corporation.

Meanwhile, the West, which reputedly places more value on personal learning and innovation, has often generated plenty of knowledge, yet struggled to capture that knowledge effectively across the organization. Even though Westerners could often come up with a big idea, keeping track of all the necessary means to implement such an idea cheaply and efficiently often remained beyond their grasp. To circumvent the problem, Western firms would develop and install massive and expensive electronic knowledge management systems. Despite these efforts, however, Western firms still often cite their principal problems as the difficulties of effectively capturing knowledge. Meanwhile, fitting new hires into the corporate culture and handling succession smoothly remain two of the most vexing challenges these firms face.

The Japanese still remain better at fine-tuning existing processes than at developing strategy in the first place—after all, total quality control was all about organizing existing data and getting everyone to do the "right thing." Japanese firms also require a definite answer before anything can be improved upon, preferring systemic thinking to conceptual thinking. These systems were built by great men who led their organizations to success.

But with droves of Japan's workforce retiring over the next decade, some worry about how Japanese managers can possibly get all that built-up knowledge out of the soon-to-be-retired heads and into those of younger managers. In our survey, about 52 percent of Japanese said that their company "effectively captures what its people know." This is compared with 61 percent of Americans who felt the knowledge capture of their organizations was effective—odd, given how American executives tell us how much of a problem they have managing information.

We all know that Japanese systems work relatively well when those who built them are still involved in them. But as this generation moves out of the workforce, Japan's Modern Day Samurai will need to lead the charge to capture the competitive skills of near retirees and adapt them for the future. Already there is evidence that the *ronin* have started down this road.

In a fortunate turn of events, the Japanese have extensive expertise in knowledge management. For the most part, Japanese management theorists are known for their work in areas like quality control and manufacturing—usually not considered areas that are key to corporate renewal. But the one other area where Japanese business scholars have been able to claim guru status for their country is in knowledge management. And we believe it is fair to say that the Japanese school of thought in this area is much more forward thinking and more compatible with the process of renewal than those that have originated in the United States.

Dialectics

Two of the biggest names in the field of knowledge management are Hirotaka Takeuchi and Ikujiro Nonaka. They champion a theory of dialectic knowledge creation—that knowledge is created when the tension between two apparently opposing concepts is resolved. This is not a particularly new notion; even ancient Greek philosophers were interested in dialectics, to say nothing of Hegel. But the way Takeuchi and Nonaka approach the subject casts an interesting light on the importance of the samurai sword and pen. These implements, of course, are usually considered opposing forces. Peacemakers sign treaties with pens; poets use them to share the emotional response to the real world. Warriors bloody each other with swords—and the results of their battles typically reshape the world itself. So to most in the West, writers and poets are effete brainiacs while warriors are macho conquerors. Yet the samurai lived with these two conflicting metaphors at the center of their everyday lives. The inspiring tension afforded by these opposites gives Modern Day Samurai a potential advantage over their competitors who think of the pen and the sword in either-or terms.

Tacitly Explicit

Another basic concept at the heart of Nonaka and Takeuchi's theories of knowledge creation is the interplay between tacit and explicit knowledge. Tacit knowledge is stuff we just figure out. No one necessarily teaches it to us; we just know and act on it. Explicit knowledge is what you're reading right now (assuming you're paying attention). It's found in books or electronically stored, or taught by experts. So far, Western knowledge management has been more focused on explicit knowledge, whereas Japan has become very good at tacit knowledge.

The interplay between the tacit and the explicit is extremely important during periods of uncertainty. This tension has to become the basic currency of the *ronin*. Samurai in a stable environment and under the tutelage of other samurai learn their craft through explicit knowledge transfer. But the *ronin*, cut off from traditional means of survival have to learn by doing in an unfamiliar environment. Each Modern Day *Ronin* will have to learn tacit knowledge in his or her own way. That tacit knowledge can then be used to serve the greater good as it is transformed into explicit knowledge and transferred to larger groups, organizations, and even the society as a whole.

Ba, humbug

The word *ba* literally means "places." If the need is to drive dialectics and spur the creation of new knowledge, then, as Takeuchi and Nonaka point out, we need "places" where the social interactions that facilitate these processes can actually happen. These places can take physical form, like shared office space, or metaphysical form, such as the sharing of ideas and experiences, or both. *Ba* at its heart allows for the free "exchanges of data, of information and opinion, collaboration and mobilization on a project to face the unknown."[1]

The kanji ideogram for *ba* is composed of two parts. The left part means "boiling water rising out of the ground," and the right part means "to enable." So *ba* is really about making ideas bubble up through thought and action, and become realities through conscious acts.

The Japanese have revered *ba* through the years, as they see it as the genesis for much of the technological advancement they've achieved. Yet a frequent misconception of the Japanese management technique is that all direction flows from the top down. On the contrary, *ba* cannot be "produced by the command and control model of traditional pyramidal management."[2] Rather, *ba* is important in linking information together in ways that had not previously been possible.

In both *ba* and the interplay between the tacit and explicit, the basic role of the social context of knowledge creation is clear. Say "new knowledge" to a Westerner, and the image that typically occurs is Newton under the apple tree, perhaps Edison, Einstein, or Madame Curie toiling alone in a workshop or study. In other words, Great Innovators alone with their thoughts. But new organizational knowledge literally cannot be created by one person alone in a room. Rather, it is always the interaction of people sharing their tacit knowledge, making it explicit, and then using that explicit knowledge to teach new ideas to others who make those ideas their own as tacit knowledge. As a result, *ba* (places designed for knowledge transfer and integration) allows Japanese organizations to keep different parts of the bureaucracy from working at cross-purposes. Instead, the efforts of disparate groups are simplified to achieve a greater cohesion among co-workers and across departments or divisions. Even though the benefits of this process seem obvious, we'll see how *ba* may be changing as Japan enters a new phase of thinking about knowledge management.

THE NEW ATTITUDES

The conventional wisdom about the difference between American and Japanese business culture has been that they would never change—that both sides were in effect hardwired to be the way they were. But when we looked at the survey data comparing the United States and Japan, we found patterns that didn't quite fit with what people usually assume about the two cultures. First, our Japanese respondents were much more likely to look toward competitors for new ideas—about 50 percent Japanese respondents preferred this approach, versus only about 20 percent of Americans.

The supposedly insular Japanese look not only to their in-country competitors but they also seek inspiration from the rest of the world—whereas the famously eclectic and exploratory Americans are doing just the opposite. Three-fifths of Japanese say to adopt systems and practices from other countries, while about the same number of Americans prefer to use traditional values and practices. Apparently, there is less "not invented here" in Japan than in the United States. Japanese will eagerly accept an idea from external sources if they think it can help them perform better. Again, Japan is willing to cast off traditions if they don't seem to be fulfilling an important need, while Americans cling to tradition as a defense against change and the unknown.

Finally, our survey also showed that Americans preferred to be as efficient as possible—perhaps taking their learning from the previous Japanese cycle to the extreme. The Japanese, on the other hand, appear to have switched places with Americans, preferring to be unique. Three-fourths of Japanese wanted to be unique, versus only just over half of Americans. Japan seems to finally be placing value on *not* fitting in, while Americans, curiously, seem to be valuing conformity more than ever.

How have these new attitudes affected Japanese firms? As we'll see, there are a few success stories linked to this "new dynamism" emerging in Japan.

I-mode

Changing how knowledge is shared was key to the reform of one of Japan's stodgiest utilities—Nippon Telephone and Telegraph (NTT). The company's mobile unit, DoCoMo, had long been frustrated in the mobile market. Morale was low, partially because the Japanese mobile market was closed to innovation and costly for subscribers. But as liberalization later took hold, DoCoMo would finally find success with a new mobile service offering called i-mode.

What made i-mode such a success was a new way of sharing information at NTT. Keichi Tachikawa, DoCoMo's president, made effective knowledge management the number one priority within the company. To support this corporate mission, DoCoMo's managers devoted themselves to facilitating i-mode penetration nationwide—one of the most ambitious projects ever attempted by the company.

Instead of staying within individual silos within the company, key players formed new strategic communities that worked across functions—from development to technology, from marketing to content. Feedback from users, sales figures, and usability metrics were all shared openly, giving birth to a variety of new knowledge that had never before been available throughout the company.

The result was amazing. I-mode became the first truly ubiquitous Internet service from a mobile phone. When the service came out, millions of subscribers became instantly addicted, using their time on the subway to check sports and news and trade pictures with friends. Users liked all of the new features so much that by 2002 i-mode was responsible for over 85 percent of NTT DoCoMo's profits. The service now has 43 million subscribers in Japan alone—about 1 out of every 3 people in Japan is an i-mode user.

DoCoMo's task was worthy of a *ronin*. Its old master (fixed-line telephone service) was dying and in need of replacement. The new Japan (more mobile, more dynamic) required a master who was ultra-flexible and could deliver innovative new services. The team at DoCoMo was up to the challenge. It then gave Japan's other *ronin* a valuable tool that struck at the very hierarchies to which the company had previously been linked.

Q.P. Corp.

Although slightly less glamorous than mobile phones, Japan's biggest mayonnaise company, Q.P. Corp., has also been reinvigorated through improved knowledge management practices. The 85-year-old food manufacturer suffered from a bland corporate culture, perhaps nearing its sell-by date, where "few people made the effort to get to know each other, and staff conversations rarely went beyond the team or section they belonged to."

Enter the mayonnaise *ronin*! A new intra-company Web site was developed, where employees could share information about sales techniques, new business development ideas, or even personal information such as hobbies and off-the-clock activities. Talk about throwing off the yoke of an old master—the hierarchical practices of yesterday would never have harbored such information sharing.

Not only has the Web site become a success at Q.P., but the employees have gotten to know one another outside the usual context. The site is updated every day, and employees receive regular e-mail updates about changes and new features on the site. A five-person team manages the site, and regularly travels "around Japan, interviewing workers at their offices and factories and accompanying salespeople on their sales calls to find out how they sell mayonnaise to restaurants."[3]

This sort of personal exchange was not common in Japan until recently, but things have clearly changed. Executives were skeptical at first, wondering how the exchange of information such as how someone's last fishing trip turned out could help the company sell more mayonnaise. But employees and executives alike have embraced the new openness.

The Web site has also helped generate new business. A new boiled red-bean product was publicized on the site, and employees were free to offer their own recommendations. "Some staff commented that the bean was good as an appetizer or side dish—a new idea, since the planning department was only thinking about using the bean in a dessert."[4]

Sensing that something was amiss at Q.P. with employee morale, and daring to go outside established channels to fix it, illustrates essential *ronin* behavior. Sharing of knowledge through an open platform such as an employee intranet may have seemed risky or unusual in a top-down environment such as Japan's. But the old way simply wasn't working any longer, and knowledge had to be shared among the people. Luckily, Q.P.'s leaders recognized this and assented to the change, before it was too late.

DARK SIDES OF KNOWLEDGE

There are, of course, downsides to the new attitudes toward knowledge in Japan's latest change cycle. One is that the eagerness to import ideas from everywhere may dilute what makes them uniquely Japanese. And this is more than a point of cultural heritage or national pride. It is their Japaneseness that many value about themselves—and that the outside world values, as well, not only for tourism but in choosing Japanese products. By suddenly being so outward facing, Japan may be unprepared for what it is inviting in. This is certainly a change from hundreds, even thousands of years of Japanese history, where the "Yamato spirit" reigned unchallenged. There is always a risk that a lack of discretion may unleash trends that the average Japanese simply isn't prepared to face.

One of those trends is a rise in individualism. Though not a bad thing in and of itself, it can certainly be taken too far. Individualism by its very nature discounts cooperation and the sharing of knowledge. If one person tries to act only in his or her own interests, it can lead to negative consequences for others. The rise of the *wagamama*, or selfish people, is causing concern for some in Japan. Instead of doing traditional things, like marrying and having children, a surprising number of Japanese singles are opting to remain just that—single. The consequences of such behavior for Japan's economy and demographics are only starting to be felt.

Then there is the challenge of innovation—how will Japan get to the next level of finding the new concepts and products that will reinvigorate its economy? How will the Japanese extend their view beyond existing customers to create new markets? Finally, how will they combine both the small problem solving, which they seem to excel at, and the big problem solving, which they seem to avoid at all costs?

Japanese companies have historically relied on the government to provide answers about the greater operating environment. During the formative postwar years, the Japanese government willingly provided big-picture data to everyone, specifically to help make Japan competitive with the rest of the world and then stay there. Yet in these days of massive Japanese government debt and a shrinking demographic base, private companies may have to do their own research. Are they up to the challenge?

Failing to respond to these challenges would result in a stagnant Japan, only eager to enter the marketplace after other people do the heavy lifting of creating new ideas. When the "other people" are outsiders, not from the Ministry of International Trade and Industry (MITI) or another government agency, the economic consequences may be very different. The need to capture and use knowledge efficiently takes on greater urgency as Japan faces demographic peril due to a low birth rate and a pending wave of retirements. If Japan is unable to move from its past information age into a true knowledge age, it is likely to be surpassed by the other Asian societies now striving to become the leaders of the region. The stakes are high if Japan wants to continue to lead in this latest Renewal Cycle.

CREATE NEW KNOWLEDGE

Japan currently seems comfortable with taking new ideas and philosophies from other countries. Japan also seems to have moved beyond a myopic drive for efficiency—with Americans increasingly sacrificing innovation for cost-cutting. Who would ever have guessed that the Japanese would be more concerned about being unique than the often all-too-solipsistic culture of the United States?

If a stolid decades-old phone company can suddenly transform itself by offering the most popular device in the country's history, and if something as ordinary as mayonnaise can be perked up through the sharing of vacation stories, then Japan really has found its way to something special—and embraced it wholeheartedly.

Understanding how to effectively create critical knowledge is perhaps one of the greatest challenges for Japan throughout this next cycle. However, if we begin with the basic premise of Japanese knowledge management—that all knowledge is created as part of a dialectic, coming into existence when a tension arises between two polar opposites and is resolved—then you can see that Japan may be poised to enter a new era of knowledge that will carry into the next round of renewal.

CONCLUSION

We can't think of a better description of our friend the *ronin*, caught between a world of loyalty on the one hand, yet on the other hand driven, even forced, to become his or her own person. Through forces beyond their control, they've been put into a world that values both loyalty and independence. As these *ronin* are forced through economic necessity to find new ways to express themselves, they will be on the forefront of knowledge creation.

Modern Day Samurai can also help in turning tacit knowledge into explicit knowledge—following in their predecessors' footsteps like the famed warrior Musashi, who spent much of his life teaching others his own style of sword-fighting. Bushido is, after all, a "way" of living in order to transform theory into action. As our survey results suggest, the mindset of the modern-day samurai is uniquely suited to this task.

To truly succeed, the *ronin* in your corporation will need to spend more time on real-world scenarios so they can formulate a menu of possible responses to what the future will bring. War gaming and simulations can provide a real insight. But it is vital to understand, and remember throughout the process, that this is far more than just crunching numbers. It's teaching yourself how to think like a customer or a competitor, and to anticipate their every move. Armed with those skills, one can finally "attack where the enemy isn't" even before they make their own move.

The *ronin* seem eager to learn. But teaching them the right lessons will be the biggest challenge of all. Japan, like any group of competitors, must be able to capture what people know while taking it to a greater level of understanding, all the while allowing new ways of thinking to emerge. If the *ronin* can accomplish this, they'll be on their way to providing Japan with all the creative energy it needs in this next cycle.

NOTES

1. Pierre-Marie Fayard, "Strategic communities for knowledge creation: A Western proposal for the Japanese concept of Ba," *Journal of Knowledge Management*, Kempston, Vol. 7, Issue 5, 2003, p. 25.
2. Ibid.
3. Ichiko Fuyuno, "Sour to Sweet," *Far Eastern Economic Review*, Hong Kong: July 29, 2004,Vol. 167, Issue 30, p. 38.
4. Ibid.

CHAPTER 17

MORAL PURPOSE

No great institution has ever succeeded without having a powerful underlying moral purpose. The notion of a greater good has often motivated the works of humanity, from the Roman Empire (which believed its mission was to civilize the world) to grown-up dot-coms like Amazon and eBay (which believe their mission is to provide ultimate levels, and models, of customer convenience). Success in Japanese history is no exception.

But with all the wrenching social changes that Japan is facing as part of this newest Renewal Cycle, its companies must find a new moral purpose to guide and motivate their samurai. In the old days, samurai were bound to their daimyo by honor and loyalty, which later transferred itself into a link between employee and corporation. But how do you motivate a samurai when the warlord can't guarantee the same level of loyalty in return?

Given the current circumstances, the relationship between employee and corporation will simply have to change. No one will put his or her life on the line for shareholder value the way the samurai did for their masters. But successful enterprises will be able to attract the right people for the right reasons, and these include a sense of moral purpose. We believe many successful samurai will become *ronin* in order to survive the changes in store for them, relying more on their own talents than on any lord or company. Instead of depending on the company for guidance about the future, employees will have to seek out a moral purpose of their own.

THE ORIGINS OF MORAL PURPOSE

Bushido derives its sense of moral purpose from a borrowed set of beliefs from Shintoism, Confucianism, Buddhism, and Zen Buddhism. Shintoism, a Japanese religion based on ancestor worship, supplied the samurais with the sense of loyalty and patriotism. The beliefs that the emperor is god, that ancestors should be worshiped, and that the land is the abode of all, have generated a devout patriotism that samurai feel toward their lord and land. Because of the Confucian influence, the samurai revered the importance of relationships in several dyads—master and servant, friend and friend, and father and child. Buddhism helped the samurai deal with impending (and, as with most warriors, most likely early) death. The thought of reincarnation helps with the acceptance of death, releasing the samurai from the overall fear of death or danger. Finally, Zen Buddhism instilled the belief in meditation to "know thyself," making the samurai acutely aware of their fears, humanity, and, ultimately, their fallibility.

In brief, the samurai adapted to their way of life the thoughts and beliefs from different religions from different nations, as they saw fit. Samurai combined these beliefs into a general understanding of the way of the warrior. Morality was not imposed from above, either, as from a pope or king, but rather, from an agreed-upon set of principles that slowly adapted over time. Japan's emperor was not the instrument of divine will, but rather, a manifestation of the divine on Earth. He was a constant reminder that there was something higher at work on Earth. Samurai made it their mission to be as close to divine as possible, while knowing none of them could ever reach perfection. But because the emperor was never called to prove his divinity, he remained pure in the minds of his subjects.

THE CHALLENGE OF MORAL PURPOSE

What are the modern counterparts of these antiquated moral compasses? How can a company bring these lofty moral values down to the operational level? In the past, companies sometimes adopted national priorities as their own in order to connect their people with something greater. This was certainly true of Japan after World War II. Rebuilding from the ruins of the war required great moral purpose, and an entire generation of managers was motivated to believe they were directly helping in that effort through their work.

But companies don't need a devastating war to motivate; the Tata Group not only focused on its business but also the greater welfare of India.[1]

It was able to merge patriotism and corporate dedication and commitment. And in China, Zhang Ruimin followed the example of Confucius by getting his Haier Group employees to believe in the importance of group unity. As the group grew, Zhang realized the need to institutionalize this moral purpose throughout any joint ventures and acquisitions, codifying the enterprise's culture and values through a company cultural center.[2]

Matsushita

As mentioned earlier, one important role model for business professionals in Japan today is Konosuke Matsushita, the founder of Matsushita. He was a tinkerer and inventor who came up with a product inspired by his sharing a tiny room with his younger brother. Electrical devices were becoming readily available in Japan in 1918. Yet while most homes and buildings had electrical light sockets, there were not a lot of outlets for plug-in devices. Matsushita solved the problem by inventing a light bulb socket with an electrical outlet built into the side of it. The popularity of the "attachment plug" was still clear in the late 1970s when it was common (especially in pre–World War II construction homes) to find electrical cords hanging from light sockets powering everything from stereos to rice cookers.

But it was not Matsushita's inventions that won him role-model status in today's Japan. Matsushita became a guru because of the moral purpose he was able to instill into his company and his workers from very early on in the enterprise's history. It all started in 1932, a key transition period as the company was moving from a small entrepreneurial venture to a medium-size company—a type of transition that has been problematic for more than a few organizations. Matsushita was persuaded to visit an evangelical Buddhist sect, Tenrikyo, by a proselytizing customer. His daylong visit to the sect's headquarters impressed Matsushita at a very deep level. He saw happy people working long hours with "clockwork-like smoothness" producing lumber for building homes, libraries as large as any in Tokyo and Osaka, and schools in which the students seemed eager to learn. As John Kotter wrote in his biography of Konosuke: "The implication was clear. If a corporation could somehow be made meaningful like a religion, people would be both more satisfied and more productive."[3]

Two months after Matsushita's visit to what is today known as Tenri City, he gathered his 168 employees together in an auditorium in Osaka. He explained his "new religion" to them. He hadn't joined Tenrikyo, but he had adapted a number of key concepts from the sect in formulating a new moral purpose for his organization. He told the audience: "The mission of a manufacturer should be to overcome poverty, to relieve society as a whole from misery, and bring it wealth."[4] His metaphor for the day was tap water, and the goal he charged his employees with was to make electronic products as cheap and available as tap water.

Matsushita said that it might take 200 or 300 years for the moral purpose of the organization to be realized, but he believed it was worth the effort. And one might argue that his goal has already been achieved. When was the last time your organization put out a mission or a goal that sounds like it could take centuries to accomplish? How often does a for-profit company suggest that "overcoming poverty" is one of the main goals of its operations? Konosuke died in 1989, but his corporate goals still live on. Today's younger employees may be a bit grudging and even embarrassed by the practice, but they still stand and sing the corporate song every morning which pledges them to improve human progress through the work they do.

Toyota

Another great example of a Japanese company built on the foundation of moral purpose is Toyota. Toyota has grown up from humble beginnings in a part of Japan not known for being the most economically prosperous. At a time when a younger group of managers was asked why Toyota has become so successful, all answered with vague business school platitudes. One elder manager stood up to rebuke them saying, "What these people do not understand is that in 1946, the people in this city were eating bugs. That is the reason, you know, the reason that we had to rebuild this company is because our children were starving to death." The manager went on to say that building a better life for the people of the region was first and foremost in the minds of Toyota's founders. Perhaps this is heresy today, but doesn't that seem like a more powerful driver than abstract concepts like return on investment?

In a parallel example, this dedication to contributing to the community spurred Cummins Engine Company in the United States to become the first member of the Fortune 500 to have a Vice President for Corporate Social Responsibility. Not surprisingly, this deeply held belief in protecting and giving back to the community is part of what has helped Cummins survive an industry shakeout—going from the nineteenth largest independent diesel engine manufacturer to the only independent diesel engine manufacturer remaining in the United States.

Retailers also have joined the moral purpose movement. The U.K.'s retail giant Marks & Spencer persists in keeping human resources policies that make customers feel as if they are shopping at the highest-quality store and receiving the best service possible—equivalent to that available to a Lord or Lady. American retailer JC Penney's stores were originally called the Golden Rule stores; the company's mission statement was chock full of Christian values, and employees were expected to have very strict moral temperaments to work there. Although there is less overt religiosity in today's businesses in the United States, this sense of contributing to some greater good is still an important tenet for many. The Body Shop, for example, illustrates retailing with a "higher purpose," as all products are billed as environmentally friendly. Even if you prefer to feed your java habit by patronizing the independents, it is hard to overlook Starbucks' emphasis on social responsibility. Starbucks is pursuing a number of such initiatives including marketing its "Commitment to Origins" coffees that are produced through methods designed to promote both environmentalism and human rights.

Although we may have trouble remembering this, even some of the dot-com boom was filled with a higher moral purpose. This was about getting rich, for many, but it was also about literally changing the world. A failed dot-com called Red Sky Interactive actually went to the trouble of creating a "history" for the startup, complete with sepia-toned photographs of what Red Sky might have been around the turn of the century. It was all made up, but it described how employees and customers would have acted had they been around in that era and how they had supported the company loyally over the years. They did not live up to this beautiful dream, true, but their hearts were in the right place. By the same token, the Hewlett family vehemently opposed merging Hewlett Packard (HP) with Compaq on "moral" grounds—believing not only that HP could create more value for shareholders on its own but also that HP was a different kind of company and should not have its mission dictated by Wall Street bankers. The company's lackluster performance since the merger seems to have proven the Hewlett family right, at least for now.

A NEW MORAL PURPOSE

Japan is searching for a new moral purpose precisely because this is a time of such tremendous change on political, social, and financial fronts. Japanese troops are now deployed overseas for the first time in half a century. Serious debates are taking place over whether or not to amend Japan's constitution to allow the redevelopment of a robust military. Japanese society is changing as the younger generation moves away from the typical family structure. More women in Japan want careers instead of the traditional mother role. In the past, when a woman married and had children, it was assumed she would no longer work. But now, as more women are starting to put their family life on hold to advance their careers, Japan's birth rate is dropping significantly. The Japanese workplace is also experiencing demographic change through increased immigration. In brief, Japan is being exposed to a new set of beliefs, work habits, and morality, and some long-standing samurai moral purposes need to go through their own Renewal Cycles in order to adapt to the realities of modern Japanese companies.

In historical times, Japan was often governed by the notion of a "clique" that identified the boundaries of where "we" ended and "they" began. This started with the family, then was later broadened to the village, then later, to corporations and the entire nation. But now the boundaries of these cliques are changing as loyalties shift. Old bonds are breaking down, while new ones form. Increasingly, cliques are forming around voluntary associations rather than forced or inherited bonds. This reformation of "the ties that bind" now even allows for the possibility of non-Japanese involvement in the affairs of a Japanese company, introducing an entirely new conceptual model for who "we" and "they" are.

Such openness can be an important force to help companies move through the change cycle. Many of the best organizations have renewed their moral purpose by "adopting" outsiders whose different perspectives open up entirely new vistas. Honda is a classic example, as it relied upon a network of foreign distributors to seed the U.S. market in the early days. Although their presence was small, these distributors developed a loyal following of car and motorcycle dealers and owners. As Honda shifts gears into the new century, it can rely on this established network to disseminate its new corporate credo of environmental responsibility. By leading the way with innovative hybrid energy offerings, Honda can help create and capitalize on a market that offers something much bigger and more important than well-priced, reliable transportation.

Samurai Purpose

Success in this next Renewal Cycle requires a driving moral purpose. And, as you can see from the historical examples, this is not something one can simply invent, or even choose; it is something that needs to emerge from the reality of the situation and deeply shape cultural and personal values. Here the samurai tradition may yet again mold Japan's response to change.

There are several main beliefs where the old moral purpose of the samurai may form the basis of a new moral purpose arising from the current challenge—and drive Japan toward meeting that challenge. Key elements include the following.

Have No Fear of Death; Take Challenges Head-on

The corporate samurai of the 1980s would strike at the competition directly, for example, undercutting competitors through price wars, product dumping, and taking exceedingly long work hours for granted. But in the new millennium, companies need to balance the instinctual innovativeness that comes from being close to danger with a more planned strategy. Modern corporate samurai need to accomplish their success through cunning and through understanding the costs associated with their decisions.

Do It for the Homeland

Although Japan's national pride suffered from the shame of World War II, the Japanese love of the homeland is returning as memories of that era fade from the national consciousness. According to the University of Chicago, Japan ranks ninth in national pride for specific achievements and eighth in general national pride (with the United States number 2 in both categories). Press reports confirm that "six decades after World War II, patriotism is making a comeback in Japan. In classrooms, barracks and the corridors of power, the Japanese are extolling the virtues of national strength and pride with greater freedom and enthusiasm than at any time since their defeat in 1945."[5] However, being patriotic is not necessarily being nationalist—in a global world, you can have pride in your homeland, but still be an active player in the global community. This is a complexity that many cultures may have difficulty understanding at first. Those who embrace it, though, seem more likely to capture the moral drive associated with love of country yet avoid the destruction that nationalism can unleash. Samurai will need to balance these competing interests to succeed in the next cycle.

Use Every Weapon Available

Unlike the old days when traditional samurai would call out their name and rank in battle so they could find an opposing samurai of similar class to fight, today there is no such thing as a structured fight, much less a fair one. As seen in the movie *The Last Samurai*, a noble reliance on tried and tested weapons and protocols of war is no match for the guns and cannons of the modern day. Enter the new corporate samurai, who will need to be flexible in the "weapons" used, no matter what the situation. While these weapons will not necessarily be designed to deliver a fatal blow to competitors, their use should hinder others' progress enough to allow *ronin* sufficient time and space to create better strategies for eventual victory.

Twenty-First-Century Moral Purpose

While samurai beliefs can serve as the basis for establishing corporate moral purpose almost anywhere in the world, we expect to find the following in any Japan-specific purposes that emerge during the next few years.

Leisure

Given the prevailing stereotype of the Japanese, it is almost inconceivable to think of this culture as one that might lead the international pack in leisure and fun. But there already is an abundance of evidence that leisure has and will motivate Japanese workers and their customers. After Atari met its demise in the 1980s, it was Japan that gave video games a second, long-lasting, and extremely lucrative life. Anime is now a regular daylong staple on basic cable channels in the United States. Prime-time American shows like *Survivor* and *Fear Factor* are based on Japanese TV predecessors. Even the Food Channel celebrates Japanese cuisine and competition with shows like Iron Chef. Nike claims that after it sells a few pairs of new sneakers in Tokyo, it is only a matter of days before those shoes show up in the "hippest" parts of New York City. The Japanese lead in trendy.[6]

There were 52,238 U.S. university and college students studying the Japanese language in 2002, up 21 percent from 1998.[7] And most of these are studying Japanese not to do business in Japan but because of their passion for Japanese pop culture. The number of non-Japanese studying the Japanese language worldwide could be as high as 3 million. Again, pop culture is a main driver for worldwide interest in Japan. In April 2004, the Marubeni Institute released a report that estimated the value of Japan's "cultural exports" (music, films, books, handicrafts, royalties, etc.) at $15 billion a year—triple the amount in 1992.[8]

There seems to be a kind of renaissance of fun and leisure taking place inside Japan as well. Japanese hotels have always been known for meticulous service, but two decades ago, even facilities in the best hotels were old and cramped. Now Japan is known for having some of the best hotels in the world—with the Golden Globe award–winning film *Lost in Translation* celebrating the design and luxury of the famed Park Hyatt in Tokyo. Not surprisingly, the public shopping and entertainment spaces in the bigger cities of Japan now rival the best in the world.

During the next 50 years, the percentage of Japan's population that is over 65 years old is expected to go from about 18 percent to over 35 percent. With an average population older than any developed nation on earth, Japan has the challenge of developing a societywide response to the coming onslaught of retirees more than a decade before the United States faces similar challenges. And of course Japan's response to challenges—such as small roads and expensive fuel—have often proved to be competitive advantages on the world market. Japanese companies (even nonleisure industry companies) who can tap into the demand for relaxation and fun—from both customers and employees—can create organizations which motivate in ways that pure economic incentives simply do not.

Family

Japan has a history of venerating the family and the elderly in a way that crosses direct bloodlines. The basic building block of Japan has always been the *ie* (translated as family or house). But *ie* was always something bigger than the nuclear family. People were "adopted" into *ie*, and other *ie* were acquired to create even bigger *ie*.

The concept of *ie* has been applied to commercial endeavors for centuries, but a company designed to serve the needs of the noncorporate family (even the extended, nontraditional family) is still an emerging concept. Caring for the elderly will be one of the most important challenges Japan faces in the next two decades, and corporations will need to build their moral purpose more around family, as opposed to nation building or profitability. If family is successfully linked to work, Japanese firms can motivate workers in very human and humane ways.

Convenience Gadgetry

Japan has been a very inconvenient society for years. When we first started going to Japan in the 1970s, it was crowded and just plain difficult to navigate. Even today, traffic is still a mess, public transportation usually only gets you halfway to your destination (you get to walk the rest of the way), store hours are limited, bureaucracy is pervasive and slow, and the financial services system remains outmoded. Even better, you have the privilege of paying through the nose for all of this inconvenience. But things are gradually getting better.

One very important by-product of all this inconvenience has been the development of a large domestic market for small electronic gadgets. During the long commutes, in storage-constrained homes, and in the constant search to find privacy in a very nonprivate country, Japanese find themselves relying on miniature electronics. No wonder that 42 percent of Japanese in our survey admit that they "get jealous" when they see other people with a new electronic gadget (compared with only 29 percent of Americans who feel the same way). Japanese also report that they—significantly more than Americans in every instance—are more inclined to spend money on technology rather than on going to sporting events; that they "need to have the latest tech gadgets"; and that they don't feel that these electronics are "a waste of money."

But in addition to the obvious miniaturization of electronics, which now take up almost no space in the average small home, there have also been truly amazing breakthroughs in GPS systems for cars, mobile telephony, and even supply-chain technologies to keep small corner stores stocked. It wouldn't surprise us if Japanese companies harness this near-primal drive toward convenience as their battle cry into the future. Their employees would certainly warm to the concept, letting the whole world benefit from this moral purpose in much the same way we have from better "made in Japan" home electronics.

Globalization

Fitting in with the world doesn't exactly describe the Japanese, except when they decide they want to be known for that. Akio Morita, the founder of Sony, moved himself and his family to New York to sell products in the United States at exactly the time that "made in Japan" had the worst reputation in history. He learned what products would appeal to U.S. buyers and came home telling all of his executives they should learn English. Today Sony's biggest market is the United States.

Japanese (42 percent) in our survey were slightly more likely than Americans (40 percent) to agree with the statement "My organization is global without ties to one location or culture." But they were far less likely to report that their organizations were good at integrating locations and cultures (27 percent for Japanese versus 47 percent for Americans). And only about 44 percent of Japanese said their organizations make them feel a part of something bigger, as opposed to almost 70 percent of Americans.

Still almost all Japanese corporations have the potential to become truly global if their moral purpose connects disparate parts of the world to each other. Japan could be the champion of developing nations in ways other developed nations cannot. Less developed countries are naturally reluctant to rely on the United States or European nations, since our history of imperialism makes them leery. Likewise, developing countries in Asia are also wary of Japan for its not-too-long-ago atrocities in developing a Greater

Economic Co-prosperity Sphere. Given this cultural "baggage," Japan's best chances of helping connect First and Third World economies may be in Africa, Central Asia, the Middle East, and Latin America—all countries that also have conflicted relationships with and attitudes toward the United States and Europe. If Japanese firms can purpose themselves to be an intermediary in these regions, there is great good and profitability in store.

Individuality

In the new millennium, modern Japanese companies can no longer be responsible for all their workers and expect to remain competitive. Japan is still struggling with this change, and both companies and employees have been slow to embrace it. Said one entrepreneur, "When we were in high school, we were told that banks and securities companies were great places to work and that we would do well to find jobs there. But as soon as we went to college, banks and securities firms started to go out of business. Now we see finances as the risky sector! In fact the whole world has become a lot riskier, and no single sector is seen as a career 'risk hedge.' The result is that more of us feel that, as long as the world is risky, we might as well do what we want to."[9] Doing what you want to do is not necessarily a bad thing. If this self-reliance can be channeled in the right directions, it will lead to tremendous innovation and creativity.

In fact, the real potential to be unleashed is in turning this individuality and "*ronin*-ness" into a moral purpose for entire organizations in Japan. As such, it could become their defining virtue. You already see some indications of this in entrepreneurial technology and media companies in Japan, which allow employees much more freedom in their attire, work times, and roles. But large corporations could also use individuality as a mantra to attract and keep both employees and customers. One obvious example of the potential inherent in greater freedom is Japanese banks which still have very limited hours; even ATMs close down at night. New financial institutions might benefit dramatically from truly opening up and giving customers the freedom to conduct business whenever they want.

THE DARK SIDE OF MORAL PURPOSE

A strong moral purpose is necessary, but it is important to see the potential failings of adopting a popular moral purpose in order to make your own personal drive stronger. We believe *ronin* will face several challenges in honing their sense of moral purpose in this latest Renewal Cycle.

Most moral purposes are appropriated from other sources. It is quite common for a company to draw its moral purpose from a founder or leader who has brought the company into a new era. Whereas that is often a terrific thing for the company, the hard part is remembering that nothing lasts forever, at least not without concerted adaptations. Japan's moral purpose may change irrevocably when those not involved in the original building of these modern corporate behemoths fade from the scene. While this can be good (by, say, allowing new blood to reinvigorate a company), it can also sometimes result in companies losing their way from their strategic mission.

In addition, implementing a moral purpose can affect a company's ability to be flexible. For example, when a person is hired into a company in Japan, he or she goes through a training course—anywhere from three days to two months—in "how to be polite." A new employee is usually indoctrinated in how to answer the phone, sit in a taxi with clients, and where to sit during meetings, just to name a few things. While politeness is definitely a worthy cause, this example shows the effort Japanese companies put into having their employees follow their doctrine. The system is already in place to let employees know the company's purpose and desired way of achieving it. However, this education will require any change in moral purpose to be dictated through a top-down approach.

Finally, there is the specter of violent ultra-nationalism lurking in moral purpose. An organization's moral purpose will sometimes unwittingly give some of its members a "moral" excuse to act in an unethical manner, from preventing an employee's flexibility in mergers or acquisitions to unwittingly placing the company in legal danger by following the moral purpose to the extreme.

Japan's Modern Day Samurai will have to watch their behavior to make sure they do not fall into any of these traps. Maintaining a connection to the original source of their moral purpose yet being flexible in order to adapt to changing conditions will be a narrow path to walk, but the most successful samurai will succeed in doing so.

MAKE MORAL PURPOSE REAL

Moral purpose is clearly a part of a corporate mission, if not always emphasized to shareholders. Like it or not, companies are engaged in a "war of ideas"—something we hear a lot about in the political world, but rarely in the business world. But think about it—a company asks its customers to take a stand, make a commitment, and vote with their money: buy *this* product or service instead of *that* one. That is an ideology of sorts. People choose their associations with brands and with companies, or sometimes even against brands and companies. But it all boils down to a war over people and their time, money, and attention.

For corporate moral purpose to be adopted and successfully implemented, it must emphasize four elements.

1. *Consistency*. The cause must offer employees clear consistency of thinking about their daily work. A singleness of purpose is inherent in a really good statement of purpose.
2. *Excellence*. If the moral purpose does not inspire excellence, it is not a particularly useful tool for the corporation. And employees who are supposed to live by a standard that does not inspire excellence will soon tire of giving lip service to the idea.
3. *Compassion*. The "moral" of moral purpose can be found in compassion. All great moral purposes inspire excellence not only in the job itself but in interactions with other people. These are goals that make us feel better about ourselves. We sleep easier at night knowing that our daily work is in the service of some good greater than just making someone rich—even if that someone is our family or ourselves.
4. *Effectiveness*. The moral purpose must be one that the corporation expects will be effective in achieving the business goals of the organization. Moral purpose and corporate mission do not have to be one and the same. But an effective moral purpose will always lead employees toward goals that make sense for the organization.

MORAL PURPOSE GUIDELINES

To make the benefits of moral purpose real, we'd recommend the following. First, any change must come through a participative process. In order to get employee buy-in, your people need to understand the reasoning behind any moral purpose you prescribe. While it would be impossible for a large multinational corporation to get all its employees to agree on a moral purpose, each group must feel as if they had some participation in the process. But if global participation is hard to implement, employees should at least be aware that a new or updated purpose is being discussed, as well as why.

Once the moral purpose is created, it has to be idealized into something nearly unattainable. Why unattainable? The best systems always create and maintain a gap between the ideal and the actual to ensure continual striving toward the goal. Companies must admit there is a gap and make a good faith effort to close it without making the effort seem futile.

Both company and employee need to understand the role of the individual in this gap. The employees' and the company's goals should both be to try to close the gap, always knowing it cannot be closed completely. Still, it is important to let the employee know that failure to close the gap should not result in shame. Sadly, there are many good executives who become ashamed of their performance in a company they love and decide to leave. The company must produce a method of coaching and "absolution" for individuals to help them pursue a new moral purpose.

It is also important to evaluate the foundation of creating the moral purpose. Just as the basic tenets of bushido were borrowed from different creeds, Japanese companies should not be wary of gaining their moral purposes from different countries, companies, or sets of beliefs. Just as the samurai slowly integrated new beliefs into their "way," companies should be willing to incorporate moral beliefs generally agreed upon by employees, and hence easily accepted into their everyday doctrine. It also might be worth looking into how other people, companies, or countries view your operation. Sometimes an outsider's view might not only show the merits of your belief, but also highlight additions that need to be made or aspects that should be dismissed outright.

CONCLUSION

Ronin may be masterless, but they are not purposeless. In fact, in many ways it is the moral purpose that becomes the ultimate master of these Modern Day Samurai. Even the most fiercely independent *ronin* will gladly submit to corporate membership if the moral purpose of the firm is something they wholeheartedly support. Moral purpose is important enough to die for and can be just as important to people as love or loyalty. People will die for the emperor; give up hard-earned cash for charity; or work twice as hard as anyone thought possible—all because they believe in the cause. Similarly, lack of a strong "buy-in" can cause havoc in companies—everything from baggage claim workers claiming to be sick during the busiest travel days of the year to rude call-center operators. In a world where the best customer service is often what makes a market leader, moral purpose still has a great amount of relevance to success.

NOTES

1. Robert E. Kennedy, "Tata Consultancy Services: High Technology in a Low Income Country," Boston: Harvard Business School Publishing, March 2001.
2. Lynn Sharp Paine, "The Haier Group A," Boston: Harvard Business School Publishing, July 2001.
3. John P. Kotter, "Matsushita Leadership: Lessons from the 20th Century's Most Remarkable Entrepreneur," New York: The Free Press, 1997, p. 110.
4. Konosuke Matsushita, "Quest for Prosperity." Tokyo: PHP Institute, 1988, p. 202.
5. http://www.dailystar.com/dailystar/relatedarticles/42654.php.
6. Christopher Palmeri and Nanette Byrnes "Is Japanese Style Taking Over the World?" *Business Week*, July 26, 2004, p. 56.
7. Ginny Parker, "Learning Japanese, Once About Resumes, Is Now About Cool; Business Majors of '80s Yield To Kids Smitten by Anime; Up at 4 a.m. for Cartoons," *Wall Street Journal*, Aug. 5, 2004, p. 1.
8. "Is Japanese Style Taking Over the World?," op. cit.
9. Japan Entrepreneur Report (December 2002), "Lunch with the $40million man," www.japanentrepreneur.com.

CHAPTER 18

CHINA-FACING

INFLUENCE FROM THE MIDDLE KINGDOM

As Japan decides how it will face the wrenching changes of the twenty-first century, one issue looms larger than perhaps any other: how to deal with its rising neighbor, China. The Middle Kingdom presents an economic, strategic, and cultural challenge greater than any faced in Japanese history. If Japan gets it right, there will be much to celebrate. If Japan gets it wrong, it will be subjugated to second-class status among the community of nations. Clearly, the one thing Japan cannot do is ignore China, especially given the intertwined history of the two countries. And it is clear from our survey that Japanese (60 percent in our survey) believe their organizations are paying attention to China. (This compares to just 51 percent of Americans.) And in this world of China's ascendance, Japan's new samurai will be tasked with the key role of ensuring the two countries work together productively over the next few decades.

A Shared Culture

Samurai have always had an interesting relationship with China. Adopting many cultural cues from China, their Confucian thought gave form to a stable and naturally ordered society. Yet China and Japan share a troubled past stretching all the way from the Mongol invasions to the Japanese military campaigns of the 1930s. During this most recent time of relative peace, the underlying cultural bonds between Japan and China have fostered the development of solid economic ties. Economists credit the growth of the Chinese market with much of the success of the Japanese domestic economy in the last couple of years. How will this current relationship affect the cycle of change for our Modern Day Samurai?

China exerted strong influence on Japan during the Taika ("great change") period in the 600s A.D. The Taika reform was modeled after well-established Chinese government practices. Land was redistributed from the great clans of the day to centralized control. Heredity no longer determined possession—all land reverted to control of the state after an owner's death. An extensive taxation system was set up to pay for public works and a military. For the first time, Japan was divided into administrative districts and prefectures, all responsible to a central power and sovereign.

Chinese influence continued with the adoption of Zen Buddhism throughout Japan. Buddhist thought permeated architecture and art. The famed tea ceremony came from China to Japan. The city plans of Japanese capitals, specifically Nara and Kyoto, were inspired by what planners saw in China.

Even more influential, the Chinese writing system became known to the learned classes, especially samurai. In fact, knowing and using the Chinese character set became the exclusive right of samurai. Until the turn of the twentieth century, most formal writing was done in the Chinese classical style, with marks added to the sentences to help readers who were not trained in classical Chinese understand the sentence structure. And even today, Chinese characters continue to be the backbone of Japanese writing systems.

But historically, there have also been many less than stellar episodes in Sino-Japanese relations. In 1879, to China's dismay, Japan annexed the Ryukyu islands. In 1894, Japan and China fought a war over Korea with the much more modern Japanese forces eventually prevailing—and taking Taiwan in the process. And the much larger Sino-Japanese conflict of the 1930s and 1940s still raises hackles on both sides in discussions about how much blame to acknowledge from that war's painful past.

An Economic Kinship

Despite the geographic proximity of these two countries, true economic ties between Japan and China have never really formed until the past decade. China has now become Japan's largest total trading partner, eclipsing the United States for the first time since Perry's Black Ships entered Yokohama harbor. Bilateral trade between the two nations has skyrocketed in the past few years, even as Japan experienced a less than robust economy. Japan's annual trade with China has grown from $25 billion in 1990 to nearly $150 billion in 2003.

Japan has experienced success in both the export and import fields in trading with China. Exports to China have risen at double-digit rates for the past four years, consisting mainly of machinery and parts for use in Chinese factories. Komatsu, a Japanese construction magnate, is typical of many firms shifting production to China. Their falling domestic sales have been offset by their skyrocketing Chinese sales, with the net result being increased value for the firm overall. In consumer sectors, the Chinese are buying Japanese goods by the truckload. A Royal Bank of Scotland analyst gives other Asian nations, especially China, most of the credit for the Japanese recovery in 2002: "There wouldn't have been any noticeable recovery if it hadn't been for Asia."[1]

One magazine called 2003 "The Year Japan Learned to Stop Worrying and Love China."[2] Japanese businesspeople—who once complained about cheap imports from China—have finally recognized the market potential lying just over the water to the west. During Japan's "lost decade," many Japanese firms refused to transfer production to low-cost centers such as China. As a result, productivity and economic growth stagnated. But since Japan decided to make the move to China, economic growth has definitely recovered. In 2003, for the first time in history, Japan's trade with China was higher than her trade with the United States. Two-way trade between China and Japan was at $132.4 billion—a 30.4 percent increase from the year before.

No wonder our survey showed such a marked difference between Japanese and American attitudes about China. Even among the Modern Day Samurai, only 40 percent of American respondents thought their nation's companies should look to China for opportunities, compared to 85 percent of Japanese samurai. But while the Japanese acknowledge the need to work with China, they are no more likely than Americans (both at 27 percent) to report that their company *is* actually "taking advantage of opportunities in China." Perhaps Japan's inability to capitalize on its cultural and geographic proximity to China stems from the traditionally uncomfortable relationship between the two. Whatever the obstacles, the individual attitudes are clear: Japan's samurai seem ready to take advantage of China's opportunities, and reap a serious reward.

WORKING WITH CHINA

There's good reason for the optimism from Japan about China—success stories about the Chinese market are being heard throughout the business world. However, these two countries have not always cooperated with each other. Part of the reason is the difference in mindsets between the two countries.

Because of these basic differences between traditional Japanese and Chinese mindsets, it is unlikely that mainstream Japanese samurai thinking will succeed in China. In fact, as Japan has gained a significant economic foothold in countries around the world, it hasn't been the bureaucracy-bound businesspeople who have been most able to connect across a variety of different societies. Instead, it has been the *ronin*—that set of masterless businesspeople—who have played a critical role in Japan's internal economic history. Again, while *ronin* remain complete adherents of bushido, they are different in significant ways. Most importantly, they are, perhaps forced by circumstances, willing to learn the teachings of a new master. This makes them natural candidates for the leading edge of Japanese expansion into any market.

For example, it was these *ronin* who took early control of Japan's corporate relationships with American consumers. Honda and Sony were both renegade companies that left the "master" of Japanese bureaucratic control and adapted to a new master: the almighty American consumer. These companies' best products were often first created for the non-Japanese market and then reintroduced back into Japan. Even Toyota followed this strategy when it founded its luxury car line, Lexus. Up until 2005 the Lexus brand did not exist by that name in Japan. Lexus cars have been designed for Western buyers and then sold under a regular Toyota nameplate in the domestic market.

Combi

The relationship between the Modern Day Samurai of Japan and the Chinese business world is likely to take a similar turn. Modern Day *Ronin* will probably have the flexibility necessary to adapt while still remaining loyal to the basic concepts of bushido. For example, Tokyo-based baby clothing manufacturer Combi was an early *ronin* company in China. Combi has been successfully operating factories inside China for more than a decade. Vice president of international operations Shoji Shibata has commented, "Chinese factories have become so proficient that we are now considering moving our most complex products like car seats and exercise bikes to China as well."[3] Shibata is not only eyeing China as a production platform but as an emerging market as well. "There are only 1.1 million babies born in Japan every year, and even that number is declining. But there are 17 million babies born in China. We are prepared to wait many years, but when a critical percentage of new Chinese parents have a high enough income to afford our upscale products, this will be a huge market for us."[4] China's relative fecundity compared to Japan has provided access to a critical new market as it matures. Looking over Japanese business history, it becomes clear that only a *ronin* would have spotted this opportunity.

Koichi Nakanishi

Japan's *ronin* have also been able to share their knowledge and to teach Chinese manufacturers about the importance of little things. Take men's suits, where the Japanese market features expensive and immaculately tailored products. As mass production from China ramped up in the 1990s, prices collapsed—even for small, independent tailors who could no longer command a premium. Yet as the price dropped, suits suffered a significant decline in quality as well.

Ronin Koichi Nakanishi partnered with others to train and equip Chinese workers to create a suit of the quality Japanese men were used to buying, while remaining within the new cost framework. The transition was hard at first. In the venture's first year, a major Japanese client took Liu Yukai, a Chinese partner in the venture, to a warehouse and asked him to identify the suits made in China. "The minute I walked into the warehouse, I could tell which ones were ours," Mr. Liu recalls. "Whichever ones were wrinkled all over."[5] By working with the Japanese, Chinese suits became indistinguishable from Japanese made. The venture was ultimately a success, as Nakanishi's sales doubled even while the suit market demand declined overall. "We have learned from the Japanese to care about tiny details," says Zhang Yurong, who now heads factory operations for the venture.

Suntory

While most of the biggest Japanese successes in China have been led by entrepreneurs that we would clearly classify as Modern Day *Ronin*, there is evidence that even Modern Day *Samurai* from the best-known companies in Japan have great potential for success. Suntory, the famed Japanese alcohol brand, ran into some cultural friction when it first tried to enter China, but persevered anyway. Several years ago, the company's sales team received a small monetary "bon voyage" gift from one of their clients—acceptable under traditional business practices, but banned under Suntory's strict gift policy. The Chinese supervisor, a Mr. Chen, immediately took charge, laying off the responsible manager and director. The next day, Chen called all directors to a meeting to admonish them. Chen's decisions seemed strict even to the Japanese, but Chen wanted to be ultra-careful about eliminating even the appearance of impropriety. Through this example, not only did Suntory give its Chinese employees new respect for wanting to avoid sticky ethical situations, but it helped provide a valuable lesson to the Japanese that they were in a world where Japanese-grown corporate policies might be implemented in some very non-Japanese ways.

Ronin Takeo Nakamura, in charge of Suntory's operations in Shanghai, is responsible for Suntory's success there through his motto: "I delegate power to Chinese workers when we do business in China." Nakamura gave front-line duties, such as sales channel development and product promotion, to local Chinese employees rather than bringing in Japanese employees to oversee everything. Nakamura's motto was, "There is no pecking order among us. [What matters] is how accurately and quickly you can grasp the main points of issues, and how drastically you can discard make-work." One of his Chinese employees heaped praise on Nakamura for this approach, saying, "He does not lead the team, rather, he works on creating a path for us to do [the] job better." This employee also gives Nakamura an appellate in Chinese which translates as "father" or "person of virtue." Nakamura's workers responded favorably to his leadership style, and thanks in part to their efforts, Suntory is now the most famous beer in Shanghai, becoming the top brand in less than three years.

Nakamura's behavior in China is distinctly not typical of Japanese corporate behavior. But he and others in Suntory have come to realize that the virtues of adaptation that are basic elements of bushido are key factors of success for Japanese firms in China.

Caterpillar versus Komatsu

One would think the world's largest market eagerly modernizing its infrastructure would provide plenty of opportunities for success. Yet two of the world's construction equipment industry giants, Komatsu and Caterpillar, have had very different experiences in the Middle Kingdom.

Caterpillar first entered China very early on, in the 1970s, back before Deng Xiaoping began letting a thousand flowers bloom. As a result, they have been able to cultivate local knowledge and contacts that served them well when China's economy began to go global. Caterpillar has now reached $1 billion in annual sales from China alone. The payoff was far from immediate. Even as recently as two years ago, Caterpillar had annual sales of only half that amount, and had only reached that level through years of slogging through the complex wilderness of China's regulations and idiosyncrasies. But by laying a solid foundation of local intelligence and practices early, Caterpillar was ready to take advantage when opportunity struck.

Komatsu's experience is somewhat different. The company only established a presence in China in 1995. And their initial entry was a bit blundering since "the need to import high value-added parts such as precision parts from Japan" prevented them from realizing the savings they had anticipated in shifting production to China.[6] Also, Komatsu used Japanese managers on the ground to facilitate its entry into China, but ran into resistance with this strategy. Now Chinese employees are assuming very visible roles in Komatsu's China operations, ranging from the divisional CEO and head of personnel to key sales and marketing positions. As a result of this *ronin*-like retooling, Komatsu expects to reach a $1 billion in sales in China by 2005.

These examples show that success can come for foreign companies in China, but with some caveats. The Chinese appear eager to learn from and adopt certain business practices typical of more developed countries, such as avoiding the appearance of impropriety or manufacturing to the highest-quality standards possible. However, for any foreign initiative to really succeed in China, it must be seen as a joint effort, with Chinese knowledge of local customs getting the ultimate respect. Komatsu learned it was not enough to merely transfer whole operations into China—Modern Day Japanese samurai need to be as flexible as masterless *ronin* if they want to succeed on this new and extremely complicated terrain.

THE DARK SIDE OF WORKING WITH CHINA

China is many things to Japan. It is both a tremendous opportunity and a potential financial black hole. Misunderstanding China can quickly wipe out any advantages of being there. So companies have to be careful of the pitfalls that may come as a result of operating in the world's largest market.

Much of the historical tension between the two countries relates back to the *bushi* mindset toward China. Samurai spirit was invoked during the Japanese invasions of the nineteenth and twentieth centuries, so the Chinese can't be blamed for being cautious about anything related to "samurai." Evidence of the rift broke into the open during the 2004 Asian Cup, where a football loss prompted riots in Chinese cities. And the unresolved political questions of both North Korea and Taiwan can trace their origin to fighting between China and Japan more than 100 years ago.

We identified several patterns among those Japanese and Chinese who have worked together over the years. The chief complaints from each perspective have a central theme:[7]

JAPANESE PERSPECTIVE ON CHINESE EMPLOYEES:	CHINESE PERSPECTIVE ON JAPANESE MANAGERS:
They always request higher wages.	They always keep wages low.
They don't like to work overtime in an emergency.	They don't easily delegate tasks.
They have bad manners.	They don't want to promote us up the line.
They quit easily despite our investing in their career.	They don't invest in our skills.

In addition, Japanese firms have been slower than most to "localize" their operations—reducing their popularity among Chinese nationals. A questionnaire asking Chinese which companies they'd rather work for showed no Japanese firms in the top 25 (Sony, the highest, ranked at Number 26).[8] Chinese attitudes about things like product liability have been aggravating to Japanese firms, as Toshiba took a severe public relations hit in 2000 when one of its laptop computer models proved to be defective.[9]

Addressing this mistrust of each other, Merle Hinrichs, founder and president of one of the largest business trade information companies in Asia, said he doubted such obstacles can be overcome quickly. "There is every reason for other Asian nations to see Japan as the "older brother" or "uncle," but it never will be seen that way," he says. Historical tension between Japan and the rest of Asia will stand in the way of creating lasting bonds between Japan and the rest, at least in the near term. China aggressively courts foreign direct investment to help it grow, while Japan discourages other Asian firms from entering its domestic market.

Those historical tensions are reflected in opinion polls of the two nations. In a 2004 poll, the Institute of Japanese Studies within the Chinese Academy of Social Sciences found that about 54 percent of Chinese had an unfavorable view of Japan, up 10 percent from just two years earlier. Almost 90 percent of those with an unfavorable view "cited reasons linked to Japan's wartime aggression as the reason for their view, underscoring the deep-seated resentment toward Japan."[10] Furthermore, many Chinese reported being worried about Japan turning militaristic once again.

With Japan relying increasingly on China's economy to steady its own, one has to wonder if the economic and political conditions during the 1890s, when tension between these two countries led to a brutal war, might repeat themselves. Do the Chinese see Japan as just exploiting their cheap labor for profit? Might the Japanese become resentful of China exerting increasing political and economic influence in the region? Or can the countries avoid the mistakes of the past and come to a harmonious balance?

One hopes for the last option, but stranger things have happened. We've talked about how cultural values play a bigger role in shaping competitive mindsets than we "rational" and modern humans sometimes like to admit. China's powerful underlying cultural values affect nearly everything in its society. It's true that samurai then imported and promoted many of these same values in Japan. But those values were shaped quite differently by the respective cultures of the two countries—particularly when it came to competition. Military power and top-down organizational thinking became an important model for business activity in Japan, but not in China. The military was not highly thought of in China, where one was much more inclined to be a scholar or a bureaucrat than a soldier. The Japanese ensured that the sword was melded with the pen. In classical Chinese philosophy, the pen *alone* reigns supreme.

This simple difference in mindset has the potential to change the entire future of Sino-Japanese business relationships. The Chinese come from a very entrepreneurial model of business—small family businesses are the norm. The Japanese, on the other hand, thrive in large, well-structured organizations. Fortunately, when the best parts of the traditional samurai mindset are combined with the entrepreneurial nature of masterless samurai, it is possible to arrive at a mutually agreeable position where the Japanese can significantly increase their chances of success in China. These business *ronin* need to seek out their new master in China in a wide variety of industries and locations. Some may look for the master in the interconnecting network of Chinese family businesses; others may look on the emerging Chinese middle-class consumer as the new master; still others will try to placate Chinese government officials (who still wield tremendous power). The most successful Japanese businesspeople will see the master in all of these places. By using their whole bushido mindset and the full set of samurai methods to support these new masters, Modern Day Samurai from Japan can create the foundations for wild success in China. Indeed, with the same mindset and methods, Modern Day Samurai from all countries can do the same.

LEARNING IN CHINA

"For more than 2,000 years, China was the parent state and Japan was the satellite," says Yoshihiro Sakai, managing director of investment banking at

Nomura Securities. "More people now believe that the best course for the future of Japan is to figure out how to maximize its relationships with the two real global powers: China and the U.S."[11] China is now such a large economic force that it cannot be ignored by anyone, let alone its closest neighbor. Japanese samurai do seem open to exploring what opportunities lie ahead inside the Middle Kingdom, while American samurai still seem to lack such vision. It seems safe to say China will play a role as Japan moves through this newest cycle, but what sort of role?

Japan has shown itself capable of absorbing lessons from China—from the Taika reforms 14 centuries ago to the relocation of their manufacturing base in this current one. As Japan moves through its current cycle, it may move to bring China closer into the community of nations. Japan's current attitude toward China is that of curiosity combined with wariness. Japan thinks it has a lot to learn from China—our data show 7 out of 10 Japanese believe this as opposed to only 6 out of 10 Americans. Yet more Japanese than Americans perceive China as both a threat (by about 30 percentage points) *and* an opportunity (by about 8 percentage points). It seems China is on the radar screen in Japan far more than in America (maybe we are a bit distracted at the moment).

CONCLUSION

The key factor that will shape the next few decades is the role that Japan will play in helping China take advantage of its rising power. There has been talk of creating an Asian currency bloc, which would instantly rival the largest common markets of the world. China may also take cues from Japan about how to transform from being a low-cost producer (Japan's role in the 1960s and 1970s) to a true technological and innovative powerhouse.

On subjects where Japanese and Chinese already agree, such as their shared Confucian heritage, Japan can use this to its advantage. Japan should focus on finding opportunities where Japanese efficiency and Chinese entrepreneurialism can work together harmoniously. And finally, where there is friction—and there has been a lot of friction over the centuries—Japan needs to be more self-aware to try and eliminate any new friction before it starts.

Japanese could start by bringing the elements of Japanese samurai mindset back to where they began—in China. By offering their expertise in this way, without being too overbearing, they may inspire China to reciprocate by helping Japan become more entrepreneurial.

As Japan and China move closer together, they may also turn away from the United States. And geopolitics always has a funny way of exerting itself on otherwise rational economic actors. China may soon face its own catalytic event, similar to or greater than those that have rocked its recent history. Whether the economic relationship with Japan will survive such an event remains to be seen. But together, China's and Japan's *ronin* may decide their best fate lies in cooperation, raising their relationship to a new level. Modern Day Samurai from the United States would do well to recognize the tremendous opportunity such a partnership holds, and try to be a part of it.

NOTES

1. Sebastian Moffett, "How Japan's Neighbors Give It a Lift—Nation's GDP Set to Shrink But Its Exports to Region, Especially China, Are Rising," *Wall Street Journal*, New York: Feb. 13, 2003.
2. Ibid.
3. Ibid.
4. Ibid.
5. Sebastian Moffett and Leslie Chang, "Pressing Reform: For Ailing Japan, A Prescription Made in China; Mr. Nakanishi Sends Out for Labor, Slashing Costs of His Handmade Suits; A Nation's Inefficient Habits," *Wall Street Journal* (Eastern edition), New York: Aug. 29, 2003.
6. Chi Hung Kwan, "The Conditions for Successful Business Operations in China—The Case of Komatsu" (2004.1.9) http://www.rieti.go.jp/en/china/04010901.html.
7. Shingo Konomoto, "Kyu-seicho suru Chugoku shijyo ni okeru Nihon kigyo no kadai to taiou," *NRI*, Nomura Research Institute, Ltd., Tokyo: 2004, p.15. http://www.nri.co.jp/opinion/chitekishisan/2004/pdf/cs20040808.pdf.
8. Chi Hung Kwan, "Why Japanese Firms are Unpopular" (2003.4.2), RIETI, Research Institute of Economy, Trade and Industry (Keizai Sangyo Sho), http://www.rieti.go.jp/en/china/03040201.html.
9. Ibid.

10. Xiao Qiang, "Anti-Japanese feeling growing in China, poll shows," *Yahoo News*, November 23, 2004.

11. Jim Frederick, "Here Comes The Sun," *Time Asia*, April 5, 2004, http://www.time.com/time/asia/covers/501040412/story.html.

CHAPTER 19

Entrepreneurs

As Japan moves into its newest Renewal Cycle, the greatest challenge its *ronin* will have is to master the art of entrepreneurship. The ability to create something out of nothing, blaze new ground, and anticipate market demand requires an ultra-savvy mindset that uses both pen and sword in just the right amounts.

After all, where does prosperity come from? When faced with near-zero growth, economies create prosperity by wringing greater gains from the same old resources. That means effectively capturing new technologies, identifying unmet demands and ways to meet them, and inspiring humans to desire things they often haven't heard of. (Latte, anyone?)

But it takes a certain spirit to capture the essence of what makes a good entrepreneur. One might assume Japan has always pursued a top-down style—Japan continues to be stereotyped as an economy dominated by big corporations and lifetime employees who are more like bureaucrats than businesspeople. And there's at least some truth behind that stereotype.

FINDING THE INNER *RONIN*

Yet entrepreneurship is far more ingrained in Japanese society than most Westerners would think. A dual economy has always existed inside Japan, where both big and small could coexist peacefully. Since many of the big name corporations were essentially coddled by the national government to ensure their success, they lacked a real need to innovate much beyond what their customers asked of them. Entrepreneurs could survive in this environment. Since the big companies had no need to develop new product lines and features, there were market niches for entrepreneurs to create and play in.

The entrepreneurial spirit is alive and well today—even inside corporate Japan. Nearly 2 out of every 3 Japanese businesspeople in our survey, some 61 percent, said that they were interested in launching a new business as an entrepreneur. Fewer than half of the American business population (48 percent) felt the same way. Americans may find themselves taken by surprise by Japanese corporate *ronin* and their entrepreneurial thinking. But if they knew more about Japan's history, they wouldn't be.

JAPAN'S ENTREPRENEURIAL HISTORY

The entrepreneurial history of Japan is long and vital. Some of the most successful, long-lived Japanese companies today are descendents of Japanese soy and sake makers. In the fourteenth century, several hundred sake manufacturers were in business, leading to important technological developments such as the use of yeast and *koji* spores, which helped convert starch to sugar. Although today the sake industry is protected by tariffs, it took root in an environment that was not only unprotected, not only wide open, but fiercely competitive.

But it wasn't just sake and soy companies that existed in the Tokugawa era. Construction companies, restaurants, trading companies, tatami manufacturers—any product that existed at the time came from entrepreneurial origins. Even before the end of the shogunate, there are abundant stories of samurai crossing class boundaries to become entrepreneurs. And when the Tokugawa era ended, former samurai moved aggressively into moneymaking ventures of all types.

When Westerners think of modern Japan's large, bureaucratic companies, they often forget that almost all of these firms were entrepreneurial upstarts at one point. Those that have survived for decades have had to remake themselves over and over again. Toyota is one shining example, developing new production techniques over time to become one of the most efficient car manufacturers on the planet. But Toyota wasn't always large or always an auto manufacturer. The company had its beginnings in building silk spinning machinery. In the 1920s, the Toyoda family could see that there was no future in the manufacturing of silk spinning machinery, and they began to look for other areas where their expertise could be used profitably. It takes a great deal of entrepreneurial, creative thinking to get from the motors used for automated looms to those that could drive a car's powertrain. But Toyota made this transformation quickly and was already a very successful auto manufacturer in the 1930s. The company executed the same type of miraculous entrepreneurial renewal again by making a strong, competitive entry into the U.S. auto market only 12 years after the end of World War II.

Even within state-supported industries, an entrepreneurial spirit took hold in post-war Japan. As Japan's war surplus economy was slowly converted into peacetime production, old machine tools were used in industries from automobiles to sewing machines. The state-run Japanese coal industry was turned over to private enterprise, where it diversified into steel and chemical concerns. In fact, contrary to our instinctive belief in the economic power of war efforts, many of Japan's conglomerates were actually *more* successful both before *and* after Japan's wartime economy of the 1930s dragooned large sections of industry into helping out with the war effort.

However, as we've seen, the age of the state-subsidized conglomerates has ended. Japan's industrial policy formed between the 1950s and 1980s actually helped to restrain some of the more inventive car companies, such as Honda and Toyota, from realizing their full potential at that time. Bureaucrats, after all, are allergic to risk, and both Honda and Toyota knew they couldn't depend on the government's help for much longer, given Japan's post-boom fiscal situation. Ultimately, though, fighting both the other Japanese auto firms and the government regulators may have created a more fiercely competitive spirit and strongly entrepreneurial mindset in these firms.

Legendary among the Japanese state's failures in the business world in the most recent decades is the Fifth Generation Computing program. Begun in 1982, this program incited fear in companies like IBM, Apple, and Siemens who saw it as Japan's attempt to corner the market on the next wave of computers. Yet after spending a decade and 50 billion yen (or about half a billion dollars), the program has been lapped by almost every shoestring initiative in the private marketplace. The program only produced one workable prototype, which was hopelessly out of date by the time it came online. And the Japanese have noticed that their Fifth Generation program did not lose to some other large-scale effort, either national or corporate. The lesson of ultimate non-Japanese entrepreneurial success in the face of coordinated government-led programs at home has not been lost on the current generation of business leaders in Japan.

TANAKA'S JOURNEY

Even one of Japan's most famous statesmen has served as an important role model of entrepreneurship. Tanaka Kakuei, who would rise to become Japan's most powerful person for two decades (and, importantly, decades when today's business leaders were developing their personal mental models of what it takes to succeed) was born to poverty in a rural town in Niigata on Japan's western coast. He spent much of his youth attending county fairs buying and selling cows for his father's dairy farm. By the eighth grade, however, he had decided to break into construction and moved to Tokyo. A chance meeting in an elevator with the head of a construction firm gave him his first big break. Later, he would enter the highest classes of Japanese society by marrying his boss's daughter.

Toward the end of the war, Tanaka's timing was incredibly lucky—perhaps, depending on what you choose to believe, a little *too* lucky. He was able to fund his political war chest by cashing in soon-to-be worthless Japanese war bonds in Korea mere weeks before Japan's surrender. He then used that money to build a political base of power. Even though he was tainted by minor scandals more or less throughout his entire political career, he persevered until the early 1990s—lasting just about as long as Japan's old state-guided model did.

Tanaka dominated his sphere despite the supposed extreme meritocracy of Japan, with its emphasis not just on performance but also on credentials. He never had the prestigious university degree or even much formal training in the ways of government. Tanaka also missed the mark when it came to consensus, conformity, and collaboration. Instead, he was a scrapper who fiercely fought to get every opportunity, sometimes breaking the rules along the way. He had no compunction about using whatever resources were within his reach. Tanaka in many ways symbolizes how Japan pulled itself up from nothing to become a giant on the world stage today.

THE MINDSET OF THE *RONIN* ENTREPRENEUR

As Japan moves into its latest Renewal Cycle, it is going to have to become ever more entrepreneurial. But what exactly does that mean? There are several elements that have to be in place before a country can raise an entrepreneurial class—a sort of *principa entrepreneuria* of conditions. Mark

Fuller's company, Monitor Group, has surveyed this across cultures and national boundaries and has noticed a few key patterns.

First, before we get into the details of the entrepreneurial mindset, there are some preconditions. A government must be in place with a reasonably healthy regulatory system and with relatively liquid capital markets. That is, investors have to be able to feel they can not only put money in safely but also withdraw it safely. The financial markets take care of the nitty-gritty, but the regulatory structure ensures everyone on all sides is happy. We may take this as a given, but occasionally we are shocked to discover how much of the world has yet to absorb this.

With those preconditions in place, profitable entrepreneurship is driven by all of the factors that we have discussed as chapter topics in this book. But we have done scholarly work on the role of attention in business. So we are convinced both academically and personally that we've given you far too many factors to remember without referring back to this book. (That may be a good thing for people trying to sell books, but it is not a good thing for people trying to help people change the way things get done.) So we'd like to leave you with what we believe, based on the findings of our Entrepreneurship Survey, are the six most important factors:

- Individualism
- Innovation
- Moral purpose
- Competitiveness
- Execution
- Flexibility

Individualism

Obviously, *ronin* are individuals by definition. And we believe that the masterless samurai is probably the right metaphor for entrepreneurship in the twenty-first century. But even samurai who were firmly devoted to their daimyo had much more individualistic spirit than the modern stereotype of samurai cookie-cutter uniformity. Each samurai had his own armor design, often with a colorful flourish to distinguish him on the battlefield. In fact, the faceplate was often a caricature of the person beneath the armor. And a samurai's sword—perhaps the ultimate expression of his identity—was individually handcrafted to a stunning degree of quality. While Western arms and uniforms were more often than not interchangeable and mass-produced, the samurai expressed their individuality through their tools of war.

Then later, when the fighting was finished, they exhibited even more distinctiveness through their skills with the pen. What is a more unique expression of self than a person's signature and handwriting? In both pen and sword, the samurai lived in a world of tremendous individuality.

Innovation

Innovation is a priori for an entrepreneur to be successful. A single innovation may lead to the first idea, but a consistent ability to innovate in process and product is exactly the stuff of which the Bill Gateses of the world are made. Modern Day *Ronin* will need to be constantly and consistently creative as they adapt to the rapid speed of change in the business world around them.

Moral Purpose

As discussed earlier, the secret to the entrepreneur's drive is often not merely a love of getting rich: most people accrue personal wealth long before they have created a truly lasting impact. And there are less painful routes to relative wealth. No, it is often about creating something new and unique that can improve the world in some way. Being driven by things greater than yourself speaks to both the power of the samurai's mission (to protect the daimyo) and the entrepreneur.

Competitiveness

The competitiveness of the entrepreneur is self-evident—you're racing to get an idea to market that is better than all the rest before someone beats you to it. One cannot be a warrior without being competitive as well—it is the essence of staying alive in battle. The greatest warriors were the "trash talkers" of their day, fighting an enemy as much with their spirit as with their sword. Some of the most competitive of today's younger Japanese professionals are actually bailing out of the corporate world. They tire quickly of the low productivity and rote work generally required of many white-collar workers in Japan. Instead they are joining the flexible employment pool—temporary workers that now number over 2 million people (250 percent higher than the number of temp workers five years ago).[1] Most twenty-somethings in Japan have known for a long time that if you want to make more money than your same-age colleagues and do relatively interesting work, become a temp.

Flexibility

This reflects the samurai's ability to reinvent himself over time—from loyal servant to *ronin* to businessman as Japan's history progressed. Even during the beginning of the peaceful Tokugawa era, samurai roles were changing as the number of powerful families rose and fell. In order to maintain their "value-add" for their masters, samurai had to accept changes in the social order. For the entrepreneur, it is no different—the idea must be tweaked many times to calibrate it to market whims. And, as we've shown in this book, the process of renewal is a cycle. It must happen over and over again. The samurai mindset and methods that we've introduced are meant to help you incorporate in yourself and in your organization a culture that will make it easier to begin the process of renewal again the next time you need to embark on the next cycle.

Execution

This is exactly how thoughts are turned into action. The ultimate question of how well the samurai survived was determined finally by execution. He could be unique, innovative, have great moral purpose, and a strong competitive purpose, but the samurai who could not execute well was a dead samurai. The organization that is striving to renew itself must ultimately pass through all four squares of the Renewal Cycle. Organizations that get stuck somewhere along the way are not managing the renewal process. And they, like samurai who cannot carry through on the battlefield, will not survive.

There is a lot to do in the process of renewal. Yes, it has four discrete stages, but we do not purport that it is a simple set of steps. Yes, the six key factors that we have pointed out above are vital—worth keeping in mind even if you forget everything else—but the renewal journey they equip you for will still be extremely complex. All of the factors discussed in this book are part of it. In fact there are probably more factors than we've written about.

The samurai and the entrepreneur have much in common, and it is easy to see why many samurai became leaders in industry after the Meiji Restoration—it really wasn't that much of a stretch. But now that Japan is reaching a new cycle, Modern Day Samurai must become something more to stay truly entrepreneurial. They must become Modern Day *Ronin*—samurai without masters.

LEADING MASTERLESS SAMURAI

Ronin took the entrepreneurial traits learned by the samurai and pushed them to the next level. Often not knowing where their next meal was coming from, *ronin* had to be extremely philosophical about life—but ready to snap into action at a moment's notice. By observing what was going on around them during life's quieter moments, the more skilled *ronin* could savor life's lessons until it was necessary to convert those lessons into action.

Without a master to pull the strings, *ronin* had no choice but to face the wishes of the marketplace. The more bureaucratized samurai—the ones who had grown accustomed to the comforts of living on an allowance from the lord—could sharpen their skills only by becoming *ronin*. We often see this same thing happening in today's large organizations when employees get too comfortable. Efforts at "intrapreneurship" are nothing more than corporate lords trying to keep their samurai razor sharp (and maybe develop a few new ideas along the way!).

We can think of examples where the men behind efforts to "*ronin*-ize" a few Western companies did so because their life experiences led them to become *ronin*. Almost from the very beginning of his tenure at General Electric, Jack Welch was turned off by bureaucratic behavior. Welch saw this sort of behavior as nothing more than people trying to protect themselves against potentially better ideas that might poke through to the surface. In his book *Jack: Straight from the Gut*, Welch talked about his early middle-class upbringing in small-town Massachusetts and a stuttering problem that threatened to hold him back. Welch fought against such impediments, and was eventually thrust into the upper echelons of leadership at General Electric, where his non–Ivy League pedigree was unusual compared to past leaders of the company. But his attitude throughout was "as simple as knowing you're never too old to learn something new or to recognize the fact that no one person ever has all the answers. There's always a better way!"[2]

This attitude drove Welch to tear bureaucracy down at the company once he reached the top. By delayering operations at the company, he was able to unleash an entrepreneurial revolution that would propel the company forward into new realms, such as finance and entertainment, that had nothing to do with GE's original mission. Welch's philosophy of pruning back underperforming parts of the company allowed new branches to spread and blossom. This is just one of the reasons why GE was able to produce more than 100 consecutive quarters of net income growth, and rise to become one of the world's most valuable corporations.

BP's Lord John Browne has a similar story. The son of a British army officer father and a Hungarian mother who spent two years in Auschwitz, he worked hard enough in public school to become sponsored into the prestigious Cambridge University by the company he would later run—British Petroleum (BP). Thanks to this opportunity to make it into the big leagues, he excelled within the company's ranks "by focusing on achieving short-term goals and...vacuuming up all the advice he could get."[3]

When he was made CEO, Browne took an entrepreneurial mindset into the boardroom. Using phrases like "virtual team networks," and "breakthrough thinking," he did not sound like the CEO of an industrial energy company. Browne created a number of different business units at the company and flattened the organization into a profitable dynamo. By putting a greater emphasis on being able to learn from itself and react quickly to a constantly changing environment, Browne was helping to create empowered corporate *ronin* throughout the organization. And by giving his employees a clear moral purpose at the same time, Browne was able to motivate employees in nontraditional ways—by pushing decision-making power down through the organization, and eliminating hierarchies wherever possible.

Welch and Browne seemed to use their relatively modest upbringings as anchors even as they ascended to the very highest heights of the corporate world. Neither was bound by any artificial social structure—class, title, or educational status—and thus, neither owed anything to anyone or had anything to lose once they reached the top. Their vision was unclouded by artificiality, and they used their positions to make life better for their organizations. They were the essence of *ronin.* Their entrepreneurial spirit, vision, and loyalty made their companies into something greater, rather than be tied down by politics or internal agendas.

One potential future corporate *ronin*-maker to watch is Siemens' new CEO, Klaus Kleinfeld. Dubbed "Neutron Klaus" by the press already, Kleinfeld is relatively young and ready to make waves within the staid German conglomerate. Full of fiefdoms, Siemens will be a challenge for Kleinfeld, who has already attempted to bust up the bureaucracy at the company at lower levels by consolidating departments and divisions, and asking workers to be more flexible. It seems that if Siemens is to make it to the next Renewal Cycle, it will definitely need more corporate *ronin* on staff. Kleinfeld reportedly has "a whole generation of young Siemens executives, keen to conquer the world and frustrated with the bureaucracy"[4] rooting for him to do just that.

Managers of today and tomorrow would do well to emulate these three, among others. More specifically, Japanese *ronin* will have to master the coming tasks of the next Renewal Cycle—handling uncertainty, preserving their adeptness at knowledge management, building a new sense of moral purpose, and mastering the enigma that is China. Above all, they must do so while respecting and maintaining their adroitness at the six fundamental skills we outlined above for the entrepreneur.

CONCLUSION

As this challenge becomes visible, we are seeing a new preference emerge from the youth of Japan as to which model they would prefer to follow. We asked Japanese which of 11 samurai archetypes they liked the most. Japanese under 35 prefer samurai archetypes from before the Meiji Restoration; Japanese over 35 tended to favor figures of leadership from after the Meiji. Why the difference in attitudes? Younger Japanese seem to be harkening back to Japan's more distant glory days, which are less tinged with the regret of recent history. Older Japanese were perhaps raised with the model of the men who helped make Japan into the modern superstate it currently is. So perhaps, as these younger workers take the stage, they will ignore the lessons of their relatively recent leaders and try to recapture some of the dynamism from Japan's early days.

But today's *ronin*, wherever they may be and whoever they look up to, have a significant challenge in front of them. Modern Day *Ronin* need to translate boredom, stress, or even failure into the opportunity to do something different and new—to go down an individual path. *Ronin* need to rise above being slaves to the basic hierarchy of needs, and follow a higher calling than just putting food on the table and a roof over their heads. They have to believe that life is more than just bureaucratic service to the warlord—it is a chance to remake yourself over and over again. And in the process, they earn the chance to experience all the variety and pleasure that corporate and personal renewal has to offer.

NOTES

1. Brian Bremner, "Is Japan Back?" *Business Week*, June 14, 2004, p. 51.
2. http://www.straightfromthegut.com/meet/meet_qa.html.
3. Rupert Steiner, "Odd Man Out Among the Oil Barons," *Sunday Times* (London), Jan. 21, 2001.
4. Jack Ewing, "Siemens New Boss," *Business Week*, Jan. 24, 2005, European Edition.

Index

About the Authors

Mark B. Fuller is the Chairman and Chief Executive Officer of the Monitor Group, a firm he co-founded in 1982. Monitor currently employs more than 1,500 employees in twenty-nine offices located in twenty-two countries and competes in three different business areas: general management consulting, principal investing, and intelligent products, such as software.

Mark formerly served as an Assistant Professor of Business Administration at the Harvard Graduate School of Business Administration, where he taught courses in strategy formulation and implementation, as well as industry and competitive analysis. While a professor, Mark was Co-Director of Harvard's Project on the Auto Industry and the American Economy. He has authored or coauthored more than fifty articles and teaching cases. In addition to sitting on a variety of Monitor Group boards, Mark serves as a Governor of the Asian Institute of Management, a Trustee of Belmont Hill School, a Foundation Member of the World Economic Forum, a Member of Harvard University's Major Gifts Steering Committee, International Studies Committee, and Board of Overseers' Committee on University Resources, as well as a Member of Massachusetts' Governor's Council on Economic Growth and Technology.

John C. Beck is President of the North Star Leadership Group, a Senior Research Fellow and professor at University of Southern California's Annenberg Center for the Digital Future, and an Adjunct Professor at Switzerland's IMD. He leads research and consulting projects on topics of strategic thinking, wireless communication, the global internet, leadership, and online communities. Dr. Beck served as the senior strategic advisor to the First Prime Minister, Prince Ranariddh, during Cambodia's first three years as a democracy. Additionally, he was Director of International Research at Accenture's Institute for Strategic Change. He has served on the Board of Directors of a variety of corporations and universities and is currently a Board Member at Choice Humanitarian, a nonprofit organization supporting village development programs in six countries around the world.

Dr. Beck has published hundreds of books, articles, and business reports on the topics of business in Asia, strategic management, globalization, leadership, and technology. His books include *The Attention Economy*, *DoCoMo: The Wireless Tsunami*, and *Got Game: How a New Generation of Gamers is Reshaping Business Forever*.